To my frie[...]
I appreciat[...]
on this project!

David D. Brown

M000295729

How Strong Is
Your Faith?

How Strong Is Your Faith?

David T. Brown

David Brown Books

Cover Design: Charles McClurkin, aka DesignerDouglas, and L.A.A.D Studio

Published by David Brown Books, Spartanburg South Carolina
Email: HowStrongFaith@gmail.com

ISBN-10: 0692691634
ISBN-13: 978-0692691632

DEDICATION/ACKNOWLEDGEMENTS

To my wife, Stacey, and our two wonderful children. Thanks for the love and inspiration that keeps me wanting to soar to new heights.

I would like to thank the following people for the love, support, and faithfulness shown to me as this book was being created: Loretta Grna, Kenyetta Hurd, Tamara Davis, Gary Nesmith, Clarence & Karen McGill, Rev. Arnold McJimpsey, Sr., Timothy Aiken, Rev. Richard Johnson, Pastor John Henderson, Rev. Paul Rice, & Pastor Tony Griffin.

1

THE COMING STORM

The *Carolinas Medical Center* in Charlotte, North Carolina is a strikingly modern building with organic curves, which employs what architecture critics called "an elegantly efficient use of space." The Center is nationally renowned not only for its aesthetics, but more importantly, its functionally therapeutic design that considers the long term wellbeing of patients. That's brochure-talk for having lots of windows, and feeling more like a four-star hotel than a sick-bay, or prison.

Reverend Theodore Church's room was no exception, and was located in a wing with an extended strip of giant windows and lofty, looming ceilings. Doctor Jefferson, a loyal parishioner of Holy Light Christian Church, of which Reverend Church was the pastor, insisted on the good Reverend's stay in his department (cardiology,) despite the cause of the Reverend's symptoms remaining as of yet, somewhat of a mystery. Doctor Jefferson had arranged for the cost of Reverend Church's care to be greatly reduced, and had been pulling more than a few strings to ensure the good pastor's health insurance barely took a hit.

As the days wore on Doctor Jefferson became worried. Even with the help of his esteemed colleagues in dermatology, nephrology, cancer and gastro, and seemingly endless batteries of tests, the cause of Reverend Church's condition continued to elude them. They'd simply never seen anything like it. He hated to admit it, but even though he hated to listen to the gossips in church, the faithful Doctor Jefferson was beginning to wonder if God wasn't perhaps bringing down a chastisement on the good Reverend, for some, yet unknown, sin.

The man was as tall as he was unusual; around six-foot-five or six-six. The sterile polished floors and generic postmodern art on the walls contrasted sharply with the grubby, ragged appearance of the bearded stranger. His shoes, once white Reebok sneakers from the nineties, were now discolored with stains of brown and grey, and the left shoe had a gaping hole in the front, from which a couple of bare toes poked out. He wore a heavy, well-used trench coat, even though it was mid-summer in a Southern State, and his filthy, stained jeans were baggy and frayed.

The man's size, coupled with his grimy appearance and less-than-pleasant odor, made him more than a little intimidating to the hospital visitors, who were giving him a wide berth as he stood gazing through the large window in the door of Reverend Church's hospital room. Despite his appearance however, the man's eyes were sharp and bright, surveying every inch of the room, and each tiny detail of each occupant. True to his appearance though, the homeless man appeared to be muttering to himself.

"Yes, I understand..." he nodded. Reverend Church and the four others were apparently too engrossed in their animated conversation to notice him.

"No, the three friends continue along their same paths of understanding. Or the lack thereof."

He paused.

"Yes, the fourth remains silent. He is listening but his growing frustration is evident."

He paused again.

"Yes, Lord" he nodded.

"No, the tragedy has affected him deeply and I can't see his heart as you can, but in my opinion he appears to have been driven further into himself. He isn't willing to change his mind."

He listened then spoke again.

"No, he still doesn't appear to have any idea of why this is happening. His three companions aren't helping much. It seems they make it worse, making him more defensive...self-righteous."

He paused again, and a somber expression crossed his face.

"Yes, Lord... as you wish," he nodded. "Yes, I will personally be stationed on watch when your Spirit begins to speak."

The homeless man eyes suddenly darted up and down the hallway with a soldier's gleam, searching for something unseen.

"Yes Lord, we will not allow them to disrupt."

He sensed her behind him, but kept looking forward. She came up slowly at first, but then found her voice.

"Excuse me? Can I help you?" the pretty young nurse demanded of the stranger. He turned and looked down at her with clear, piercing eyes she had not expected.

"No, thank you," he replied with a warm smile and turned back to the window.

"Ss...sir," she stuttered then found her voice. "Are you visiting a patient? If not, I'm going to have to ask you to leave."

The man nodded again, and as the nurse was about to ask which patient, when he muttered again.

"Yes Lord. If the rebuke doesn't pierce his heart, should I be prepared for stronger measures?"

"SIR! I'm going to have to ask you to leave now, or I will call security!"

The stranger's eyes grew wide and he stood completely upright. The nurse took a step back.

"I see. Yes, without question Lord. We will begin preparing the vicinity for you in that event. Praise be to the great God Jehovah."

He bowed his head slightly and then turned to address the panic evident in the woman's eyes.

"Have no fear. I'm leaving," he said without a trace of hostility on his face.

She stared at him speechless, and could only watch as he loped away. Some of her courage returned as he disappeared around the corner and she decided to walk after him to make sure he was leaving. She turned the corner to be greeted by an empty hallway. Confused at first, she walked over to the only door that he could have gone through. She jiggled the handle of the locked sanitation closet and looked up in surprise. The next door was all the way at the end of the hall, before the doors to the exit. She jogged down the corridor to search for him, but there was no trace of the homeless man. Unnerved, she called security and informed them to be on the lookout for the tall stranger. As she gave them his description she had the strangest sensation that it was a waste of her time. She couldn't forget his piercing, calm eyes as he looked down at her. She'd never seen anything like them in her life.

2

THE APPROVAL OF MEN

The Honorable Reverend Doctor Henry Williams, was an imposing figure, even from the stage where it was difficult to tell one's true size. He scratched his graying temple, pausing as he searched for the perfect words. He then spoke slowly and deliberately, but gently.

"It is my great privilege today to honor a man with whom I've had the joy of being friends since childhood."

He paused to look at Reverend Church and slipped him a warm smile.

"This is a man all of you know and love...and with good reason. He has been a pillar of our community for more years than I care to count, never hesitating to sacrificing his time, sweat, tears and sometimes even quite literally, his blood."

Several in the congregation agreed with a few "Amens" and a "Bless Gods."

"As many of you know, Pastor Baker, Bishop Davis and myself have long been blessed to share in the ministry and life of our dear friend Reverend Church. Our individual congregations are in fact, more like extended families across this great city of ours."

He inhaled and looked up from his notes.

"A city that has many challenges, but far more grace abounding. And grace comes in many forms...one of which, God has provided for us in our dear pastor, friend and, many would say, blameless man of God... the exceptional Reverend Church."

All the guests, visitors and the congregation of Holy Light Christian Church thundered applause. They stood to their feet, clapping and shouting and singing. In the front row, Sandra Church, the petite and striking first lady leaned into her husband, squeezed him tightly and kissed his cheek. He hugged her back but only waved down the applause, looking at the carpet with a bashful smile.

When the applause showed no signs of subsiding, Reverend Williams spoke again, and a hush eventually fell over the crowd.

"At this time, I would like to invite the mayor of our great city, Charlotte, to the podium. Mayor Greenburg, if you would please do us the honor."

Mayor Greenburg, a small, spectacled man, left the front row and walked up the stairs to Reverend Williams. Dwarfing the mayor, Reverend Williams leaned over, shook his hand and took his leave of the stage.

"Thank you for the introduction Reverend Williams, and I couldn't agree more. We serve one of the finest cities in all the world." More applause rippled through the church, as the mayor took out a sheet of paper from his coat, and adjusted his glasses.

"Well, Reverend Williams stole, many of the wonderful traits of our dear Reverend Church from my notes..." he began. The congregation laughed in unison. "But there are many more we can truly say about a man so generous, so insightful... so...I will say I love that word *blameless* Reverend Williams used?" The church agreed enthusiastically.

"In this city alone, Reverend Church has founded no less than two orphanages, three soup kitchens for the homeless in various low income neighborhoods, and most recently, a ground-breaking recovery center for those suffering the agony of addiction. Where nationwide relapse rates are at a whopping seventy-five percent, under Reverend Church's leadership and spiritual insight, the *Coulwood Newness And Rehabilitation Center* has consistently achieved an astonishing and unprecedented rate of less than fifty percent relapses."

Mayor Greenburg adjusted his glasses as several in the

church couldn't refrain from offering their appreciation.

"That's why nothing makes me more proud than to present to the Reverend Doctor Theodore Church, one of the fathers of our community, a key to the great city of Charlotte, North Carolina."

The church erupted again and the keyboard player, who had so far been waiting patiently on standby, seized the moment with a volley of elaborate arpeggios and booming bass lines. Passionate church members danced, and jumped and ruined expensive hair-dos. They clapped and sang and some even broke out into Holy Ghost hops in the aisles, as the choir belted out individual, impromptu melodies. If Reverend Church had no idea before, he certainly knew in that moment he was loved and admired by not only his church, but his community and city at large. Representatives from every city district, pastors from the poorest neighborhoods, and the richest, even several city officials had all turned out to honor the pastor of Holy Light Christian Church. The church rumbled with gratitude and admiration as Reverend Church made his way onto the stage.

Mayor Greenburg shook the Reverend's hand as he reached the podium, and presented the giant, ornate key, which was seated in a luxuriously carved wooden box, lined with rich blue velvet. Inscribed into the lid were the words:

This key to the great city of Charlotte, North Carolina is presented to the honorable Reverend

Theodore Church; a man blameless in all his ways, a servant and leader to all, pillar and bedrock of our communities. May God bless him and his family, through every challenge and every blessing, forever more.

Reverend Church graciously accepted the key, and shook the mayor's hand. He dabbed his eyes with a handkerchief and a hush fell over the church as he started to speak. For a moment, the great man's voice cracked and he took a moment. After a few seconds he gathered himself, and spoke.

"First, I want to thank each and every one of you for sharing this very special day with me," he boomed. His head was cleanly shaved, and his salt-and-pepper goatee was cleanly trimmed. He wore a pristine black suit, with wide silver pinstripes and a red, satin tie that matched the handkerchief he dabbed his eyes with again.

"Y'all know me as a man who says what he thinks, even if I say it in the most loving way possible."

A teenager yelled "Wooo!" from the back of the church, and laughter rang through the church.

Reverend Church smiled, "I'm glad you appreciate that Anthony. If anyone knows my straight shooting son, it's you." The congregation laughed again.

"The truth is," he continued, "None of this...none of these great things we do for this city, and even other cities, would be possible without the endless support and sacrifice of so many of you."

A silence fell over the church, and more than a few ladies dug into their purses for tissues.

"I look across this crowd of beautiful faces and see so many stories...so many changed lives...so much hope. I see tremendous love, and selfless service to others. Now I know we're still growing, each and every one of us, but we're a lot further than we've ever been. And this wonderful honor Mayor Greenburg has bestowed on us - and I say *us*, because I consider this key a symbol of all of our combined work - of *all* y'all's work to bring the life, light and love of God to the communities of Charlotte. So I thank you all today, and say it is the greatest privilege I could ever have dreamed of, to serve you and hopefully continue serving you for many years."

The church broke out in a roar of approval again, and everyone was back on their feet. The keyboard player let rip again and people danced, sang and shouted. After longer than he'd expected, Reverend Church was able to quiet them down.

"Now don't think you all are getting away without hearing the Word of God today." The church laughed together again, and then settled down as Reverend Church began his message.

At the back of the church, in one of the few pews that wasn't crammed full of worshippers, a man in a pure wool, meticulously tailored *Armani* suit stared intently at the Preacher. The suit was complemented by an immaculate pinstriped Egyptian cotton shirt, a sky-blue *Salvatore Ferragamo* tie and a pair of *Tanino Crisco* shoes. The man wore an expression somewhere between a smirk and a subtle snarl, as he absently twirled a *Montblanc* pen through his fingers.

As he listened to the Preacher, the man's thoughts were interrupted as the back doors of the sanctuary opened, and a disheveled, dirty, extremely tall homeless man shuffled into the building. His eyes darted around looking for a place to sit as members instantly avoided eye contact. Brother Samson, the largest usher in the church instinctively stepped forward to intercept him, but stalled when the homeless giant made a beeline for an empty space at the end of a pew in the very last row. Brother Samson wasn't sure what to do and looked at a fellow usher who just shrugged.

The homeless man sat down and didn't appear to be doing anything crazy for the time being, so the ushers exchanged an unspoken agreement to keep a close eye on him. The homeless man settled in, nodding to the people in the next pew down, who had turned around, apparently trying to locate the odor. They immediately swung their heads forward without acknowledging his presence. He then looked down to the other end of the pew and was met with a gaze of pure contempt. The homeless man held the stare of his *Armani* clad neighbor, who when they made eye contact, flinched for a second but then wouldn't back down.

The two held an intense stare for several seconds until the church doors opened again, and a young man in baggy jeans, an *X-Large* hoody and a *Nike* ball cap in one hand, walked around the end of the pew, pushed past a few people who scrambled to move their legs in time, then he flopped down next to the man in the suit.

"Gerald!" he whispered in surprise. "Good to see you, son!"

"What's up Rev?" the twenty-something held out a fist which was bumped by the older man. "What you doin' all the way in the back of the bus? Shouldn't the great Reverend Black be up front with my dad and his esteemed pastor buddies?"

"I have to leave early for another engagement, but I wanted to drop in to congratulate your dad on his special award."

"Mmm, yeah. Isn't it somethin'?" the young man snorted.

"Now, now you know he's done a lot of good work in this community," Reverend Black said, with a grin.

"Yeah, so much good work he has no time for his own kids," Gerald said acridly.

Several people in the next row down turned to see who was talking, and Reverend Black mouthed an overly sincere "Sorry."

When they had turned away again Reverend Black whispered, "You've sure gotten less... inhibited," nodding to a half jack poking out of Gerald's hoody pocket.

"Ha, oh yeah...my bad," the younger man snickered, but he tucked the bottle out of sight. Reverend Black shook his head but gave Gerald a fatherly smile.

"Gerald, I have to leave now but swing by this week. You know there's no judgment in my house."

"Oh no, Rev, I don't want to endure this service alone. Stinky over there doesn't seem like he'll be much fun?"

Gerald nodded to the homeless man, who appeared to not have heard him, as Reverend Black only let a wicked grin crack through.

Gerald wasn't done though. "What kind of riff-raff are they letting in this church these days anyway?" he demanded, as a woman in the row in front of them turned around again. Both men ignored her.

"My, oh my... soon we'll have a junkie leading choir and a hooker leading Sunday School!"

Reverend Black was still grinning but he shook his head again, and kept his cool. "You're killing me man."

Reverend Black looked past Gerald and realized the homeless man was staring at him again. This time he snarled at the man and mouthed an aggressive, "What?" The homeless man's gaze remained transfixed.

"These people are all fake anyway so who gives a rip," Gerald mocked, oblivious to the sudden moment between the two strangers.

Reverend Black, broke his gaze and chuckled, "You're crazy son, but I love you! I wish I could stay... I gotta run, but please... come and see me. Whatever you need, you can count on me. You know to always just come as you are."

"Word, you know I will Rev. I actually need to ask your advice on a business offer an associate of yours made me."

"Oh yeah, which one?" Reverend Black asked.

"The one who takes his coffee black, because he's sweet enough," Gerald replied, knowing better than to mention the man's name.

"Ah yes. Hmm...he's a heavyweight but we can talk." Gerald nodded.

They gave each other a seated man-hug and then exchanged some dap, and Reverend Black stood and left. It was Gerald's turn to catch the homeless man's gaze, who was studying him with a sad, disappointed expression.

"What's your problem?" Gerald growled. The homeless man just turned to the front of the church.

Through all of this, Reverend Church had been preaching up a storm, and his red, satin hanky was drenched as it mopped his brow.

"The church, my brothers and sisters, is a place where we ALL can come together and worship! If Christ is your savior you need to praise Him and share in your praise. You see, some of you look at church in a way that I can't understand."

He paused, to wipe another rivulet from his forehead. "Amen's" and "Preach It's" filled the silence.

"Watch your toes now... I started off wearing slippers, but now I think it's time I put my boots on."

"Preach!" someone yelled.

"Don't mind if I do, brother... some of us feel like we're better than the person that's not here, just because you are in the church. But the Lord knows what others don't know..."

"Tell it!"

"You see, the Lord knows you lied to daddy on Monday, but you-are-in-the-church. You stole from momma on Tuesday, but you-are-in-the-church. You cheated your friend on Wednesday, stepped out on your partner on Thursday but you my brethren... you-are-in-the-CHURCH. You cussed out a co-worker on Friday, hit the club on Saturday... and now you wanna come in here acting like you've been praising God all week long!"

The congregation erupted again.

Reverend Church lowered his voice, but he wasn't done. "All the while, you're convincing yourself that you're a good Christian, because you-are-in-the-church. My brothers and sisters... we have to strive to be like Jesus Christ every day of the week. We have to strive to be like Him, no matter what we suffer. No matter what life throws at us...we have to endure and stand strong as He did. Being tempted in all ways as we are, He was without sin. Let us never grow weary in doing good, and follow in the example of our great Lord and Savior. Can I get an AMEN?!" The entire church echoed an amen.

"I love y'all, that's why I would be doing you wrong if I just accepted this wonderful award, without preaching some truth. You know there's always love in this pulpit, but there's truth too. We love you, that's why we all have to help each other walk closer to Jesus."

The crowd accepted that word, and echoed their appreciation again.

Reverend Church drew the message to a loving close, then gave an altar call. Finally he offered up the benediction, then an associate pastor made an announcement inviting everyone to stay for a special lunch prepared by the members of Holy Light Christian Church. Sandra Church had already overseen the preparation of the two largest fellowship halls, which were decked out with rows of tables set and decorated with colorful flower arrangements, place settings, glasses and napkins. At the front of each hall, a row of tables presented huge, buffet-style serving trays overflowing with all kinds of mouthwatering catering. This would be a celebration for the history books.

Reverend Church and his family waded through the

crowd, trying to make their way to the back of the church. They were intercepted quickly by an exclusive list of Charlotte's who's-who, to say they had hobnobbed with the great Preacher. Reverend Church was really trying to make his way to the church doors to greet all of his church members as they left, and almost found the socialite's interruptions exasperating. He kept his patience, however, and smiled as all the immaculately dressed folk made empty promises to come back and attend his wonderful church. He had to silently wonder if they'd taken a word of his chastising to heart.

Eventually he and Sandra made it to the large, ornate church doors and the first person in line to shake hands with Reverend Church was Deacon Jeffrey Lee. Jeffery was not a deacon at Holy Light but instead served at New Day Church of Faith, under the relatively new Pastor Reverend Black. He was however, a longtime family friend of the Churches. Jeffery was six feet tall, and of medium build but a physically fit college wrestler. His mild-manner belied a meek, yet astonishing intelligence that Reverend Church had come to rely on and appreciate more than he would ever probably realize. As an accomplished programmer in a former life, Jeffery had made a small fortune by selling a QuickBooks plugin, yet he still lived modestly and gave away more than half of his monthly income. Although Jeffery had long served in a ministerial capacity at New Day, he was also Holy Light trustee, and although fifty-five years old, volunteered tirelessly to oversee many aspects of both church's ministries, including grounds work, new construction projects and most importantly, both church treasuries.. Jeffery also refused any salary from either church.

"Awesome sermon, pastor!" Deacon Lee leaned in and gave the illustrious Reverend a hug.

"Thank you my brother. You know this key belongs to you as much as it belongs to me."

"Aw not at all, you're the leader we can all get behind pastor. I'm proud to serve under you."

"It's only because of men like you, Jeff." They exchanged a joyous smile and hugged again. "Love you man!" Reverend Church said with all his heart.

Suddenly a larger than life, middle-aged woman bounced over and bumped a startled Jeffery out of the way.

"Oooh Pastor! Pastor Church! Oooh boy, you know you can preach Pastor!"

"Thank you sister Haywood." Reverend Church replied with a warm, polite smile. "I hope you catch a blessing on this wonderful day, in the name of Jesus."

"Mmm yes, I'm already blessed just being here Pastor! But I receive that!" Sister Haywood lunged in and bear-hugged the good Reverend before he could stop her. He wriggled free and patted her arm. "Sister, you better save some of this fervor for the Lord now," he said nervously, looking around desperately for his wife.

"Pastor, how would you like to come by my house this week for some of my famous fried pork chops with *aaall* the fixin's?"

"Sure! We'd love to!" Sandra popped out from behind the large lady, and winked at the mortified preacher. "We'd love to come by Sister Haywood. Do you need us to bring anything, dear sister?"

"Got CDs here! Get today's power-packed and memorable sermon already on CD. Only three dollars!" a teenager announced loudly from the Book and CD Table.

"Oooh, hey Sister Sandra! Yes, I'll be in touch with you. Oooh, you know what though? I'd better get me one of them CDs before they all get gone. Let's catch up later, mmkay?" Sister Haywood wore the expression of a kid caught red-handed trying to get at the cookie jar.

"Excellent... just let us know..." Sandra sang as Sister Haywood scuttled away surprisingly fast for her frame. Sandra turned to her husband and raised her eyebrows. He rolled his eyes and they both cracked up like teenagers.

"What *are* we going to do with her?" Reverend Church grinned. "Jeff, you okay brother? You got a concussion from that bump?"

Jeffery laughed but gave the thumbs up he was okay.

"The question is, what does she want to do with you?" Sandra said mischievously.

"Oh hush!" her husband chided.

After all the hands had been shaken, the business cards pocketed, and the backs patted, Reverend Church's three noble friends walked over to him and Sandra.

"Whoa that brother can PREACH!" A handsome, well-built man in his mid-fifties, with a light complexion and green eyes slapped hands with the Reverend, and came in for the man hug. He wore a sharp navy suit, but with a starched open collared white shirt and silver cuff links

"Tobias! Thank you for coming my brother! Representing the King in style as always!"

"As are you with that oh-so fine suit, Brother Church!" He bobbed and weaved and threw a lazy jab and a cross at the Reverend's solar plexus. Reverend Church laughed, blocked instinctively with his elbows and then slapped his friend on the back.

"Is the good Pastor Tobias Baker picking on his elders again?" a small, round man exclaimed as his dimples sank into his cheeks like two joyful wells.

"Jim, who you calling old, bro?" Reverend Church laughed and leaned down to hug his jolly friend. "Why didn't you sing today? And play us a number on the piano?"

"Well, I wasn't asked to," the round little man hung his head forlornly.

"Aw man, who scheduled the program? I can't believe we

didn't have you sing!"

"Oh please, I'm just kidding!" Bishop James Davis shushed his friend. "My throat is all hoarse anyway from shouting at your mighty message!"

"We could have had you sing before you got hoarse..." Reverend Church insisted, but grinned at his friend. "Man, I can't believe my boys are all here to have lunch with me. This is great. The astute Bishop James Davis, The mighty Pastor Tobias Baker, and certainly not least, the dignified Reverend Henry Williams!"

He looked around at his friends visibly overjoyed when Sandra spoke up.

"Well now, some pastor gets a golden key and everyone forgets their manners!"

"Oh Miss Sandra, please forgive us!" Tobias spoke quickly. "How have you been? We all know you should be the one getting a golden key for putting up with Theo's trouble every day." Reverend Church's stomach bounced as he laughed, loving the roast.

"Oh I need a whole set of keys for that!" Sandra chirped. The men roared.

"Oh God knew what he was doing when He gave you this woman!" Tobias laughed. "She's the power behind this throne." Reverend Church nodded vigorously.

"Seriously, it's so good to see you all. I'm so glad you could make it out today," Sandra smiled sincerely.

"Wouldn't miss it for the world," Reverend Williams nodded with a smile. "Our Reverend Church is something special, isn't he?"

"Indeed, he is," she agreed.

Reverend Church was still shaking his head and smiling, when he noticed something just past the parking lot. He cocked his head, and then looked to his friends and wife and asked, "Hey, can you all excuse me for a minute? Go on and grab yourselves a plate of food, I'll be right in."

"Honey? Where are you going?" Sandra asked, but he had already started walking. She looked to where he was heading and saw a homeless man sitting in the shade, against a large oak on the church's front lawn.

"Theo, mind yourself," she said in a loud whisper. She had never become used to the Reverend's instant willingness to embrace anyone and everyone he felt needed his help.

Reverend Church strolled up to the large tree to greet the shabby vagrant resting in the shade. As he approached, the man stood up and Reverend Church was taken aback at how tall he was.

"I'll be on my way. I was just tryna cool off for a minute," the man announced.

"Oh no, take your time. There's no rush," Reverend Church said gently.

"Oh... well I appreciate that!" the homeless man said, cautiously lowering himself back down.

"What's your name brother?" Reverend Church knelt down to the man's level.

The homeless man just looked away.

Reverend Church cleared his throat, but followed up with a warm "Would you like to join us for a meal? It's catered by Smoky Ray's. It's the best barbeque in the state, you know."

That got the homeless man's attention. "Oh, I don't know... maybe after everyone's left, but thank you Reverend. Many folks in there probably wouldn't appreciate it if I sat next to them."

"Oh they won't care," Reverend Church replied with a tinge of sadness. "They're good people, but regardless you can sit with my family and me." The homeless man looked off in the distance again.

"Say, I've never seen you around here before. Where are you from?"

The man looked Reverend Church square in the eyes and replied, "Heaven."

Reverend Church was caught off guard. He'd encountered mental illness often in his work with the homeless and downtrodden, but it always seemed to take him by surprise. The men looked each other in the eye for a long moment, then the homeless man broke into a slight grin. The

Reverend's eyes lit up and he started to laugh. The homeless man laughed with him.

"Did you enjoy the service?" The Reverend asked, still smiling.

"Yeah, I really enjoyed the singing at the end. A good praise team will carry you a long way."

"You're absolutely right. We have a great praise team. They're truly a blessing." The homeless man nodded, chewing his lip.

"What did you think of the sermon?" Reverend Church asked pointedly.

The man looked off into the distance again. "I think you did alright for a shepherd who still has some serious flaws."

Reverend Church flinched, trying not to show he'd taken offense. Before he could stop himself he replied, "Well maybe we can grab lunch sometime, and you can give me some tips?"

"It won't be me Reverend, but the Lord will send a counselor when your heart is ready, and the time is right."

Reverend Church was rarely speechless, but he suddenly found himself off balance by the homeless man's articulate conversation and direct opinion. The man stared off into the distance again and Reverend Church had a sense the conversation was over.

"Well it was good to speak with you friend." He extended his hand.

"Likewise," the man replied, and shook the Reverend's hand.

"If I can't persuade you to come and eat with us, I'll send someone out with a couple of plates of food and a to-go cup?" Reverend Church made one last attempt.

"Gabe," the man replied.

"I'm sorry?" Reverend Church replied, confused.

"The name's Gabe."

"Ah..." Reverend Church recovered quickly. "Well very good to meet you Gabe! And please come back and see us."

"I sure will Reverend."

Reverend Church nodded, almost in amusement then turned and started walking back to the church. He suddenly realized how hungry he was, yet his mind raced with the homeless man's strange words.

"Reverend!"

He spun around.

"How strong is your faith?"

"My faith?" The Reverend was confused.

"In God. How strong is your faith?"

Reverend Church raised his fist and clenched it tightly.
"Solid as a rock, my friend. Solid as a rock."

The homeless man narrowed his eyes slightly, and stared at the preacher. For an instant the Reverend thought he saw a trace of what appeared like sympathy on the man's face, but he was already too far away to be sure. He kept his fist in the air for a moment, then turned back to the church and kept walking.

3

THE BEGINNING OF SORROWS

"Mom, any more food and this table is going to break in half!" Tavaris protested. He widened his eyes dramatically at the piles of food shaking his dreadlocks back and forth.

"Oh please, don't tell me you're not going to eat half your own weight in protein alone," Sandra rubbed her youngest sons head. She searched for room on the table to place the two pitchers of lemonade. Dishes of roast beef, grilled chicken, macaroni and cheese, potato salad, green beans, okra and bread covered almost every inch of the table.

"Ma, there's no room for these table settings?" Jewel asked, jumping on the bandwagon with her younger brother.

"Oh just find some room!" Sandra scolded her middle child loudly, taking the bait. Tavaris laughed at his partner in crime, who giggled back.

"Hey, how about you two helping your mother out instead of harassing her!" Reverend Church boomed, from the head of the table, covering a smile of his own. He absolutely loved family time.

"I'm looking for room y'all but we're apparently too blessed!" Jewel laughed.

The Reverend shook his head. "Hey now, we should never take our blessings for granted. Not even jokingly. Tavaris, help your sister clear some places for these settings." Tavaris drooped his broad shoulders as if the oppression was too much to bear, but obeyed his dad and started clearing some room.

Jewel's beautiful face lit up as she heard the front door open.

"Honey! You made it! How did you get off so early on a Monday night?" she said, as her husband walked into the dining room. She pounced on him and threw her arms around her man's neck. Dexter could have been a real lady-killer if he wasn't so mild-mannered. He was good-looking, without an ounce of fat on him, but by nature he was an analytical man. Everything about him screamed "conservative."

Dexter wore thin, executive-looking glasses every day and his hair was perfectly cropped in a side path. Even though work did not require it, he dressed in a collar and tie every single day.

"Ooh, I just love this new vest my babe!" she crooned, pointing at the tartan threads. "I'm so glad you're home!"

"Hey angel!" he said, kissing his wife. "I finished up those numbers on the Livingston account early. Just for you girl!"

"Awww!" she blushed, and took him by the hand to the table.

"Evening Rev!" Dexter greeted Reverend Church with a broad smile.

"Glad you could make it son," the Reverend smiled.

"Me too!" he said, eyeing the mountain of food hungrily.

"Tavaris, what's up man?"

"Aw you know... just keeping my chill like I do bro," Tavaris slapped hands with Dexter and bumped his fist.

"Of course! Man, have you bulked up even more? You're not juicing are you?" Dexter joked.

"He better not even think about using that garbage!" Reverend Church interjected sternly.

"Don't you see all this food right here? I just turn it into pure muscle, baby!" Tavaris flexed a large bicep and Jewel rolled her eyes.

"So what's the scholarship situation T? Who's looking good?"

"I don't know man. South Carolina wants me to play baseball and football."

Dexter nodded and raised his eyebrows. "Nice!"

"U.C.L.A called him last week, but I told him to forget it," Sandra announced as she walked in from the kitchen, carrying a steaming apple pie. "There's no way my baby is moving across the country."

"Mrs. C!" Dexter greeted his mother-in-law as he moved to clear some room for her to put the pie.

"Hey Dexter! I'm so glad you could make it."

"Wouldn't miss it for the world," he smiled.

Sandra placed the apple pie on the table, then tottered slightly, staggering into Tavaris' chair. Dexter and Jewel sprung forward to steady her, but Tavaris caught her. "Whoa, mom are you okay?" Tavaris asked, fear flashing in his eyes.

Reverend Church rose up out of his chair, but Sandra found her feet and patted Tavaris' hand.

"I'm fine, I'm fine," she said placing a hand to her head. "Just have a headache, and got a little dizzy is all."

Tavaris and Jewel exchanged glances, and then looked at
their dad. Reverend Church averted his eyes, then looked
up at Sandra.

"Mom, you've had these headaches for weeks now. Have
you been to the doctor yet?" Jewel asked quietly.

"Yes honey, I've been to the doctor. I'm going for tests in
the morning. Don't you worry about me, okay?"

"How can we not worry?" Tavaris exclaimed, standing up
and dwarfing his mom. He wrapped her in his huge arms
and hugged her gently.

"Everything will be fine, you all," Reverend Church said.
"God is good, and your mom is fine. Maybe it's something in
her diet. A deficiency or something. She'll be fine. God is
good."

"Amen," Dexter nodded and Jewel and Tavaris echoed him.

"Anyway! Getting back to Tavaris' scholarship..." Reverend
Church tried to change the subject. "We all just need to
trust him to make the right choice. I'm sure he wouldn't
break his mother's heart by moving halfway around the
world." Sandra smiled, and walked back to the kitchen.
Reverend Church's eyes followed his wife, making sure she
was ok.

"Oh! This coming from the man who practically forged my
signature for medical school?" Jewel snorted.

"Hey now... let's just say I knew intuitively what you really
wanted honey," The Reverend said, suppressing a smirk.

"And I would say that you love it and it's paying off. Dexter
couldn't afford that huge house you're building, on his
own!"

Everyone looked at Dexter, who had just happened to
snatch a piece of bread while they were all distracted, and
had stuffed it in his mouth.

Tavaris laughed loudly, covering his mouth and pointing,
"AAHAHA BUSTED, YO!"

"Whatever man," Dexter mumbled through hamster cheeks. Reverend Church's considerable belly bounced as he squeezed his eyes shut and cracked up with Tavaris.

"Oh leave the poor man alone!" Sandra chided but she was also smiling. "Dexter could be the president if he wanted to."

"Thanks Mom!" Dexter mumbled again, swallowing as Jewel giggled but scratched his back.

"Okay, okay let's give thanks to our Father before anyone else's hunger drives them to theft," Reverend Church chuckled, not letting his son-in-law off the hook that easily. "It's okay Dexter, but you know the Word says if the thief is caught he has to pay sevenfold."

"Okay Rev... how much will seven pieces of ciabatta run me?" Dexter grumbled, finally swallowing the last of the dry bread.

"Oh the last thing we need is more bread bro!" Tavaris taunted. "But you can rinse the dishes and load the washer!" Everyone cackled again.

"Hahaha," Dexter faked amusement.

"Okay, leave my husband be you all. He's worked hard today, and he's entitled to an *hors d'oeuvres*." Jewel batted her almond eyes at Dexter, and he instantly forgot his tormentors.

"Besides, we're really appreciative we can stay with you all until our dream home is built BUT don't harass him too much or we won't let you come over and watch movies in our state-of-the-art home theater!"

"Oh you mean come over and whip him at Madden on his own state-of-the-art turf?" Tavaris jabbed.

Dexter was about to be roped into an all-night video game challenge when the Reverend wisely intercepted, "Alright, everyone grab their seat, and let's join hands."

Tavaris was still grinning wickedly but they all gathered around the table, and joined hands.

"Dear heavenly Father, thank you for this wonderful food, the beautiful hands that prepared it, and for my precious family. We love you and appreciate all you have done for us. We ask You to lead and guide us in all our decisions, and we trust You to continue providing for us in all areas. Our strong faith in You will lead us through any and all trials. In Jesus' name we pray. Amen"

Everyone *Amened* loudly and wasted no time diving into the food.

"So honey, how did *your* tests go today?" Sandra asked Jewel.

"What do you mean?" Jewel said, flipping her shiny, long hair.

"You know what I mean," Sandra replied pointedly.

"HEY how about this lame weather huh? I hope it doesn't rain tomorrow." Tavaris interjected. "I don't wanna miss any more football practice."

"Sandra..." Reverend Church furrowed his eyebrows at his wife.

"I'm just asking," Sandra defended herself. "I'm concerned about my daughter. And her husband."

"Aw... do we have to do this now?" Tavaris complained.

Sandra looked at her plate, and just chewed her food, but Dexter took her hand and squeezed it gently.

"You can tell your mom," he said.

"Tell me what?" Now Sandra definitely wasn't going to let up.

"The tests came back negative again... and Jewel says she is done taking the pills and fertility shots," Dexter announced like a five year-old telling on his girlfriend.

"Whaaat?" Sandra cried in dismay.

"You got a big mouth, you know that?" Jewel said to him.

"I'm just trying to get some help in talking sense to you," Dexter shrugged.

"Look, the doctor even admitted after these tests that the chances are slim to none, okay? Even if I take a thousand shots."

"Jewel, honey, is that true?" Reverend Church asked softly. Jewel was looking down at the table again but nodded.

"Now now," Reverend Church spoke, and everyone became quiet. "Just use what they say as information only. We know who the Great Physician is, so you know who to talk to."

"That's right," Jewel muttered, her moist eyes narrowing at Dexter.

"Yeah, but we've been praying for so long. She needs to keep taking those shots," Dexter replied sullenly. "Success may be around the corner."

Reverend Church sighed and rubbed his face, but looked over at Dexter with compassion. He was weighing up what to say when the front door opened.

Everyone looked at the hallway as Gerald walked into the dining room, wearing baggy *Ralph Lauren* jeans and the ripped and bloody tatters of a *Dangerous Elite* t-shirt.

"Oh yeah, I forgot you all were having your family thing tonight."

"Gerald! Oh my God, what happened to your face?" Sandra cried, as she rushed to touch his swollen cheek. Gerald pulled away roughly, and looked around the room saying nothing but slowly took an *Altoid* mint box out of his pocket, and popped one in his mouth.

"I'm good, Ma! Don't sweat it."

"You don't look like you're good," Reverend Church replied, studying the cuts and swelling on the young man's face.

"That hustlin' caught up with ya today?" Dexter prodded.

"You oughta check yourself Carlton," Gerald said without even looking at Dexter.

"Honey, we need to get you to a hospital right now! Tell me what happened!" Sandra was on the verge of hysteria, visibly restraining herself from touching her sons face again.

"Nah, I told you I'm fine. Bernice already took care of me. I just came to pick up some clothes."

"You're running with Bernice again?" Reverend Church said, irritation building in his voice.

"Ah see and you all wonder why I don't do these cheery family dinners. You should call 'em Spanish Inquisition dinners. Or maybe Divine Judgment dinners."

"Gerald! Don't test my patience boy. Tell me now. What happened to you? Who did that?"

"I fell off my bicycle." The young man threw a fake smile.

"You haven't had a bicycle since you were sixteen Gerald," Sandra replied naively.

"Oh yeah, I forgot," he said sarcastically.

"Boy..." Reverend Church said putting his hands on the side of his chair. "Don't make me come up out of this chair." Gerald just squinted and gave a small nod to no-one. "Oh don't get up. I won't be joining you."

"Man, why can't you just be chill and hang out with your family for a change?" Tavaris said with uncharacteristic stress and fear in his voice. "Why you always gotta bring the drama? We care about you, man. Just believe that."

"Yeah... you love me with the love of the Lord right? But how about the *acceptance* of a family?"

"Oh Gerald, you know that's not true," Jewel replied, dabbing her eyes. "You can't come in here all broken up and expect us not to be concerned."

"I guess my life is just too full of drama for you all," he sniped. "Like I said, don't sweat it. I'll grab some leftovers from the happy meal later." He swaggered out, and they heard him clomping up the stairs.

"What are we going to do Theo? Did you see his face?" Sandra's voice quivered with grief.

"That looked like a pistol whippin' from where I'm sitting," Dexter chirped.

"Dude! Not now man," Tavaris chided. "We all got problems okay, and everyone's already stressed."

"I'm just saying..." he mumbled.

They all turned to Reverend Church to hear the verdict. He was sitting with his elbows on the table, and his hands over his face. After several seconds of uncomfortable silence he rubbed his face hard, and then slowly opened his eyes.

"We need to pray. We need to pray hard for this family. I refuse to let Satan tear us apart. We need to pray for whatever is causing Gerald to go astray, to be defeated and for him to return to God. We need to pray for Jewel to overcome these - infertility issues, and..." He paused and clenched his jaw. "...for your mother's test results to come back completely normal."

Jewel bowed her head, and Tavaris nodded. Dexter just looked down at the table. Sandra, fighting back tears, put her hand on Reverend Church's shoulder and whispered "Amen."

"Alright. I guess that's that. Thank you Sandra for the delicious dinner. You're a true Proverbs thirty-one woman." Reverend Church stood up and hugged his wife, who buried her head in his shoulder and whimpered, unable to hold back the tears.

Tavaris stood up and hugged his mom, while Jewel and Dexter got up too and without a word, began clearing the table.

***

After helping her mom clear and load the dishes in the dishwasher, Jewel walked upstairs and opened her bedroom door. Dexter was flopped on the bed, still in his work clothes and typing on his phone.

Jewel kicked off her shoes, and slid up next to Dexter.

"You've got a big mouth Mr. Fertility Shots," she whispered in his ear.

Dexter put down his phone, and then turned to look into his wife's eyes. He stroked a lock of hair behind her ear. "I just figured your mom may be able to talk some sense into you."

"I've got plenty of sense honey. I'm just so tired of taking pills and getting stuck with needles." She inhaled deeply and tilted her head wearily. "What's the rush anyway? We're young. We have some time."

"I know, but I'm worried. If you don't do what the doctor asks you to now, you may never be able to fall pregnant."

"Oh, Dexter. It'll happen." Jewel stroked his arm gently.

Dexter's face dropped and he pulled away roughly, turning on his side, staring at the wall.

"What?" Jewel asked in surprise.

"I understand we have to have faith..." he said.

"But?" she asked, anticipating a condition.

"But I believe God also wants us to have common sense." He felt Jewel deflate, so he turned back to her. "You're infertile! You need the shots. Take the freaking shots!"

"So because I'm tired of being poked and feeling sick from these pills and because I believe God can give us a child without all that, I have no common sense?"

"Oh boy... here we go. You know that's not what I meant."

"That's what you said."

"You know what? I can't do this tonight. I've had a hell of a day, and you just want to argue." He swung his feet off the bed, slipped his shoes on and then stood up and grabbed his jacket from the dresser.

"Where do you think you're going?" Jewel frowned.

"To Nate's. Don't wait up." He walked toward the door.

"Dexter! Please... you can't just run away from this."

"Oh I'm not running. I tried discussing it but you just want to talk in circles, so I'm heading out for some fresh air."

He walked out of the door, didn't look back and shut it behind him.

Jewel stared at the closed door as her mouth creased up and her sadness turned to anger. She turned and fell into her pillow, cuffing it aggressively.

4

GOD AND MAMMON

Reverend Church rolled his chair back from his large, oak desk, and blinked. His home office was usually a place of solitude and uninterrupted focus, but he hadn't slept well, and his double espresso wasn't kicking in. He contemplated chugging another, but decided to heed his wife's chidings. *I have to be missing something* he thought, as he stared at Holy Light's online banking. Two huge transactions didn't make sense.

Tuesday mornings were Reverend Church's admin time, and everyone knew it. Through his years of ministry he'd learned that no matter how busy a shepherd is, the most dangerous thing he could do to his flock was neglect even a fundamental understanding of the ministry's finances and operations. It was the easiest way to lose control, and in time, it guaranteed being blindsided. It had happened once when he was younger, and the fallout almost ruined him. He swore it would never happen again, but some Tuesdays were undoubtedly more challenging than others.

   He picked up the landline's receiver and long-pressed the number two key, the phone responding by speed dial.

"Good morning Reverend!"

"Jeffrey! How are you, my friend?"

"Just getting out of my prayer time, so I'm on top the world brother. How about you?"

"Well... I'm not sure yet. Have you happened to see the *First National* account this morning?"

"Not yet. Is something wrong?"

"I'm looking over the First National account and there has been a transfer of $42,000 out of the account."

Deacon Jeffery paused. "What? When? I checked the account yesterday morning, figuring up payroll and even wrote some checks for the youth building contractors..."

"Dear Lord... so you haven't moved the money to another account or something?"

"Heck no. I wouldn't do that without clearing it with you Pastor."

"I know you wouldn't but I have been busy lately..."

Reverend Church was silent for a second thinking of what to say next. "Jeff, this is bad. This is really bad."

"Have you gone through the account details?" Jeffery asked with the first trace of panic in his voice. "Are there any line items that show a withdrawal or fund move? It has to be a mistake?"

Reverend Church sighed. "I was hoping so but there are two unusual line items. Both say only *International Wire*, and the first is for $42,000 and the second is for $108,000."

"You're kidding me? Are there any more details other than *International Wire*?"

"Nope. Not that I can see online. I wanted to call you before I called the bank."

"Okay, I'm headed straight over to the office to take a look."

"Okay... Jeff, you know this cleans us out. This could sink the church if we can't recover this money?" "Oh, believe me, I know... but let's see if we can figure it out."
"You're right... I don't mean to panic. There has to be some explanation. The Lord wouldn't let that happen to us."
"Whew... let's hope not Reverend." Jeffery groaned. "Say, have you said anything to Sister Willis yet?"
"No, you're the first person I've spoken to." Reverend Church sighed. "Who oversaw the counting on Sunday?"
"It was Sister Willis this last Sunday. We're still switching every other week. I counted the Sunday before."
"And she deposited the cash and checks?"
"Yeah..."
"Hmm.... okay. Jeff, can you please find out who all knew the balance of that account? Those withdrawals were clearly based on some knowledge of what was in the account. I know you'll be discrete. I never want to point any fingers prematurely, but even more so, I never want to neglect due diligence in stewardship either."
"Absolutely Reverend. And I just had a thought..." Jeffery paused.
"Go ahead..."
"Well... I've thought for a while now, we need to begin auditing all of our books....and employees."
"Speak clearly brother." Reverend Church was not one to waste time.
"When last did Sister Willis take a vacation?"
"Hmm..." Reverend Church pondered that for a second. "I know she took a few days about six months ago, but I don't believe it was a full week. Now that you mention it, I

actually can't remember when last she took a good chunk of time off. I certainly don't recall anyone filling in for her duties." The fact hung in the air like a dark cloud, neither man wanting to say it.

"Well, I never want to insinuate anything either, but I think we should consider who else - if anyone - has access to even the balance of that account, and meet with them. I place myself on that list too Reverend." Deacon Lee spoke softly, but with a conviction and firmness.

"Yeah... that's probably a good idea." Reverend Church sighed. "Okay, thanks. Listen, why don't the three of us meet in about an hour?"

"Okay Rev you got it." Jeffery exhaled loudly. "Oh, one more thing..."

"Yeah?"

"It would probably be a good idea not to schedule the meeting either..." Jeffery waited, confident Reverend Church would catch his meaning.

"I agree."

"So Rev, you're at home now?"

"Yep. But I'll head over to the church now."

"Sister Willis is working today right?"

"Yeah. At least she should be."

"Okay, I'll see you in a bit."

"See you then."

Reverend Church hung up and stared at his laptop screen, trying to ignore the sinkhole in his belly. After a few seconds he stood up to get that second double espresso. As he did, his vision narrowed into a tunnel, and he staggered. "Daddy!" Jewel cried, running to steady him. He tottered sideways and was going down but managed to get a knee onto his armchair, his weight driving the chair back into the wall. Jewel caught his arm and stabilized him, but her eyes were wide with fright.

"Dad!" she said again. "Are you okay?"

Reverend Church took a few deep breaths and then rubbed her hand. "I'm okay angel. I'm okay."

"What happened?" she said not moving away from him. Reverend Church rubbed his face again, and took another deep breath. "Aw I think I just stood up too quickly," he said. "Just a head rush I think."

Jewel's face said she wasn't convinced. "That looked like a little more than a head rush! Let me check your pulse..."

"No I'm fine honey... don't sweat it." He patted her hand again, stood up straight and walked over to his desk. "What's up?" he asked, trying to change the focus.

"I was going to ask if you wanted a sandwich. I'm uh... making one for mom." She eyed her dad with lingering concern.

"No thanks. I'm not feeling too hungry. Plus, I still have a good few pounds to burn from Sunday," he smiled.

Jewel smiled weakly. "Okay. Let me know if you change your mind."

"Listen, I have to run down to the church for a while. If you're not called in to the hospital, please keep an eye on your mom."

"You should be taking two full days off daddy! I'm heading over to see Dexter in an hour or so, but I will keep an eye on her and she'll be fine."

Jewel kissed her dad on the cheek, still worried, but he grinned like the Cheshire Cat.

"Love you angel. I'll be back soon."

Reverend Church was just pulling up to the church when his cell phone rang. He glanced down and saw it was from Jeffery. He decided not to take the call, and just talk to his deacon in person, but as he parked he noticed a black Chevy Tahoe right at the entrance. The plates were government issued. The Reverend's mind whirred for a few seconds, then he said a quiet prayer before getting out of the car. He took a deep breath and walked inside.

"Reverend!" Sister Taylor, the church receptionist's eyes were filled with apprehension. "I was just about to call you."

"It's okay Sister," he replied somberly. "FBI?"

Sister Taylor nodded, looking scared. "How did you know?"

"Hunch," he grimaced.

The Reverend poked his head into Jeffery's office, but he was nowhere to be seen.

He walked over to Sister Willis' office. The door was closed, so he knocked and then opened it. Seated in front of her desk were two men in dark suits, while Jeffery and Sister Willis sat behind her desk.

"Good morning! Seems like I almost missed the party!" The Reverend smiled.

"Reverend Church, Jeffery told us you were on your way in..." Sister Willis said quickly. She looked very nervous but her body language was a touch defiant. As always, Sister Willis' appearance was pristine. Her hair was quaffed immaculately, in a short but stylish cut, tinted slightly auburn. Today she was wearing her *Hugo Boss* glasses, with the thick black frames. She liked to switch up between those and her tortoise-shell *Burberrys*. She was also dressed to the nines as usual, wearing a silk blouse printed with giant colorful flowers, and several pieces of tasteful gold on her fingers and around her neck.

"Reverend this is agent Jameson and agent Willoughby. They're with the FBI." Sister Willis announced.

"I tried to call you Theo," Jeffery interjected.

Reverend Church nodded, and kept smiling. "I'm assuming this about our missing funds?"

"You're aware that funds are missing?" agent Jameson asked with casual suspicion. His face was freckled and muscular and his dark orange hair was close-cropped and square, military style.

"As of this morning, yes. Tuesdays are my admin day," Reverend Church replied.

"Any reason you haven't reported the missing funds Mr. Church?" agent Willoughby asked. He had a friendly face, but his tone suggested otherwise.

Reverend Church raised his eyebrows. "Wow, I'm not sure I appreciate your tone Agent... Willoughby was it?"

"There's nothing in my tone," the agent smiled. "We're just here to ask questions."

Jeffery stared at the man but kept his cool. "Here's a question...when did *you* notice the missing funds Sister Willis?"

"Now you listen here Jeffrey," she began, but the Reverend cut her off.

"Okay folks, the last thing we need is for anyone to begin pointing fingers and fighting. I'm sure the good agents here will soon figure out what has happened, and hopefully who is responsible."

Sister Willis nodded, and cleared her throat.

"Okay, well just so we're clear, I noticed the missing funds about forty-five minutes ago and called my treasurer, Jeffery over here," he gave an exaggerated nod to Jeffery . "And I was on my way in to discuss the issue with him and our bookkeeper, Sister Willis."

The two agents glanced at each other and then looked over at Sister Willis. "Sister... uh... Miss Willis," agent Jameson said. "When did you become aware of the missing funds?"

"Last night," she said.

"So why did you wait to report the funds missing this morning?"

"Because I figured the FBI was closed after business hours... I don't know?"

Jeffery gave an *Oh come on*, expression but Reverend Church maintained a poker face. "Why didn't you call me, Mary?" Reverend Church asked quietly.

Her defiant look returned, but she addressed the agents. "Well, I wasn't sure what to do, since the only people authorized to make wire transfers are..."

Jeffery cut her off, "The Reverend, myself and *you*. And you know we have a two-person rule for any withdrawals over five thousand dollars." Sister Willis tilted her head to the side and raised her eyebrows.

"Okay everyone, relax. No-one's a suspect...yet," Agent Willoughby spoke up. "Again, we're just asking questions at this point."

"Agent Willoughby," Reverend Church said quietly. "May I ask how you were aware of this crime so quickly?"

The agent nodded at Reverend Church, "The wire was sent to the *First Caribbean International Bank*, on the Grand Cayman Island. We're getting more information from the Cayman bank, the transfer was sent to an account we have uh...red-lighted."

"Red-lighted? For what?" Jeffery asked more loudly than he intended

"For money laundering..." Agent Jameson spoke up with an accusing frown. "And they say the withdrawal was signed for by two authorized parties...so they have to hold the funds until we can prove otherwise."

"What? Which two authorized parties?" Reverend Church exclaimed.

"Well that would be you two gentlemen." Agent Jameson responded flatly.

"WHAT?" Jeffery cried. "There's no way. We don't even know about this account, and that would require I.Ds and signatures for both of us."

Agent Willoughby eyed Jeffery carefully for a moment, then said, "The wire was authorized with digital signatures."

"You're kidding me?" Jeffery replied.

"Nope. Not kidding." Agent Jameson said smugly.

"Agents Jameson and Willoughby," Reverend Church took a deep breath and then continued. "Do you really believe that Jeffery and I would embezzle a hundred-and-fifty thousand dollars like this... our church's entire operating fund? With our own digital signatures, and then stick around and wait for the fallout? Think about it?"

"We don't know what happened Mister Church," agent Jameson said eyeing the Reverend. "Things get screwed up all the time. That's why we're here. What we know is Miss Willis here noticed the funds missing this morning, and then called the bank, who are required to report an amount this large to us. Yes we had actually red-flagged the transfer, so here we are. Now I guarantee we will figure out who took this money. The question is, how cooperative is everyone going to be?"

Reverend Church closed his eyes for a second and leaned his head back. He breathed in deeply and exhaled every last ounce of the air out of his lungs. While he did this he counted silently to five. Then he spoke. "Agent Jameson, with all due respect...you're coming into my church, saying you're just investigating but your attitude tells me otherwise. You've implied more than once that my treasurer and I are guilty in the case of this missing money, and quite frankly I expected a lot more from government agents. I *assure* you I want this money returned to the church - in fact, we'll sink without it. If you know anything about my reputation, you'll know I've served this church for decades. I also assure you, any and all church employees will cooperate with you as far as possible. If you don't mind however, I would like to have a word alone with my staff. If that is not suitable to you, I will continue this discussion through our attorney."

The two men stared at Reverend Church for several seconds then agent Jameson smirked at his partner. "Fair enough," he said and slowly stood up. Reverend Church stepped out of the doorway into the hall, and ushered them out.

"Sister Taylor at reception will get you coffee or a pastry if you're hungry, gentlemen," Reverend Church said congenially. Then he walked into the office and closed the door.

"Sister Willis? Can you please explain to me what exactly is going on?"

"Reverend, I didn't know what to think! I saw the money missing last night, then I called the bank first thing this morning and then they said someone will be contacting us shortly. Next thing I know the FBI shows up." She had eased up on the defensiveness but was still on edge.

"It slipped your mind to call your Pastor?" Jeffery asked, his eyes bored into hers.

"Jeff, the bank said the wire was authorized by you and Reverend Church. What was I supposed to think?"

"You only spoke to the bank this morning, Sister Willis. Why didn't you call me last night?" Reverend Church asked, somehow still maintaining a non-accusing tone.

"Reverend I figured it had to be some kind of mistake, and didn't want to bother you at home. I figured I'd check it out this morning, and I'd tell you if something was amiss." Her voice had become a little louder.

"I don't know Mary... something just doesn't feel right," Jeffery said, shaking his head slowly but keeping his eyes on her.

"Oh here we go with your hyper-righteous 'God is talking to me' babble," she replied, her face twisting into a scowl.

"Sister Willis! That is no way to talk to a brother in Christ, especially one that has been called to serve," Reverend Church rebuked her sharply. "Now, no-one is accusing anyone else of anything. What I am going to do however, is remove our access to all bank accounts - yes, that includes me - and assign our attorney as executors over the church's financial matters until I deem it fit to return access."

"What? Why would you do that? How are we going to pay bills? Receive offerings?" Sister Willis threw her hands in the air. Jeffery narrowed his eyes while watching her.

"Mary, there really isn't any money left to pay any bills is there?" Jeffery replied. "And you can bet your bottom dollar, we'll be making some changes at the offering counting and deposit."

"Oh, now I'm stealing offerings?" Sister Willis waved her hand dramatically.

"Jeffery is correct," Reverend Church replied. "We will be making some changes all around. For now, I want to cooperate with the FBI, but something in my gut tells me we should be engaging the services of our attorney, Mr. Lewin and his team while this investigation continues."

"I'll get him on the phone," Jeffery said, and began to get up.

"Uhh... if it's just you all under investigation, should you be using a church member as an attorney?" Sister Willis said quickly.

For the first time Reverend Church squinted at her, and didn't answer for a few seconds. Just as Sister Willis opened her mouth to speak again he said, "Sister Willis, you can be assured that everyone who touches that accounting system, and our bank accounts will be under investigation. On that you have my word."

"That's fine," she replied. "Whatever. I sure have nothing to hide. Heck, we were obviously hacked, or scammed or something."

"Mmm," Jeffery said with a last look at her as he got up, and walked out the door. Reverend Church followed him, leaving Sister Willis in the office.

"We need to pray Jeff. We really need to pray. This could be bad. Something just feels really wrong."

"I know boss. I will be hitting my knees shortly. You okay?"

"Yeah, I'm good. But get Lewin on the line and have him send someone down here pronto okay?"

"You got it Rev."

Reverend Church walked to the reception area with his treasurer. Agent Willoughby was munching on a giant Danish and holding a coffee mug with a printed *Holy Light* logo, and caught a glimpse of Jeffery walking back to his office, "Yo! Where is he off to?"

"Agent Willoughby, I have all the respect in the world for the FBI, and we are going to cooperate with your investigation by all means possible. Jeffery is going to call our attorney now to speak with you further, and to name their accounting team as executors over our financial affairs until this investigation is done. Myself, Sister Willis and Jeffery will have our access removed to all accounts and Holy Light accounting software as well within the hour."

Agent Willoughby gave a snort, through a mouthful of pastry. He took a big swig of coffee and then nodded, smiling. "Wow. I can see why your reputation precedes you.

I knew you were hailed as a holy man, I didn't realize you were shrewd too."

"Well, believe it or not, I do try to follow the tenet of being wise as a serpent, and harmless as a dove."

Agent Willoughby smiled again. "I like that... wise as a serpent, harmless as a dove. I really like that! Let's hope the harmless part is true, right?"

Reverend Church just looked at him with tired eyes.

"Okay Reverend, we'll wait until your lawyer gets here, and then we can talk more. But as holy or as shrewd as you are... don't you or any of your accounting staff leave town anytime soon okay?"

The agent winked at Reverend Church and stuffed the rest of the Danish into his mouth.

5

TROUBLE IN PARADISE

Dexter sat at his large mahogany desk, frowning at one of his dual twenty-one inch monitors in concentration, and tapped furiously on the number pad of his keyboard. The shelves on the opposite wall were matching mahogany and lined with all sorts of books on number theory, statistical analysis and risk control. A rich, burgundy sofa lined one wall with an Afghan rug adorning the carpet in front of it.

Two brief knocks rapped at the door, to which Dexter replied, "Come in!"

"Surprise baby!" Jewel sang as she poked her head in.

Dexter looked up in surprise. He smiled and finished his calculation quickly, then hit Control and S on his keyboard.

"Hey! What have I done to deserve a visit from my beautiful wife?" he asked, scooping his hand around her waist and pulling her into a hug.

"Oh I just thought I would surprise my honey with some real food for lunch," she said holding the basket up to his nose.

"This right here... you can't buy in a restaurant! Smell that, buddy!"

"Oh girl! That smells delicious," he said following his wife to the sofa like a puppy. "Did you make that?" he asked.

"Boy you know Mama made this!" she flirted, putting the basket on the coffee table.

"Well I sure appreciate it," he smiled as he kissed her on the cheek and then pulled away to inspect the basket.

Jewel pulled him back. "Thank you babe."

"For what?"

"For the kiss, silly. You've been so busy lately. It feels good to be close to you." She tilted her head to one side and brushed his hair with her fingers. Suddenly the door swung open.

"Dex, you wanna grab some lu-" A young blonde, with a short, flowery and very low cut dress burst into the office. Instinctively, Dexter and Jewel broke their embrace.

"Oh I'm sorry... I didn't realize..."

"It's okay Kathy. Come on in," Dexter said straightening his tie. "Jewel this is Kathy, one of my colleagues. We work on a few projects together. Kathy, this is my wife, Jewel."

"Oh hi!" Kathy said as if she were catching up with her best friend. "Dex talks about you all the time."

"He does, does he?" Jewel asked with a snip of attitude.

"*Dex*, you didn't tell me you had a new co-worker?"

"Yeah, uh... JT moved on and Kathy has taken his spot. We were really lucky to get her on such short notice. She's highly qualified." He regretted his words the moment they spilled out of his mouth.

"Aw, thank you Dex. Isn't he just a teddy bear?" Kathy batted her eyelids.

Jewel raised her eyebrows, and Dexter had a sudden urge to crawl under the desk.

"But I'm sorry! I didn't mean to intrude. I was just gonna invite Dex to lunch. Why don't we all go?" Kathy sang.

"Actually Jewel brought lunch," Dexter wisely replied before his wife could.

"Aww... okay, well maybe I'll just grab a salad or something," Kathy said, exaggerating a sad face.

Dexter looked into the basket, and reverting to his less wise self, he blurted, "Well, maybe there's enough here for all of us?" Kathy's face lit up, and Dexter turned right into the polar opposite expression worn by Jewel.

"Uhh..." Dexter said, slightly terrified and looking back in the basket. "Oh, you know what...I may have misjudged how much there was... and you know I have such a huge appetite," he laughed nervously. "Maybe we'll have to do it another time."

"Aw, really?" Kathy's pouty face returned.

"Yeah, we'll all plan something," Dexter said as he tried to usher her out of the office. Jewel was still shocked.

"Okay... well let me know," Kathy said. "Oh and Jewel, good luck with the baby situation," she said with a heartfelt smile. "I know how brutal it must be to be infertile."

Jewel's jaw dropped open, and she turned to Dexter who now wore an expression of sheer terror.

Kathy wasn't done though. "I mean, I'm not infertile, so I guess I don't actually know how tough it must be," she babbled looking up at the ceiling pondering the thought. "Gosh, I think I'm *overly* fertile," she giggled. "But I do have friends with that same problem. So I really sympathize."

"Oh Lord Jesus help me!" Dexter whispered.

"If you ever nee-" Kathy began again, but Dexter practically pushed her out of the office.

"Thanks so much Kathy! I'll catch up with you later!" he said, and closed the door.

Jewel stared at her husband with a mixture of rage and disappointment. "You told her about my personal life?" she said hoarsely.

"Well... no. Sort of?" Dexter replied, trying to gauge which answer would be least likely to cause him physical harm. "She asked if we had kids and I said we're trying..."

Jewel looked out the large window, shook her head and straightened her skirt. She then picked up the lunch basket and walked to the door.

"Aw c'mon babe. Don't do that. What am I gonna eat?" Dexter protested. "Stop, let's talk about this."

"I'm sure you and Miss Fertile can figure something out. After all, you're very lucky to have her.... *Dex*!" Jewel stormed out before Dexter could respond, slamming the door behind her. She tried to ignore the stares of the cubicle staff, and marched to the elevator. She prayed desperately that God would make sure that Kathy creature was nowhere near her exit path. The last thing she needed was jail time.

Dexter flopped into his chair deflated, and threw his head back, staring at the ceiling. "Why Lord? Why me?" he asked. He looked down, and then pulled a magnet out of his drawer, and dialed the number on it.

"Mario's Pizza, home of the Mighty Meat Supreme. Will this be pickup or delivery?"

"Delivery...."

***

Tavaris lay on his rumpled bed staring at the black skid marks on his vaulted ceiling. He dropped his gaze, and squinted at the far wall then flipped the sponge basketball in a high arc, sending it sailing through the air, swishing perfectly through the wall-mounted net.

"That's seven in a row baby! All air, yo!"

Tavaris frowned at his buddy, Smoke. "Dude I can hit a hundred like that."

"A *hundred*?! Aw it's on! You hit a hundred and I'll..." Smoke looked around the room. "I'll help you clean up this bomb shelter."

"A bomb shelter wouldn't be hit by a bomb, bro," Tavaris grinned.

"Man, whatever. You know what I meant you overgrown Bob Marley looking..." Smoke trailed off. He picked up the ball and launched it at Tavaris, who easily blocked it with his giant arm. Where Tavaris was the hulking quarterback, Smoke was his diminutive sidekick. Smoke was also a good-looking kid though, if slightly chubby, but he had a cleft-chin a few cute girls seemed to get all dreamy over, and he always dressed in the latest oversized street-wear. Smoke was only five-foot-nine however, and was afflicted with an acute Napoleonic complex, often speaking before he thought. As a result, even when unintentional, Smoke was hilarious.

"Okay okay, hold up... I want to read that article again," Tavaris said, flipping his laptop open.

"Aw man... ain't you read it enough?" Smoke sighed as if completely exhausted. "I know it by heart you've told me about it so much."

Smoke began to recite it from memory while looking at the ceiling. "*The Charlotte Observer* is proud to recognize Tavaris Church as an elite pick in the collegiate football world, like few this city has seen before..." Tavaris chuckled. "Tavaris Church has won countless medals, awards and trophies since childhood..." Smoke waved formally to the wall of shelves, heavily laden with all manner of trophies and medals.

"We even suspect Tavaris Church might have had a virgin birth...." Tavaris laughed out loud.

"The Charlotte Observer however, only recognizes athletic talent and not virtuoso singers who are more skilled vocally than any football player that has ever lived." Smoke was now sitting upright and talking rigidly like a news anchor. Tavaris was now cracking up and shaking his head.

"Pssh... when John Legend is opening for the great Smoke Carter we'll see who's turning down the *Charlotte Observer* for interviews." Smoke finished his report, cracking up with his buddy.

Tavaris kept cackling and then sat up quickly when his laptop dinged. "Yo, hold up homes I just got an email from Keisha."

"An *email*? From Keisha... Aw that cannot be good T. You see? Karma is already coming atcha."

"I don't believe in karma, Smoke," Tavaris grinned.

"What's it say?"

Tavaris started reading out loud. "Dear Tavaris, I didn't mean for this letter to be so long, but I just had to let you know, number one baby, I love you!"

"Aw man, I don't want to hear all this..." Smoke said, looking at the door.

"And, because I love you, I have to... leave you?" Tavaris frowned. "What?!"

"WHAT?" Smoke echoed. "Oh no way dude... is she for real?" He sat up shocked, but Smoke had a look of amusement on his face.

"You sorry, no good, three-girlfriend having..." Tavaris looked up at Smoke. "What?! What's she talking about? She's tripping man."

"HAHAHAHA," Smoke roared. "Oh she's definitely tripping dog. She couldn't be talking about that time you spent the whole night talking to Kiara at that pool party, or maybe she saw you flirting with Jasmine all day at school or..."

"Ah whatever man. Just because I talk to other girls don't mean I'm trying to get with them!"

"Oh you don't need to tell me bro... you need to tell *her*!" Smoke busted up again. Tavaris just shook his head and finished reading the email.

"She's crazy man,"

"Aw I don't know if she's *that* crazy T," Smoke laughed, and winked at Tavaris. He suddenly noticed his friend was a little bummed out. "She dumped you for real, man?"

"Yes!" Tavaris said, as he dialed Keisha's number on his cell phone. It went straight to voicemail and he was about to leave a message but he stopped and hung up.

"Hahahaaaa you didn't even leave a message. You are THE player!" Smoke was clearly relishing the moment.

"Man, whatever. I'm not gonna leave her a message with all your crazy hollerin' in the background." That just made Smoke howl even more and Tavaris couldn't help but smile. The phone lit up.

"Yo, it's her!" Tavaris said with a panicked look in his eyes, as though he hadn't just tried to call the girl.

"Ooo I'm out T," Smoke said, jumping up. "I really don't want to hear this. I'll catch you tomorrow."

"Keisha... what's up?" Tavaris nodded at Smoke with a nervous smile and bumped his fist as he left the room.

Tavaris' loud protests faded behind him as Smoke clomped down the stairs and Reverend Church walked through the front door.

"Rev, what's happening?" he held out his hand to give Reverend Church some dap but the Reverend just stared at him.

"Saving souls and dealing with devils, Smoke. What's happening with you?" The Reverend replied.

Smoke was a little taken aback at the latter half of the sentence but didn't skip a beat. "I came to check on the Quarterback. Make sure he eatin' right and got this head on straight, and all that."

Reverend Church usually enjoyed the young man's humor but tonight he ignored the silly comment and said, "When are you coming to join the choir? God gave you all that talent, Smoke. You need to put it to good use. The studio is alright, but church needs to come first."

"Rev, you exactly right," Smoke grinned like a naughty five year old. "The problem is all these fine Jezebel's chasing me, man. I can't think straight with them hunting me down."

Smoke had a long history of having one foot in the church and one out, but Reverend Church had long believed he'd someday serve in the ministry. Smoke's sense of humor, although somewhat irreverent was never disrespectful, and somehow endearing. The Reverend just shook his head.

"They got me all messed up Rev. I can't think straight." Smoke said with conviction.

"Son, if you had any sense, you'd be dangerous," the Reverend couldn't help but smile. "I want to see you at church on Sunday. You know the wrong woman can cost you your life, right? You never read Proverbs chapter nine?"

"I'm recording Sunday Rev, but I'll try to make it soon, a'ight? And I'll go find my Bible and read Proverbs nine tonight!" He tried again for the dap, and this time Reverend Church slapped some on him.

"Be careful driving home Smoke."

"I'll be more careful of them honeys, Rev!" he grinned, and shut the door.

6

FALSE PROPHETS

"I just can't believe the audacity of the-"
"Don't say it honey..." Sandra cut her daughter off, with a pained grin.
"Mom, you should have seen her. *'Isn't Dex just a teddy bear?'*" Jewel pantomimed, brushing her mom's arm. "It was all I could do not to lay her skinny butt out right there, I swear."
"Now, now dear," Sandra said with a chuckle at Jewel's fiery temper. "She might just be completely oblivious to what's appropriate. You know how some women are?"
"Well she's gonna learn real quick."
"Jewel, I really don't think you have anything to worry about. Dexter worships the ground you walk on."
"I don't know mom...but this whole..." she paused, hesitating to say it. "...this whole infertility thing."
"Jewel is there anything else you want to tell me?"
Jewel stared at the traffic ahead, absently. "No..."
"Jewel Theona Miller, this is your mom you're talking to. Don't play me like that."

"Mom, how have you and dad kept it together for all of these years?"

"Child, nothing but the Lord himself, kept us together. It wasn't always good between us but God makes a way if you're willing to work hard. Not to mention we love each other very much. Why baby?"

"Well, I don't really know. I just feel like there is a growing disconnect between me and Dexter." She sighed. "I don't know, you're probably right. It may just be me"

"Well it sounds like you and Dexter need to talk. Just tell him what you're thinking, and remember there is tremendous power in prayer."

Jewel stared ahead again and subconsciously rubbed her belly. "I used to believe that mom, but I don't know anymore."

Sandra grimaced, and rubbed her temple. Jewel caught it and asked, "Mom, are you okay? I'm sorry I didn't mean to stress you out."

"No I'm fine honey. It comes and goes. In Jesus' mighty name the doctors will have some good news and this is just a nutritional imbalance or something."

"Amen," Jewel replied but her expression betrayed her doubt.

Jewel pulled into the parking lot of the *Carolinas Medical Center* main entrance. "Did the doctor say anything when she told you to come in?"

"No, it was just a message from the attendant. She said come in as soon as possible but they always say that."

Jewel sighed, and walked around to help her mom out of the car. Sandra smiled but gently shrugged off her help, getting out of the car and closing the door. Jewel locked the car and they walked into the hospital.

They were only waiting for five minutes after signing in when the doctor poked her head out. "Mrs. Church?" she said, with a weak smile. "Come on back."

Sandra and Jewel exchanged a glance, as they stood up and followed the doctor into an examination room with several X-rays already posted on the light board.

The doctor stood at the light board and motioned to the chairs, "Please, have a seat."

Jewel closed the door behind them and looked at her mom nervously.

"Mrs. Church, I'm afraid I have some troubling news... but there is also some very positive news." The doctor took care to deliver the statement without any stress and without false hope. Sandra deflated a little, and Jewel frowned at the doctor with scared, angry eyes.

"Mrs. Church, even from our initial X-rays we can tell you have a tumor on your brain," she said pointing to a negative on the light board. "If you see here, this dark-grey area is an abnormal tissue mass."

Jewel covered her mouth, and whimpered like a little girl clutching her mom's hand.

"It's okay honey," Sandra tried to reassure her, but she was visibly shaken.

"Now, we're obviously hoping it's benign but we're going to have to do a biopsy," the doctor interjected. "The good news is even though it's a fair size, it's located in an area that is a little less risky to operate on."

"Oh my God," Sandra said, dropping her face into her hands. "This is the last thing we need right now."

The two other women were silent for a moment, then the doctor spoke, "Mrs. Church, please try to remember that we can't predict when illness may strike. All we can do is try to cope the best we can, and recovery will be more likely if we stay positive."

The doctor was gentle, and sounded optimistic. Then again, she was trained and experienced in delivering news like this. It wasn't much comfort to Jewel or Sandra. Jewel just put her arm around her mom and wiped away a tear from her own eye.

***

The pastor's office at *New Day Church of Faith* was a sight to behold. Two doors led into the suite; one on either side of the great room. The room had once been two offices, but the center wall had been knocked out. Now cherry shelving lined two of the walls from floor to ceiling, with all manner of books resting on them. Theology, counseling, Christian history, financial textbooks, stock market advice and even some books on Islamic and New Age thought. Two Burgundy leather loveseats sat perpendicular to each other, around a wrought iron and glass coffee table in the front of the room. They faced an eighty inch projection screen that was connected to a surround-sound system, wired throughout the office. The volume was muted but stock tickers rolled across the wall on the Bloomberg Financial channel.

A ten-seat mahogany table with leather-cushioned chairs occupied most of the far side of the office; the only other fixture there being a mini stainless-steel refrigerator. In the center of the room, in front of one of the walls of bookshelves was a huge, matching cherry, ball-and-claw desk, adorned with a deep burgundy leather top. A luxurious burgundy leather chair rested behind the desk upon which sat Reverend Black in a heathered Armani suit.

His right leg was crossed over the left, and he leaned back, as he growled into his headset.

"Listen Sims, I'm only going to say this once. Do not mention my name. Do not mention *your* name. And deal only with Sugar."

Reverend Black paused as he listened to the other end of the line.

"You can't miss him. He's big, black and scary. But don't, for a second, underestimate his brain. Give him the account details and be sure he gives you a timeline of when the funds will be transferred to a clean account."

He paused again as the receiver squawked.

"Obviously don't give him your phone number. That's why we doing this face to face. If you need a burner phone, I'll give you one. And do not leave without a time to meet again. Sims we've been over all this!"

Another pause.

"Alright, well don't mess it up. There'll be literal hell to pay if you do."

The receiver squawked again.

"Don't worry about Lee... I'll take care of him." The Reverend looked up as he heard a door close from one of the outside offices. "Listen, I've gotta go but see me after the Bible study tonight and if you need anything - which you *shouldn't* - keep ringing my cell until I pick up."

He touched the blue button on the side of his headset, and took the ear piece and mic off as a man poked his head into the left door of the office and knocked to get the Reverend's attention.

"Jeffery! What can I do you for my brother?" he smiled, oozing charm.

"Reverend have you spoken to Deacon Sims? I've been trying to reach him all afternoon."

"No," the Reverend shook his head innocently. "But I'm sure he's taking care of some church business somewhere. What do you need him for?"

"Well..." Jeffery paused and scratched his head. "It may be nothing to be alarmed about just yet, but I noticed some unusual activity in the books and wanted to get his take on it."

"Unusual activity?" Reverend Black frowned.

"Like I said, I don't want to alarm you before I had a chance to check it out. It may just be some funds were recorded in the wrong accounts." Jeffery chewed his lip and studied the Reverend's face.

"Well, keep me posted okay?"

"I will Rev," he promised.

"Say are you okay?" Reverend Black inquired.

"Uhh...yeah...just some stuff going on at Holy Light that's a little stressful, is all."

"Oh really? Anything I can help with?" Reverend Black asked, almost sounding sincere.

"No...I don't think so...but thanks. Man, we're really being attacked by the devil over there."

"Wow, that doesn't sound good. I'll be sure to pray for you." Reverend Black offered, with a smile. "You know, I know you volunteer over there, but if you need to cut back on any of your *paid* responsibilities over here, I wouldn't mind."

Jeffery ignored the barb, but shook his head slightly, "Say are you leading the Bible study tonight?"

"Yep," Reverend Black replied.

"Oh great. What you teaching on?"

"Matthew 7:15..."

Jeffery frowned and shook his head, "Don't know that one by heart,"

"Beware of false prophets," Reverend Black grinned.

***

Reverend Black stood in front of his congregation with arms outstretched, his prayer so beautiful, and so eloquent it bordered on poetic. At his Tuesday night Bible study, he lifted up the single mothers, the teenagers struggling with temptation, the fathers out of work and the downtrodden. He promised the Lord he would do his best to lead this flock into ways of success and joy and the good life. In God of course. Finally he asked the Lord to help him lead his flock in avoiding error, and most importantly to avoid the way of false prophets. When he concluded, Reverend Black received a volley of enthusiastic Amen's and applause. He smiled charismatically at his audience and said gently, "Let's open our Bibles to Matthew 7:15 my brothers and sisters."

"This past week has been a most interesting one," he proclaimed thoughtfully, almost melancholically. "There has been a significant spotlight on our Christian communities, with the celebration of some of Charlotte's long time Christian leadership... and that's a good thing." He said quickly, then paused, as if agonizing over the words to follow.
"I pray however that the leaders of other flocks around this great city... are never caught up in self-promotion and self-celebration. Truly I do pray for them... and you should too." A hush fell over the congregation as most knew who Reverend Black was talking about. Those who didn't looked to others for clarification.
"Have you found Matthew 7:15 my precious flock?" Reverend Black asked graciously. "Let's read together...."

As the Reverend led the passage reading two ladies a few rows back from the front whispered loudly back and forth. Both were about fifty years of age, and both were dressed immaculately, even for Tuesday night Bible study. One was twice divorced, the other long since widowed, and between them, they were well renowned as the keepers and disseminator of all news, which some blatantly called gossip. These two had little birds in every corner of the city, and were often ground zero for any rumors that were spread, be they true - or shades of truth as they called it, long before news was announced publicly.

"Mm mmm, such a shame about *Holy Light*," Sister Jenkins pursed her lips at her friend.

"Oo I know...Sister Willis' niece over there told me someone done looted all they church funds." Sister Jordan was eager to one up her neighbor.

"Well, word in the pews is everyone know who has been embezzling for years..." Sister Jenkins was not to be outdone.

"Who you saying?" Sister Jordan barked. "Brother Church?"

"Mmhmm....it's just what I heard."

"Aw you're crazy honey. That is a good man. There is no way." Sister Jordan was actually shocked, which was saying something.

""Think about it!" Sister Jenkins whispered back, almost louder than her spoken voice. She looked up and smiled sweetly at Reverend Black as he glanced over at their disturbance in distaste. "Sandra Church drives a late model Mercedes. Always dressed to the nines. Hair always done. Ol' Rev don't dress like no slouch neither."

"That just doesn't make any sense. He sells his book and all that, so that's where his money come from." Sister Jordan replied hoarsely. "But I heard the FBI is investigating.

Reverend Church is anything but stupid enough to do somethin' worthy of the FBI's interest."
"Darling, you think people mean to get caught when they committing crimes? Everyone is smarter than the law until they mess up."

Sister Jordan shook her head, not convinced at all. She too smiled at Reverend Black who was barely tolerating their whispers.
"Well since *Holy Light's* Tuesday night Bible study starts thirty minutes later than hours, and Brother Church is a little more long-winded, why don't we swing by there on the way out and see your niece, Alisha. We can get a feel for things firsthand?"
"I think that's an excellent idea," Sister Jenkins smile at her friend. "They have better pastries too."
"Well they may not be able to afford it tonight, if you know what I mean," Sister Jordan winked at her friend. Sister Jenkins covered a spontaneous giggle with her hand. "Mmm I guess so. *Holy Light* may be a on a budget for a while yet," she snickered.

After Reverend Black's subtle yet meticulous exposé of his so-called friend's ministry, he led the church in a solemn time of prayer for their city. He prayed solemnly that *New Day* would never be led astray by the distractions of fame, the opinions of men and worst of all... the corruption of riches. About a third of the congregation agreed with a reluctant *Amen*, but a few yes-men and women went up to congratulate Reverend Black on his timely message.

Right after the service dismissed, the two women slipped out quickly and drove over to *Holy Light*. The entire drive was spent speculating on the sordid, delicious details of *Holy Light's* calamity. They pulled into the parking lot, got out of the car, straightened their dresses and confirmed each other's hair looked good, then they strutted inside. The service had just wrapped up and the congregation were milling around, so the duo couldn't make an entrance, but they quickly spotted their first victim. Sandra Church was standing near the front of the church, gathering brochures left in the seats.

"Well how you doin', Sandra?" Sister Jenkins slid up to the Reverend's wife.

"Oh Sister Jenkins! Hi, I'm fine thanks." Sandra squinted at her a little. "Hi Sister Jordan. Have you come to see Alisha? I think she's still back with the kiddos."

"Are you okay Miss Sandra?" Sister Jordan asked, noticing the squint.

"Huh? Oh... uh yeah. Just have a headache. That's all," Sandra said a little more defensively than she would have liked. The two women exchanged a glance.

"Oooh, that's a lovely dress Sandra... is that Gucci?" Sister Jenkins asked sweet as caramel.

"No, Sister Jenkins. I can assure you it's definitely not." Sandra was no fool, and knew the reputation of the two old bats.

"Mmm, and those shoes!" Sister Jenkins wasn't giving up. "My Lord, you sure know how to dress. You sure them ain't some Jimmy Choos sister?" Sister Jenkins giggled and gave Sandra a little nudge.

Sandra smiled tightly and replied, "Positive."

Jewel spotted the two women talking to her mom from across the room, and made a beeline over, knowing nothing good could be happening. She arrived in time to hear the last backhanded compliment.

"What brings you esteemed ladies to *Holy Light*?" Jewel asked with a warning smile.

"Oh we're just admiring your mom's fine taste in clothes, honey," Sister Jordan patted Jewel on the back as though she were in elementary school.

"Come to think of it, you all have that gift," she said, eyeing Jewel's designer jeans and blouse up and down.

"Well, we learned a long time ago how to trust the Lord to find the sales and..." she stopped, not falling into the trap.

"Well, my folks wisely invested in my education so thank God, Dexter and I are not broke by any means."

Sandra put a hand on Jewel's arm and smiled sweetly at the two women. They smiled back like two hyenas.

"Ladies, if you don't mind it's been a long day and we have a lot to do to clean up. You can always lend a hand if you like?" Sandra wasn't without social maneuvering herself.

"Oh no, we just wanted to visit with you for a while, but we have to find Alisha. So good catching up with you ladies," Sister Jordan's words dripped with honey. "You all should come out and have dinner sometime."

"Thank you Sister Jordan!" Sandra smiled, sidestepping any sort of commitment. "Be sure to grab some coffee cake!" Jewel turned to her mom, her eyes ablaze, but Sandra just rolled her eyes and shook her head.

7

THE VALLEY OF THE SHADOW

In the early hours of Wednesday morning, Sandra Church jumped at the cry, instantly awake.

"Honey! What is it? Are you okay?" She reached over to her nightstand and flipped on the lamp.

Reverend Church groaned and was holding his face. She gasped as she saw streaks of blood on his pillow.

"My face..." he grunted. "Last night there was just one little bump but now it feels like my whole face is on fire..."

"Move your hand honey, let me take a look," his wife ordered. Her husband gingerly moved his hand and she gasped again. "Oh my Lord Theo, you have sores all over your face! They're bleeding!"

Reverend Church's eyes widened and he swung his legs over the side of the bed. He tried to stand and walk to the bathroom but he staggered and had to grab the doorpost.

"Theo!" Sandra cried, and sprung out of bed and ran over to steady him.

"I'm okay, I'm okay..." he shooed her off, but his voice was raspy and his breaths heavy.

"You don't look okay!" she protested. He ignored her, turned on the bathroom light and shuffled over to the mirror.

""Dear God," he whispered at the sight. His face was swollen and covered in, what he counted as seven, bleeding boils.

"Theo, we are getting you to a doctor right now," his wife said with no room for debate in her tone.

"Sandra, I have to get to the church... the FBI..." he protested but he could tell immediately she wasn't in a negotiating mood.

"Theodore William Church! I am running a bath for you, after which we are getting you straight to the doctor!" He knew better than to argue any more, and Sandra leaned over and felt his forehead. "Oh my Lord, you're burning up. I'm getting you some ibuprofen, watch this bath okay." Her voice switched to one of concern.

"Sandra, you need to rest! I can do it..."

"Theo, don't test me! You'll have all the opportunity to help me when they do the biopsy, okay?" She was ready for another objection but he just stared woozily into the mirror. Then he staggered a few paces over to the commode and sat down on the closed lid.

"Stay right there Theo. Don't move okay? I'm going to have Tavaris come in and help you." Reverend Church just sat hunched over, looking at the ground.

***

Jeffery stood outside the office door and breathed deeply. "Father I pray you give me wisdom. Help me to maintain my patience and may Your perfect will be done in this situation. In Jesus' name amen." He knocked on the door.

"Come in!" Reverend Black hollered. Jeffery opened the door and walked inside. An analyst on the Bloomberg channel was raving excitedly about some new development in a biotech stock, and tickers were scrolling and flashing madly all around the huge screen.

"Good morning Reve-"

"SSHHHH! Hold on!" Reverend Church held up a finger, not taking his eyes off the screen. Jeffery gritted his teeth, took another deep breath and waited for ten seconds.

"I can come b-"

"Hang on Jeffery! This is huge... We bought into this stock at pennies, and it's blowing up."

"Yeah... about that..."

"Dangit Lee! What is it man? Can't you just let me hear this?"

Jeffery shook his head slightly, weighing up whether or not he wanted to fight the battle right then. He decided he had no choice. "Reverend I have a few important matters to discuss with you."

"So important that it can't wait five minutes until I hear this stock report?"

"Well..." Jeffery paused, closed his eyes and prayed for wisdom. "That's part of what I wanted to discuss."

"Oh really?" Reverend Black barked. "Okay Jeff, go ahead. Whatever can't wait a few minutes, just go ahead and get right off your chest now." He muted the surround sound volume and slammed the remote down on his desk.

"For starters, there are several purchases and fund allocations in the books that I was concerned about. I had made notes of them and-"

"Yeah, don't sweat those," Reverend Black interrupted. "We're re-organizing the accounts and there is more than enough money to cover anything we're working on. We're blessed beyond measure right now."

"That's another thing. Where is this money coming from Reverend? I know our congregation have been uhh... compelled to give more, but what I'm seeing is these extra funds are being injected by anonymous donors, and although at first they're allocated for new church programs they're being shifted into different accounts, and spent on unrelated items." Jeffery cast a glance at the huge LED screen.

"What exactly are you saying, Jeffery?" Reverend Black asked.

"I'm saying that not only is misallocation of a nonprofit's funds unethical, it's illegal."

"You're accusing this church of stealing people's money?" Reverend Black's tone suggested Jeffery was Judas come back from the grave.

"Reverend, I'm saying I've noticed several irregularities and wanted to run them by you... and so far, all I'm getting is more concerned."

"Well I'm saying don't be concerned Lee," Reverend Black replied. He stepped back and folded his arms. "I'm sure you're also here to ask about your role change?"

"My *what*?" Jeffery narrowed his eyes, and the hair rose on the back of his neck.

"You've probably noticed your access to Peachtree has been limited?"

"Limited? I can't get into any of the building fund financials."

"Yeah..." Reverend Black smirked. "Deacon Sims is taking over your financial responsibilities. I need your help in guiding the Children's Church programs."

"Are you kidding me?" Jeffery's jaw dropped open. "I'm a licensed CPA."

"I know," Reverend Black grinned. "But you're also a Bible school graduate, which Deacon Sims is not. You're the perfect candidate to ensure the next generation gets on the right track!"

"And you were blowing off telling me this to watch some stocks?" Jeffery visibly wrestled with anger.

"Brother Lee... these stocks are going to change the future of this church. We're going to prosper beyond anything we could have dreamed of and lives are going to be changed."

"That is exactly what I'm worried about," Jeffery said.

"Listen Jeff," Reverend Black said in a lowered voice. "You'd be wise to roll with the changes. It's going to happen okay and *New Day* is going to be an example of hope and blessing for many in this city. Right now we have several city officials wanting to visit, and those with the local news and media. *New Day* is truly about to experience a new day."

Jeffery pondered this statement, as well as Reverend Black's plastic smile, then he spoke. "You know I've been involved at *New Day* for over ten years in one way or another," he said. "This has been my home church... my family's home church... and in all humility and love Reverend, since you've taken the role of pastor here, more than a few people are concerned about the paths you're taking this congregation down."

"Oh is that right?" Revered Black snorted. "Like who?"

"Don't you worry about that right now, but believe me there remains faithful bedrock of believers in this church. What's more is that I'm not sure if you've just drifted from the Lord's paths or if you just conned everyone into giving you this role, but one thing I know..."

Jeffery paused as Reverend Black's sneer turned to a snarl.

"You sure as hellfire aren't bearing Christ-like fruit... and that's what we're supposed to know our brethren by."

Reverend Black looked down at his desk and slowly put the cap back on his favorite *Montblanc* pen. He pushed his chair out, stood up and looked at the carpet as he strolled over to Jeffery. When their shoes were practically touching he looked up, nose-to-nose with his deacon and said, "Are you challenging my authority Jeff?"

Jeffery was not a small man by any means, and unknown to Reverend Black, he had been a Division One college wrestler. He was the last type of man to resort to a physical confrontation but he wasn't even slightly intimidated. Jeffery kept his eyes neutral and replied, "Whatever you want to call it...*Reverend.*"

"Lee, what does the Bible say about rebellion?"

"Don't try to twist scripture, Black. I came to you with all respect to discuss matters of financial misallocation-*since that's my job*, but you are more concerned about your stock prices than you are in discussing some serious church business."

"Those stock prices *are* church business Lee." The derision in Reverend Black's eyes was piercing.

"Think about that statement Reverend, and let me know if anything sounds wrong to you."

The two stared at each, other nose-to-nose for a long few moments. Reverend Black's cell phone rang suddenly.

He broke eye contact and looked at his desk, "If you don't mind, *brother*, I have to take this call."

"The church will need to know about those funds *Reverend.*" Jeffery warned as Reverend Black turned and walked over to the desk.

"Close the door behind you," Reverend Black replied. He picked up the handset and said "Give me just a second okay?" He held the phone to his chest and glared at Jeffery.

Jeffery shook his head and strode out of the office, closing the door on the way out. He paused at the door for a moment and listened. Then he changed his mind and started walking again.

"What have I told you about calling me in the day? Use that *Skim* app like I said," Reverend Black growled in a low tone.

He listened as the voice chirped on the other end.

"How much do you need?"

Another pause.

"Jeez, how do you go through money like that woman?"

He waited and a smile crossed his face.

"Yeah you do have expensive taste."

The voice chirped a comment that made the man laugh.

"Yeah I guess I do have expensive taste too. Come over to the house later and I'll take care of you."

***

Tavaris sat in the *Carolinas Medical Center* hospital waiting room trying to read a *Cosmo* magazine but threw it down on the end table. He looked for a men's magazine and only saw one catering to vintage car enthusiasts, and at the moment it was the last thing he felt like reading. He stood up and walked over to the nurse's station.

"'S'cuse me ma'am, when can I go back to see my dad?"

"Son I promise you, either your dad or the doctor will come out as soon as the tests are done. I can give you the TV remote if you like." The nurse tried to be polite but it was the third time Tavaris had asked, and her patience was thinning.

"No thanks," he grumbled and walked back to the waiting area. He pulled out his phone and started playing *Candy Crush*.

"Tavaris Church?" a doctor called from nurse's station.

Tavaris jumped up and put the phone in his pocket. "Yes. That's me."

"Hi I'm Doctor Jourgensen," the tall man introduced himself. "We've just run a battery of tests and taken blood work from your dad. He's resting now and we have him on intravenous fluids to ensure he's hydrated and some mild pain relievers as well."

"Huh? What's wrong with him? He can't go home?" The scared kid couldn't help but respond out of the strapping eighteen year-old quarterback.

"Well, until we have the test results back it's probably best if he remains here. He's fine, and we have a few ideas but we're not entirely sure what the cause of his condition is." As soon as the doctor said it, he knew his work was cut out for him reassuring the young man.

"What do you mean? He was fine last night. Well, he was feeling a bit run down and he has a ton of stress at the church as always, but he was fine." Tavaris' eyes were wide and scared.

"Tavaris, I'm sure your dad is okay, and will be all rested up and on his way soon. For now, all that is apparent is he has lesions - umm... boils that have formed into clusters called *carbuncles*, which is basically a staph infection. What is concerning me is the possibility of sepsis setting in."

Tavaris eyes had glazed over.

"Where is your mom Tavaris?" Doctor Jourgensen asked.

"She's setting up an appointment for herself," he replied.
"For herself?" the doctor frowned.
"Yeah man. My mom just found out she has a brain tumor. She got a call and walked over to neuro-oncology or whatever with my sister to set up a biopsy because she couldn't stand to wait around out here."
The doctor was speechless for a second at the news of both parents being ill, and the sight of a strong young man on the verge of tears.
"I'm- I'm really sorry to hear that. I'm sure she'll be fine Tavaris," was all the doctor could manage. His apprehension scared Tavaris even more.
"Can I go see my dad now?" Tavaris said, desperately battling back the moisture in his eyes.
"Yes... Yes, of course...." the doctor nodded, snapping back into the moment. "I must warn you though, he's fairly sedated and we've had to apply a balm and gauze to the lesions." The blank, fearful expression reminded the doctor he needed to break it down.
"Your dad may be asleep and he has bandages on his face."
"Whatever doc, I just want to see him," Tavaris replied, angrily wiping away a tear.
"Okay, please follow me," Doctor Jourgensen waved and headed down the corridor.

8

WITH FRIENDS LIKE THESE

Reverend Church wore only a hospital gown as he stood in the center of the empty parking lot. He squinted at the dark green sky and shielded his eyes as a gale whipped trash and papers and plastic bags past him. He tried to figure out why he was standing there but his head was swimming. He turned slowly to look over his left shoulder, and saw the looming wall of windows in the critical care wing of the *Carolinas Medical Center* behind him. In the center of the building a lone room was lit, and he strained to see who the tall figure was, standing over a patient in a bed. The wind howled and tore at his gown, whipping it around like a sheet, and forcing him sideways. He stumbled slightly but held his gaze and narrowed his eyes more. It looked like a homeless man leaning over the bed, with his hand on the patient's chest. He staggered closer, fighting the violent gusts, and suddenly he recoiled. He somehow knew the figure lying in bed was himself.

"Honey, it's okay... ssshh... Theo, I'm here! It was just a dream...." Sandra clutched his hand as he pushed against the pillows behind him, sitting straight up in the bed. A nurse ran in, alerted by the frantically heart-rate monitor and restrained Reverend Church's hand as he clawed at the I.V in his arm. Reverend Church's eyes darted around the room wildly as the nurse echoed Sandra's pleas. "Mr. Church, please try to remain calm... there is no cause for concern, you're at the *Carolinas Medical Center.* Your wife and friends are right next to you."

"Hey, buddy... we're here. Your boys are here... don't stress," Pastor Baker squeezed his hand.

"Yeah Theo, it's all good," Bishop Davis patted his friend's foot, but the Reverend continued to struggle against the nurse's hand.

"Honey please... just lie back," Sandra begged. Reverend Church stiffened and then stared at the four of them with wild eyes, realizing where he was and slowly relaxed his hand. He removed it from the nurse's, realizing she had been fighting him from pulling out the needle, taped into his arm.

"It was just a nightmare honey... it's okay," Sandra soothed, as he relented and lay back, closing his eyes again. The women exchanged a nervous glance and the nurse checked the I.V to make sure it was still securely in his arm.

"He wasn't this bad yesterday," Sandra whispered to the four men. They shook their heads and reassured her how tough their friend was.

"Let him sleep. It must be the meds. We'll hang out for as long as he needs us," Reverend Williams said.

***

Jewel stood over the kitchen sink, held up by her outstretched hands. She stared at nothing, her eyes still red from a night of lost sleep and an onslaught of emotions. She flinched as the toast popped up and a moment later, the back door creaked open. Jewel leaned over and saw Gerald's head poke through. Then he shuffled in and he closed the door quietly behind him.

"Yo!" Jewel called, and he jumped.

"Man... what's your malfunction Jewel?" he snapped. He turned on his heel to leave but staggered a little and caught the door jamb.

"Hey, you get back here right now!" Jewel commanded. She was in no mood for Gerald's attitude, and she'd been wanting to give him a piece of her mind since Monday night's dinner. Gerald was clearly intoxicated from God knows what, so she decided there was no better time. Her older brother sighed and leaned against the wall.

"What?" he said.

"Look at you. You're a mess. What are you high on G?" Jewel asked bitterly. "You were raised better than that."

"Oh here we go!" he said, throwing his arms in the air. "You gonna preach like mom and dad, telling me I was raised to be like the great Reverend Theodore Church?" He said his father's name pompously.

"Maybe," Jewel replied putting her hand on her hip. "You know you're called."

"How I was the smart one, and had so much potential?" Gerald continued. "And you're gonna tell me I need to rededicate my life to God and be righteous?"

Jewel stared at him just shaking her head slowly. "Don't flatter yourself, but I do have to wonder who you've become? And what did you do with my big brother?"

"I got news for you..." Gerald continued. "I don't believe anything I can't see anymore."

"GERALD!" Jewel shouted. "Don't even talk like that!"

"Ooh... I'm sorry," he said quietly, contrasting her anger. "I'm not Daddy's precious little princess, or superstar jock quarterback. I'm just bad little Gerald... but that ain't enough, is it?"

"Gerald... I can't deal with this right now, okay?"

"Oh, there's never a good time to deal with 'it' is there?" Gerald made air quotes with his fingers. "'IT' is just the stain on an otherwise sterling family. 'IT' never got the attention or love that 'IT'S' brother and sister did. 'IT'-"

"Gerald you know that's not true!" Jewel's eyes showed her pain.

"All I ever wanted was the same kind of love big sis..." he whispered, staring into the distance. "I tried...I tried real hard to be Dad's good son..."

"Gerald, I seriously can't deal with this right now..." Jewel shook her head.

"Yeah... I know... I was just leaving. Just don't act like you care okay."

"What's going on down here?" Dexter asked as he stomped into the kitchen. He was half dressed, wearing slacks and a white tank top.

"This don't concern you pretty boy," Gerald sneered. "Go on and finish dressing for your corporate masters."

Dexter squared up with Gerald and looked into his eyes, "You high again? You know you're a selfish little piece of-"

"What you gonna do big man?" Gerald pushed his face up to Dexter's, rage filling his eyes. Dexter didn't back down.

"STOP!" Jewel screamed trying to get between them. She had seen her brother's insane temper and had begged the cops to spare him on more than one occasion, as some little thug or other fell victim to his lightning-fast and extremely brutal fists.

"He's not going to speak to my wife like that," Dexter said, his eyes still locked on Gerald's.

"She's my sister, jackass!" Gerald mocked. "Blood is thicker than water...you gonna let those soft, little accountant hands go or what?"

"GERALD! DAD'S IN HOSPITAL IN CRITICAL CONDITION, MOM HAS A BRAIN TUMOR AND I CANNOT DEAL WITH THIS RIGHT NOW!"

The inferno slowly ebbed out of Gerald's eyes and he turned away from Dexter to look at his hysterical sister. "What are you talking about?"

"Dad collapsed yesterday morning, and guess what? Mom has a brain tumor too."

"Get outta here..." Gerald tried calling his sister's bluff, but the stress on her face told him she wasn't playing.

"It's true you punk." Dexter added, his lip still quivering with anger. "While you've been running the streets, your family has been going through hell,"

Gerald paused for a moment then stepped back, shaking his head, and snickering.

"How could you possibly find that funny?" Jewel said, tears now streaming down her cheeks.

"Oh it's not funny..." Gerald replied, his eyes going distant again. "It's ironic."

"What you babbling about?" Dexter said.

"WHERE'S GOD NOW?" Gerald raised his hands in the air, and looked around theatrically. "WHERE ARE YOU GOD?" he shouted. "ALL THOSE YEARS OF SERVICE AND THEY'RE BOTH IN HOSPITAL! HOW ABOUT THAT GOD!"

"Gerald... don't..." Jewel sobbed.

"What's going on down here?" Tavaris walked in to the kitchen, rubbing his eyes. He looked at Gerald and frowned, "What up G? Why you hollerin' man?"

"Oh, I'm just trying to see if God is anywhere to be found? But only you came down the stairs... are you God, T?" Gerald laughed crazily.

Tavaris looked at Jewel in confusion. She just shook her head.

"Does nobody else see it?" Gerald asked. "All those years of ministry. Of neglecting their kids for that stupid church... time for everyone else's problems except their own family's... and now they're BOTH in hospital."

"G, it's not like that..." Tavaris said rubbing his face. "Mom and dad were busy but they've always raised us well. These things just happen. If you want the truth, you wanted to be wild man...that dope you started smoking changed your whole outlook bro. We're all stressed man, please don't do this."

"Aw listen to the up and coming preacher man," Gerald sneered. "Should I call you Tebow?"

"Why don't you just get outta here Gerald?" Dexter said.

"Nah wait, Dex... he's just hurtin'," Tavaris defended his brother.

"Yo, I'm saying for the last time, you best put that dog on a leash, before she gets bit," Gerald warned Jewel, the fires returning to his eyes.

"What you talking crazy for man?" Tavaris said, stepping between Dexter and Gerald. "Don't you understand mom and dad could both be really sick? Why don't you just chill and come to the hospital with us. You can take a quick shower, and we'll get you a burger on the way."

Tavaris' voice was full of compassion for his big brother. He lowered his voice and said, "Look, I can see you're spaced man, but get cleaned up and rest a while and you can see them in a couple of hours? That will do the world of good for them."

Gerald paused for a few seconds and then shook his head. "Naw man, I can't do it... if God is real He'll make sure they're still there tomorrow. If they aren't, then I don't even want to hear His name again."

"Dude..." Tavaris said in shock.

Gerald turned and opened the door.

"Gerald! Come on...you don't mean that," Jewel called after him. He ignored her and walked out the door.

"Let him go," Dexter said. "He'll come around when he's sober or needs money. For now we all need to make sure *we're* strong for your parents."

Tavaris stared at the empty doorway. He turned away and trudged back upstairs with slumped shoulders. Jewel was sure she heard him sniff, and saw him wipe his eyes quickly.

***

"Heeey! There's our boy!" Pastor Tobias Baker grinned as Reverend Church sat up blinking and frowning. "*Water*," he whispered dryly and motioned to the cup on the nightstand.

Bishop Davis handed him the Styrofoam cup and smiled. "You feeling better? You gave us quite the scare this morning...do you remember that?"

Reverend Church was puzzled for a second. "The tornado..." he remembered, his voice still hoarse.

"It was a tornado? In your dream?" Bishop Davis asked.

"And the homeless man... scary..."

The four men exchanged glances but Reverend Williams tried to reassure his friend, "It was just a dream. Don't fret my brother."

Jeffery remembered the homeless man from the church, and figured his friend was becoming delirious. He made a mental note to mention it to the doctor.

Reverend Church shook his head. "It was more..." he whispered.

Reverend Williams patted his friend's arm, "Aw you'll be okay Theo. The mind is a powerful thing."

"Where's Sandra?" he asked.

The friends looked at each other, but Bishop Davis spoke first, "She's in the hospital. She'll be back in a bit."

Reverend Church lay back on his pillow and stared up at the ceiling. "Dear God, I feel like a thousand razors are running through my veins, and the fires of hell are all over my skin." His friends remained silent, not knowing what to say.

"The doctors know what's wrong yet?" Reverend Church asked.

"They're working on it," Reverend Williams replied softly. "They're leaning toward some kind of auto-immune deficiency...perhaps burning the candle at both ends for too long and some mechanism in your body is just refusing to cooperate."

Reverend Church grimaced, "Oh please... I was feeling completely fine, and took a vacation three months ago. I might have picked something up on one of my recent trips. Do they know about my recent trips out of the country?"

"Yes, they do. You can rest assured Sandra gave them every little detail brother."

Reverend Church tried to sit up and gave a sharp cry. Pastor Baker jumped to his aid.

"Easy there Tiger... those sores have spread everywhere." Reverend Church gave him a horrified look.

"I... I can't even sit up," he whimpered.

"Like I said..." Pastor Baker smiled in pity. "*Everywhere* buddy."

Reverend Church groaned.

"Oh man... I've never felt so wrecked in my life. Where is Sandra? I *need* her right now."

"She's...busy bro," Reverend Tobias replied. "She'll be back."

"Wait a second...what aren't you guys telling me?" Reverend Church demanded, knowing his friends too well. The look he gave them, said he wouldn't take no for an answer.

Reverend Williams sighed. "She's having a biopsy done Theo. On the brain tumor. Tavaris, Jewel and Dexter are waiting in oncology right now."

"Oh my God..." Reverend Church whispered. "They cutting on her?"

"She'll be fine. It's a routine procedure, and we're believing God for a miracle."

"It's her BRAIN man," he half-yelled and immediately winced in pain.

"Brother... chill," Pastor Baker placed a strong hand gently on his friend's arm. "She's in the Lord's hands. She's gonna be fine."

"You know, I could handle our struggles with Gerald. I've been praying and I believe God is speaking to him. I could even handle this craziness with the church's money been stolen. I could handle my health going haywire... but if anything happens to Sandra, I'll wish I was never born. I'll wish I never started in the ministry, nor never agreed to pay the price for serving God. This isn't fair. It's not right!"

His three friends stood there in an awkward silence, and Jeffery frowned as he sat in an armchair next to Reverend Church's bed, but he still didn't say a word. Things had clearly taken a turn for the unexpected. The great Reverend Theodore Church had always been a rock. The pillar of the community, the strength when everyone was down. He didn't always have the answers, but he always, *always* had faith. He was the one with the impeccable record, and was able to comfort anyone when they were down. Suddenly Reverend Williams had a thought. *What if Theo has always been able to be strong because he's never faced any challenges?* It hit him like a tsunami.

"Now Theo... you're just stressed brother. Don't say anything you'll regret." He tried to comfort his friend, but he wasn't listening.

"Man...it's not the time for preaching. All this hitting me at once...I'm feeling hedged in Henry. And now Sandra is going through it. My reputation, my family, my finances... All my worst fears are coming true. How can this be happening? How and why?"

"Theo... please," Reverend Williams continued, trying to reason with him. "I know you're not going to be impatient if we try to speak a good word to you? How can we not say anything, my friend?" He looked at the other two men who nodded somberly.

"Think about how many people you've instructed, and how many weak arms you've strengthened. Your preaching has encouraged tens-of-thousands who were stumbling...yet now trouble falls on you and you're just folding?"

Reverend Church tilted his head back and was listening to every word through a surprised frown.

"Shouldn't your holy living be your confidence?" Reverend Williams continued. "Shouldn't your righteousness and good deeds be your hope out of this?"

The others were silent, and Reverend Church wasn't responding, so he kept going. It became evident there was a lot he wanted to say.

"We all know none of us are completely righteous Theo. In my long tenure of ministry, one thing I've seen is those who sow any kind of sin reap it, and we all sow sin. God only takes it for so long, then with a breath, He decides their day has come. Even if someone considers himself as strong as a lion, God can break that lion's teeth. What I'm saying is people have hidden sins...things they haven't brought to light before God or before others, but God sees and rewards each person accordingly, sooner or later."

Now Reverend Church wore an expression of pure shock. It appeared Reverend Williams was only getting started. For a moment he thought he might be coming on too strong, but he had wanted to tell Theo for some time how it was, and he pondered again how Theo had only been strong because he'd never really faced any challenges.
"I'll tell you a little secret, Theo. I had a vivid dream one night. All the hair on my body stood straight up, as a shadow, a *spirit* glided past my face and then stood before me. This apparition asked me;
 'Can a man be more righteous than God?
 Can even a powerful man be more holy than his Creator?
 If God puts no confidence in his angels, and even holds them accountable,
 how much more does He hold mere human beings accountable, who are made of dirt,
 who are squished more easily than a bug.
 Every day men are broken to pieces,
 and they descend into the pit.
 Is not the life pulled out of their fragile body,
 and pass away without true intelligence or knowledge?'
Theo...that vision was showing me that resentment kills a fool. *Suddenly* a fool's house is cursed, and his children are far from safety. But you already know God brings down the proud, and exalts the humble. My brother...you know the man whom God corrects is blessed, so please don't despise this discipline of Almighty God. He wounds, but He also

heals. He will rescue you from these calamities, but you must discover any hidden sin in your heart, and take it before Him. Then He can restore you, and bring you even more blessings. The three of us have even discussed these things, and we know they are true."

Reverend Church looked at the other two in surprise, to confirm he had in fact, been the topic of much discussion between the three of them. Bishop Davis only offered a little shrug while Pastor Baker looked out the window. Reverend Church pushed himself up on his pillows, his face contorting in pain but he pushed Bishop Davis away as he stepped forward to help.

"You speak from your place of ease and comfort," Reverend Church said. "You've been with me for decades. What sin do I have in my life? Yes, we're growing every day, and the little things are being dealt with but how am I deserving of all this? If my suffering could be weighed, it would outweigh the sand on all the earth's beaches and even the ocean floor. Yes, maybe my reaction is a little impulsive, but you grill me like this? Yes God's terrors are against me, and why I have no idea...in fact I wish God would grant me a petition, and take my life instead of allowing me to waver in faith in this time of weakness!"

"Theo..." Reverend Williams tried to interject, but Reverend Church wasn't having it.

"I'm not invincible... I'm human. I've done my best, God knows I have, and that still isn't good enough apparently. How can I help myself, now that everything I've worked for is crumbling."

He paused for a few moments, weighing up carefully what he was about to say. Reverend Williams cleared his throat and was about to speak when Reverend Church held up his hand silencing him.

"I'll tell you one thing...anyone who keeps compassion from a friend, has no fear of God," He looked each of his friends in the eye. "It would appear that my lifelong brothers are as unpredictable as the Alaskan rivers we've fished together. When the ice melts, they overflow and flood, bringing salmon and wildlife with them. Then during the dry season they stop flowing and are cut off from any life-giving sustenance. The Inuit we minister to, rely on these streams. They're disheartened because the erratic rivers bring no food. No comfort. They relied on these rivers, and now they are shocked because in the time of need, the river is dry. You three are *dry rivers* right now!" Reverend Church was angry, and glared at his three standing friends. Reverend Williams shook his head as his friend spoke, and stared at the floor. Jeffery wisely remained quiet.

"You guys see something horrible like a fellow minister being laid waste, and you get all antsy, and use it as excuse to rant. Have I ever asked you for anything significant? Have I ever asked you to bail me out of anything? No, I haven't. So teach me now you great ministers, and I'll be quiet. Show me where I've sinned, and where I'm wrong and I'll repent."

Reverend Church paused as his face grew sad, and wiped a tear from his cheek. "You guys...you just couldn't wait to chastise me. Henry, your words have been so painful...but tell me honestly? Have I ever lied to you? Could I lie to your face if there was sin in my life? Consider carefully and don't be unjust. My reputation is at stake."

All three men averted their eyes, so Reverend Church raised his gaze to the ceiling again and continued speaking, "I pray

God remembers my life is but a breath, a vapor on this earth...I may soon be gone, so I have to speak the truth. Unfortunately I'm speaking out of pain, but it's still truth. Even though the Lord brutalizes me with these afflictions, if I have sinned why doesn't He forgive me? Soon I will be gone, and you guys will regret how you've treated me."

As he finished speaking, an exhausted-looking Tavaris and Jewel walked into the room. Jewel was dabbing her eyes with a tissue, but Tavaris sensed the tension in the room.

"Hey... you're awake!" he said to his dad, after nodding to the four men who were practically his uncles. "What's with the grim atmosphere?"

"Oh we were just reminiscing about all the stuff we've been through together," Reverend Church replied snidely. Tavaris looked inquiringly at the three standing men, not convinced. They maintained their poker faces.

"How's your mom Tavaris?" Reverend Church asked.

The young man sighed, "Doc says she's okay...stable but they were just going to do a biopsy but they ended up removing all of the tumor they could find." His eyes welled up again, and he wiped away the tears furiously. "They're hoping it hasn't metastasized to her lymph nodes or anything." His voice was shaky.

"She's going to be fine dad," Jewel cut in, realizing the last thing her father needed to hear was any potentially troubling news. "In fact, the doctor said he's going to try to get her a bed here in your room with you."

Reverend Church's face lit up.

"Then you two can drive each other nuts," Jewel added.

Everyone chuckled at that, and the icy atmosphere melted.

"Theo, we're going to let you enjoy time with your family," Pastor Baker said.

"Yes, rest up and we'll be back to see you soon brother,"
Bishop Davis added. "If we can, we'll bring you some of
those Belgian chocolate cookies you like too much. You
know the ones from that gourmet cookie store!"
Reverend Church just nodded.
Jeffery stood up, deciding to leave with the three friends,
and squeezed Reverend Church's hand.
"Take care of him," he said to Jewel, who agreed with a
weary smile.

9

SHEEP AND WOLVES

Sergeant Reggie Stone had been employed at the Charlotte-Mecklenburg Police Department for over twenty years, and was in many, but certainly not all, ways an exemplary member of the armed forces. He was not in outstanding, but reasonable physical shape, and standing only five-and-a-half feet tall, Sergeant Stone had been accused of a Napoleonic complex more than a few times. His defensive, even insecure demeanor however, belied his inclination to sudden and swift violence.

Before he was promoted, in the last review by his overseeing lieutenant, Officer Reginald Richard Stone was described as "an exceptional officer, aside from a few complaints of excessive use of force." When asked about it off the record, he would laugh and often blame his tactics on the combination of his "brutally efficient" German and English heritage. When questioned in an official capacity, however, he maintained the suspect had *always* been the aggressor.

Sergeant Stone knew his job as a uniformed officer, but his most significant talents was the ability to get close to, and befriend people in higher stations of life. Some called it kissing up, but Sergeant Stone called it being shrewd. No, he could never be mistaken for the sharpest bayonet on the rack, but he was loyal to those he served, and coupled with his skills as an enforcer, he became a very useful tool to some of the keener minds in Charlotte.

"Say Reggie, you still have any sway with S.W.A.T?" Reverend Black asked, as he reclined in his chair, flipping the channel from CNN to Bloomberg.
"I sure do," the diminutive man replied, as he leaned forward on the leather couch. "Kenny is actually one of my finest Krav Maga students. He's even teaching the Saturday Krav classes now and practically runs S.W.A.T. Kid's a prodigy."
"A kid is running Charlotte S.W.A.T? My, don't I suddenly feel safer," Reverend Black replied acidicly.
"Weeell, I say kid," Sergeant Stone grinned goofily. "He's thirty five at least. Anyone under forty is a kid to me, hehe." His chuckle was childlike. "Why, what you scheming up Rev?"
Reverend Black studied the cop for a few seconds, "Oh there's just some of our mutual business associates who may or may not get a little uhh...difficult to work with." Sergeant Stone dropped his chin to look at Reverend Black under a raised eyebrow. "You talking 'bout Sugar and his crew?"
"Now I thought you were smarter than to speak so candidly on these premises..." Reverend Black bit back. Sergeant Stone frowned but didn't argue. "We know who we're talking about."

"Listen, Harvey...S.W.A.T isn't some personal task force of yours, to keep your business associates in line."

"*Our* business associates," Reverend Black corrected. "And I know that, but who's to say an anonymous tip to the esteemed Charlotte P.D, informing them that some career thugs are packing military grade hardware in a certain warehouse, couldn't be a little insurance?"

Sergeant Stone stared at Reverend Black for a few seconds, wondering if the man was a genius or lunatic, or both. "I don't know man. Why do you need me to know anyone in S.W.A.T though?"

"Because if it becomes necessary, you're gonna receive the anonymous call, and make sure your buddies go in extra jumpy and trigger happy."

"What do you mean, extra jumpy and trigger happy?" Sergeant Stone asked nervously.

"You're going to tell them the anonymous caller was freaking out and that they should be ready for some counter fire Reggie. Damn! Must I explain everything for you?"

The desk phone rang and Reverend Black punched a button while still eyeing Sergeant Stone with contempt, "Yes?"

"Deacon...uh... Mr. Lee is here to see you," the receptionist squawked over the speaker phone.

Reverend Black paused. "I'll be about five minutes. Can you ask him to wait in the conference room for me?"

"Yes sir." She hung up.

Reverend Black nodded at Sergeant Stone. "You wanna have a word with Lee?"

Sergeant Stone's eyes were already begging the question. "Absolutely," he smiled, straightened his duty belt, and headed for the door.

"Stone," Reverend Black called. "Just a word, okay?"

Sergeant Stone snorted as if to say *Of course!*

Jeffery was already being ushered into the conference room when Sergeant Stone walked up. The cop grinned malevolently and held the door open for the receptionist to leave.

"Officer Stone," Jeffery said calmly, placing a single document on the table. "How has the Lord been blessing you lately?"

"Sergeant," the cop replied.

"I'm sorry. Sergeant Stone..."

"What do you want Lee?"

Jeffery looked down, put his phone on the table and looked back up at Sergeant Stone, "I'm afraid that's between Reverend Black and I. Is he going to be along soon?"

Sergeant Stone slowly walked around the conference room table. Jeffery turned his chair and followed the stocky man with curious eyes. Sergeant Stone stopped when he was standing right over the deacon.

"Now I think we both know your days at New Day have drawn to a close," Sergeant Stone drawled.

Jeffery, cool as a cucumber, nodded his head. "That may be the case, but I still need to talk to the Reverend."

"I want you to listen closely Lee," Sergeant Stone sucked his teeth. "It would be a really-and I mean really-bad idea to start blabbering things you know nothing about when you leave."

"Do you mean things that require the pastor of this church, and his henchman to try to intimidate me physically?"

Sergeant Stone smiled slowly. "Aw you know nothing about being intimidated physically my friend."

Jeffery returned the grin and let it go.

"You hear me clear, right? You go spreading lies about the smart way people use money in this place, and who knows what will come sneaking up on ya out of nowhere."

"Are you threatening me Sergeant Stone?"

"What if I was?"

"Well, let's say that might sneak up on *you*."

"Aw *please*," the sergeant begged. "Make a move and make my day." He squared his shoulders up to Jeffery's chair.

"Oh, the Word of God admonishes against violence Sergeant Stone. And I'm pretty sure Jesus said something very specific about law enforcement not intimidating citizens either...but I digress. If you were actually a believer, you'd know the law of sowing and reaping."

"You tryna take the mickey outta me?" Sergeant Stone growled.

"Not at all. On the contrary, I'm trying to help you. You see, I believe the good Book. And the Book says 'Yea though I walk through the valley of the shadow of death, I will fear no evil.' You can't scare me Sergeant Stone."

"Well you're not very smart then, boy. You got a momma and a daddy?"

Jeffery gave no response but his eyes hardened.

"See...you might not be scared...but I guarantee you're not the only one who should be."

Jeffery stared into the man's eyes for several seconds. Then calmly said, "See now, that's where no knowledge is dangerous."

"How do you figure?" the sergeant sneered.

"Well... I pray every day for my family's safety and God promises me that angels are encamped-the Bible literally uses that word-it's a military term you might be familiar with it... but these angels are *encamped* around my family and I. So God help the person who tries to harm any of them...although I doubt He's going to be very motivated to do so."

Sergeant Stone chuckled. "Aah, you know the difference between you and me?" He looked as though he expected an answer, but continued when none was forthcoming. "You're a religious nut, and I'm someone God understands. Reverend Black is too. You go all literal, thinking there are invisible angels and demons running around. I've got a secret for ya...we're the angels. *And* we're the *demons*. A bit of each in all of us. This world balances itself out in the long run. That's how God designed it. Guys like me...we bring justice to scumbags who would otherwise get off on a technicality. Guys like you, maybe try to convince people not to be scumbags-and that's appreciated."

Sergeant Stone took a deep breath and grinned wickedly again.

"But don't you sheep *ever*, and I mean *ever* try to get in the way of a big, bad sheepdog like me."

Jeffery studied the man for several seconds, mesmerized. Then he said, "Well thanks for the theology lesson, *Reverend*. You know I took a few psychology classes in college, and I've gotta say...just at a glance, you've got more complexes going on than a Vegas strip man."

Sergeant Stone snarled and pointed his finger, "See now that's the wrong answer."

"I don't think you could comprehend the *right* answer Sergeant Stone."

Sergeant Stone's face was turning bright red, and his finger started shaking.

"You ever fight for your life *Deacon*? Coz we could arrange that right now? Man to man. Hell, I'll even lay all my weapons on the table."

Jeffery leaned back in the chair and raised his eyebrows. "Straight back to the violence?" he asked, unperturbed. "Don't pass go, don't collect $200?"

"By gawd..." Sergeant Stone muttered through gritted teeth, and start unbuckling his belt. "Okay, you done it now boy!"

Jeffery remained in the chair and watched the sergeant with amusement, infuriating the man even more. The sergeant threw his belt on table and stepped forward.

"STONE!" The door swung open. "Exactly what are you doing?"

Sergeant Stone snapped back to his senses. "Mr. Lee over here was about to initiate a physical altercation, and resist arrest sir."

"Really? A church deacon, with no history of arrest or violence, and a congregation full of members who'll testify that he doesn't have an aggressive bone in his body?" Reverend Black barked.

Sergeant Stone was still seething but ground his teeth and his eyes cast daggers at Jeffery, who appeared even more amused.

"I'll take it from here Stone." Reverend Black commanded.

"He's trouble you-"

"I'LL TAKE IT FROM HERE!"

Sergeant Stone sucked his teeth again at Jeffery, picked up his belt and walked back to Reverend Black's office, glaring at the deacon through the windows.

"What do you want Lee?" Reverend Black said when they were alone.

"Wow, that was quite the save Reverend. I didn't know you cared?"

"What. Do. You. Want?"

"I came to officially hand in my resignation. Effective immediately."

"Well that's perfect, because I was about to officially fire you."

"So I heard."

"Jeff...let's shoot straight. I know you know better than to run your mouth," Reverend Black warned.

"Run my mouth about what?"

Reverend Black eyed him for a moment, and then nodded, "Exactly."

"You need to do right by this church Harvey. You're stealing their money." Deacon Lee, for the first time became visibly angry.

"Lee because of your faithful service, I'm going to give you three months of severance pay..."

"I don't want one cent of yours Harvey. You think I'm a fool? You need to stop doing whatever it is you're doing with these godly people's money."

"Godly people?" Reverend Black exclaimed. "You think this mess of whiny, lazy screwed-up people are godly?" He guffawed loudly. Lee shook his head.

"I think we're done here," Lee said, and stood up grabbing his phone.

Reverend Black's face snapped back to its sinister self. "Fine, you don't have to take the severance, but you'll be very wise to keep your lying mouth shut, do you understand?"

"My resignation, Harvey." Jeffery pushed the document across the table, then pushed past his former boss, to leave.

Jeffery was fuming, but didn't want to show it yet. He also didn't want to walk past the receptionist, knowing she and anyone else would be gawking. He loved these people, but who knew what they'd been told. He headed out of a side door, to the back parking lot. It was where the staff were instructed to park to keep the front of the church clear for visitors and congregation members during evening services. As he stepped outside, Jeffery looked around to be sure he was alone, and then pulled out his phone. His recording app was still open, and he hit the big red button, ending it's documentation of the entire time he'd spent in the building. He inhaled deeply, then exhaled. As he did, a familiar car pulled around the corner, and parked next to Reverend Black's Mercedes. He quickly slid the phone back into his pocket, and headed toward his car.

"Sister Willis?" he asked, as the woman was wiggling her way out of the car, greatly handicapped by her skintight, black dress and stilettos. She jumped in fright. "Oh! Deacon Lee! You startled me," she said, with a hand dramatically holding her chest.
"I'm afraid it's just Jeffery now," he replied.
"Oh yes. I hear-" she stopped short of finishing her sentence. "Uh, what happened?"
Jeffery eyed her suspiciously but only said, "Time to leave I guess. What brings you to *New Day*?"
"Oh me, I'm just... wanting to find out when the new Wednesday night Bible studies start. I've been needing a double dose of Word since the investigation," she laughed nervously.
Jeffery nodded. "You know to use the good parking at least," he smiled. "But it's a long walk around front...unless...do you have a key for the back door?"
"I guess it is a long walk, isn't it?" she grinned. "Silly me, I thought this is where visitors are supposed to park in the day. I saw all the cars..."
"Ah, of course," Lee smiled. "They really need to make those visitor parking signs up front bigger."
She smiled tightly, and closed the car door.
"Well, I guess I'd better begin my long trek around front. Hope you have a great day Brother Lee."
"You too Sister Willis. I'm glad I saw you."

10

THE BRIGHTEST STARS

Sandra lay staring at the ceiling, just a few feet from her husband. She fought the urge to wake him, and prayed silently instead, wrestling her thoughts to a place of quiet. The hospital bed was narrow, the mattress was hard and her head throbbed dully, even with the painkillers in her I.V. On any other Thursday morning she'd be meeting with the church event planning committee to figure out what was coming up, or ensure everything was ready for events approaching the following week.

Sandra loved those meetings but today she lay thinking about how drastically life could change in a moment. She tried to thank the Lord for His grace, and told herself the worst was behind them. They could deal with this. She would recover, no matter what, she knew the Word's promises on healing and she would stand on them without wavering. And Theo... well Theo was a fighter, if she'd ever met one. She looked over at his chest rising and falling and lay back down, muttering another quiet, fervent prayer.

Sandra wouldn't have heard the footsteps outside, if a sneaker hadn't squeaked loudly from a misstep on the shiny, polished hallway floors. She looked over at the doorway, doubting the visitor was for them, especially so early in the morning. They'd sent messages through the church elders to request some privacy for the time being, but thanked the congregation sincerely for the flowers and cards and food (even though they couldn't eat most of it.)

Sandra thanked God again that Jewel and Dexter could live with them during this time, so Jewel would at least make sure Tavaris was eating and taking care of himself. She sighed as she thought of Gerald, and whispered a determined prayer for him too. She smiled as she looked at the opposite side of the room, which was blanketed with bouquets and ornate "Get Well Soon!" cards. All those prayers. This would all be over soon, and they'd have another testimony to tell of God's grace and salvation.

A handsome young face poked inside the door, and then another almost-goofy one followed closely behind. "My boy!" she whispered, thrilled. She held her arms out to her son, and then put a finger on her lips with a nod at her husband.

"Mama," Tavaris said quietly with adoring eyes. Those big, brown eyes that tried desperately to hide the fear she'd been able to see since he was a toddler, too scared to go down the playground slide. He gently hugged his mom and glanced over at his sleeping dad. He was instantly happier. "Hi Miss C!" Smoke whispered loudly, and gave his second mom a kiss on the cheek. She smiled brightly at the two young men and clasped each of their hands.

"How you feeling Ma?" Tavaris grimaced, inspecting the gauze and bandage on her head.

"Just fine baby. A dull ache and that's all, and my hair will grow back. They should have the complete diagnosis sometime today."

"We prayin' for y'all twenty-four-seven Miss C!" Smoke added, with his own brand of concern.

Sandra raised her eyebrows and said with a smile, "Well that's good to hear Justin!"

He grinned widely and said, "Now you know to call me *Smoke,* Miss C... but I'ma let it slide on account of you being fuzzy on them painkillers, okay?"

Sandra rolled her eyes and couldn't help but giggle at the involuntary mischief of the boy.

A rustle to their left made the young men turn around. "Aaay... Pops!" Tavaris said with an apprehensive smile. "We didn't wake you did we?"

"No, son... I was just dozing in and out. Glad you here." Reverend Church cleared his throat and blinked his sleepy eyes. He turned in the bed to reach his water on the nightstand, and Smoke jumped forward.

"Here we go Rev!" he said, reaching the cup first and gingerly holding it out for the Reverend.

"Thank you son," Reverend Church whispered, taking a sip. "Did I hear you saying something about praying?"

"Aw maybe Rev..." Smoke replied, the impish twinkle returning to his eyes. "Still praying for the devil to take all them fine honeys out of my path." Tavaris snorted with laughter, while Sandra just shook her head.

"He never will son. He'd have to take you out of this Earth for that..." Reverend Church grinned back. "You have to get yourself around some godly women at church, so one of them can set you straight."

"Whew..." Smoke sighed dramatically, as if the prospect was a prison sentence. "A'ight... I'll be back at church soon," he promised, much to Tavaris' surprise.

"I'll hold it all down for y'all until you're back in the saddle." Tavaris held a fist over his mouth as he stifled his laughter.

"You have my eternal gratitude, Smoke. Truly," the Reverend smiled back.

"Anytime Rev," Smoke nodded seriously, but his face eventually broke into another naughty grin.

"Tavaris, have you heard from Gerald?" Reverend Church asked, changing the subject. "He hasn't been by...and that's okay...I'm just concerned about him."

Tavaris rubbed his head and stared at the floor for a second. "Yeah, he swung by yesterday. He wasn't doing too well but Jewel told him you were both in the hospital."

"He wasn't doing well?"

Tavaris just shrugged, averting his eyes. "He's okay dad. I'm praying hard for him. Don't stress about it, he'll come around. "

Everyone was silent for a moment. "He's going to preach the gospel. Mark my words," Reverend Church said.

"Amen," Sandra agreed, and Tavaris and Smoke added their own doubtful *amens*.

"Let's pray for Gerald real quick. I feel led," Reverend Church decided, pushing himself up in the bed. "Smoke, take my hand, and Tavaris hold your mom's hand."

The four of them made a chain across two hospital beds, and Reverend Church prayed a deep, heartfelt prayer for their son and brother. After they had prayed, and Sandra had dabbed her eyes with a Kleenex, the four hung out and chatted while a nurse came in and checked the charts. Smoke and Tavaris discovered and annihilated some gourmet cookies, macaroons and other gifts that had arrived only the day before. Reverend Church eyed them enviously as another nurse brought Reverend Church and Sandra a menu for either bland grilled chicken and mixed vegetables, or bland grilled fish of some sort, and collard greens.

After about an hour or so, they heard a gentle knock, and another head poked in the door.
"Jeffery!" Reverend Church called. "Come on in."
Their family friend came in and made his rounds, kissing Mrs. Church on the cheek, fist-bumping Tavaris and Smoke, and squeezing his friend and pastor on the shoulder.
"How're you two holding up?" he asked sincerely.
"We're holding..." Reverend Church smiled.
"We don't have to discuss business at all, but I just wanted to let you know that things are going a little better at the church," Jeffery said nodding knowingly.
"Boys can you give us just a moment?" Reverend Church asked. "Take those cookies with you before I eat a box."
"Sure dad," Tavaris grinned through a stuffed mouthful.
"Actually, do you care if we go shoot some hoops for a bit, if y'all don't need anything?"
"No, that sounds great. You guys should be having fun and relaxing. Get your mind off stuff. Enjoy your break!"
"Okay, cool Pop. See you guys later."

Tavaris kissed his mom goodbye, and gave his dad the biggest hug his hospital bed would allow. He and Smoke headed out whispering something about trying to spot a pretty young nurse that had come into the room earlier.
"You've got a great kid, guys," Jeffery smiled at the couple.
"Yeah, he's alright most days," Reverend Church grinned.

"Oh hush, he's an absolute gem!" Sandra chided her husband, with a smile.

"Not too many boys will get up this early to see mom and dad at the hospital," Jeffery added.

"Very true. I couldn't ask for more," Reverend Church agreed happily. "So what's shakin' Jeff?"

Jeffery put on his business face, and Sandra sat up anxiously.

"Sooo, this is just my opinion but it seems the FBI investigators might be leaning away from trying to implicate you in anything, Rev."

"What makes you think that?"

"Well, they've been cross-checking everything with the time of the money transfers... and y'alls phone records and hospital visitation records indicate you have clear alibis. Of course they're not ruling anything out entirely, but initially they seem to think it's checking out."

"What about you?" Reverend Church asked pointedly. He knew his friend and right hand man wouldn't misunderstand him.

"As it turns out, my credit cards transactions, and several reliable eyewitnesses put me at Outback Steakhouse and then Pinkberry Frozen Yogurt during the time of the transfers."

"The transfers could have been scheduled," Reverend Church replied, playing the devil's advocate.

"True, and that's why they're not completely dismissing us as potential suspects. However, it's a step in the right direction," Jeffery smiled. He was trying desperately to find some source of good news for the couple he loved and respected so much.

As they spoke, another knock came at the door. This time it was three smiling faces.

"Whoa!" Reverend Church chuckled. "Who knew the party was at the early morning shift at the hospital right?"

"Haha, I know man!" Pastor Baker laughed back. "We just saw Tavaris and his buddy leaving." Pastor Baker was flanked by Reverend Williams and Bishop Davis.

"Jeffery," Pastor Baker nodded, and his nod was met with a greeting to all three from the younger man.

"We heard you're allowed to eat as many *Ferrero Rocher* chocolates as you can keep down?" Bishop Davis grinned, holding up an intimidating box of the gourmet hazelnut delicacies. Reverend Church just shook his head at his tormenter.

"Hi Sandra!" Reverend Williams said, as he walked over and kissed his friend's wife on the cheek. "How're you holding up dear?"

"Oh, you know the Lord knew if I just had myself to worry about it wouldn't be a challenge, so he gave me this one to worry about while I'm in here." she smiled. All six laughed together.

"Well?" Reverend Church looked at Bishop Davis. "You just threatening or you gonna bring those bad boys over here?"

"You can have ONE Theo!" Sandra interjected immediately, as Bishop Davis looked over at her for permission.

"Yeah, that's gonna happen," Reverend Church grinned and rubbed his hands together. They all laughed again.

***

On one end of the city park, kids yelled happily, chasing each other around a well used set of swings and climbed up and down what was supposed to be a pirate ship. The painted grass fields had six different teams playing friendly games of soccer, while the track wrapping around the park bustled with runners of all shapes and sizes.

People walked their dogs, a dad was practicing T-ball with his daughter, and a few others ate secluded lunches on their own park benches. The real action was going down at the basketball courts though. Three pickup games of four-on-four buzzed back and forth across each court, with the intensity of an NBA final. In the parking lot next to the courts, several highly-modded street racers were thumping beats, just barely out of noise complaint range. About thirty young men and women were hollering and hooting at the players as they all took turns to shout encouragement to their friends, and talk all kinds of trash to the others. The scene appeared friendly, with nothing more than a few typical taunts but off to one side, a few heavy-duty characters sat in front of a cluster of cars. They surveyed the scene, less interested in the score of the games and more interested in potential customers in the crowd. Anyone who knew anything knew these guys were slinging everything from boosted phones to multiple felony amounts of controlled substances.

As the boys strolled up to the courts, one game ended and Smoke asked if he could jump in on the next one. The group who were up next immediately accepted him, benching their grumbling, lowest man. Although shorter than most, Smoke was renowned in streetball.

"Aw y'all switchin' players at the last second?" the lanky leader of the opposing team complained. Smoke knew him as G-man, a high-school dropout with a formidable reputation.

"What you can't handle a little Smoke, playa?" an equally tall youth from Smoke's team replied. He appeared to be the unofficial team leader.

G-man sneered and spat off the court. "Fine... bring your smoke and mirrors. I got something for that."

"Ooooh!" several of the spectators jeered.

The game started, and Tavaris strategically sat next to a group of pretty girls who were already giggling at him and whispering among themselves.

"This you?" one of the girls smiled, batting her eyelids while holding the latest copy of *Charlotte Magazine*. Inside was the full feature on the gifted, young athlete as one of Charlotte's rising stars.

"Oh hey... that article is out already?" he replied, with a modest smirk. "Let me see that. Looks like they got my good side," he winked at her, and she turned, swooning to her friends. Before he knew it, he was surrounded by the group of girls oohing and aahing over the magazine article. Tavaris, of course, ate it all up, grinning and flirting with every single one of them.

On the court, Smoke was already tearing through the opposition's defense, scoring two baskets while still making time to yell "Aw, save some for me T!" Tavaris waved him off, chuckling and explained to the young ladies how tough a photo shoot and interview was. Getting all padded up under the blazing studio lights. They readily consoled him and the boldest even asked if she could feel his bicep. He obliged and happily endured a frenzy of girls feeling his bulging arms. Smoke continued to grumble while laying up basket after basket, much to the joy of his new team mates. Before long even the benched kid was smiling.

The opposing team, however, were not taking so kindly to both Smoke's ridiculously fast offensive game, and Tavaris' equally speedy flirting game. To add insult to injury, Smoke started getting bored of dribbling rings around the other team, and began faking, and passing shots to his new buddies so they could rack up a few goals. After two more baskets for Smoke's team, G-man muttered a few curses, and spat in Tavaris' direction. Tavaris ignored him, and continued entertaining his adoring fans.

The game continued when one of Smoke's team intercepted a pass, and instantly bounced it to Smoke. He made a beeline for the net, and went hard in the lane for the layup. G-man had been waiting for this moment, and came running in at full force, slamming into Smoke's torso, spinning him around violently and sending him crashing onto the pavement. Tavaris jumped up and ran onto the court to confront G-man.

Smoke got up gingerly and intercepted Tavaris, who had fire in his eyes, "I'm good, T. I'm good," he said, holding up his hands. Tavaris sidestepped him and pushed his face into G-man's.

"What's your problem?" he snarled.

"You the problem fool. Look around you. This ain't church," G-man sneered, as his cohorts snickered.

"Yo, let's just go, T. Whatever man, who needs this?" Smoke said, looking around for assistance just in case. Amazingly, his new teammates had melted off to the other side of the court.

"I ain't backing down from this punk," Tavaris replied, pushing his face into G-mans.

"Oh you better listen to your little boyfriend, church boy. Keep that football career on track," G-man growled, his eyes icing over.

Tavaris clenched his fists and almost imperceptibly shifted his onto his back foot, loading his right hand.

"G-MAN! FALL BACK!" a monster of a man roared as he swaggered over. He was at least six-foot-four, and two hundred-and-eighty pounds of solid muscle. He was older than the group and appeared to be in his late thirties.

"Fall back? What you mean fall back?" G-man protested, but kept his eyes on Tavaris.

"You heard me," the giant replied, with a tone that made everyone believe he would not speak again. G-man took a quick glance at the man who didn't even make eye contact, and then reluctantly backed away.

"I'll see you again, church boy," G-man sang to Tavaris as he walked away.

"I look forward to it punk," Tavaris replied.

"That's right, you better walk away. We *run* this city!" Smoke added, suddenly finding his courage. The behemoth of a man just turned around and walked back to the cars, thumping beats.

Tavaris grabbed Smoke and started walking after the man to thank him. "C'mon, you wild man," he said to Smoke, shaking his head with a smirk. "What a piece of work huh?"

"I thought you were gonna drop him there and then dawg," Smoke yipped excitedly.

"Oh I was," Tavaris said, with another steely gaze after the vanquished G-man.

As they caught up to the giant thug, Smoke said, "Yo, T, ain't that yo' brother?"

Tavaris squinted and then smiled. "Yeah, that's him." They walked up to the group, swaggering and smiling.

"Yo, G! How come I always know where to find you?" Tavaris smiled at his older brother.

Gerald grinned and shook his head. Judging from his slightly glassy eyes, Tavaris figured his brother had been smoking a little weed. Gerald couldn't sincerely call the hulking quarterback his *little* brother anymore, but he threw in a jibe anyway. "I guess we just on the same wavelength baby bro?"

They bumped fists, while Tavaris gave and received solemn nods to and from several of the other crew. He gave some dap to a few of the better known characters.

"What you up to?" Tavaris asked his brother.

"Watching you get ready to catch a beat down. It was like seven on two out there," Gerald replied with a disapproving frown.

"Yeah, but Michael Clark Duncan over here rolled up and smashed the whole thing."

"Good thing I know people, huh?" Gerald winked.

"No doubt..." Tavaris replied somberly. "Yo, thank you Big Man. For real," Tavaris shouted to the giant, who was two cars over. The giant simply nodded back.

"Hey Tavaris!" a pretty young girl with hot shorts and a bikini top crooned, eyeing the young man up and down before snapping her gum.

Tavaris replied casually, "Hey Jada." He'd had enough flirting for one day.

Smoke decided to jump into the conversation, "Y'all taking odds?" he asked Gerald.

"Nah not today man. Took some heat from the park Po-Po last week, so we layin' low for now."

Smoke frowned like a seasoned gambler, while Tavaris just shook his head.

"So when you coming back home, G?" Tavaris asked his brother seriously.

Gerald threw his hands up as if he didn't want to hear it.

"Not today T. I can't depend on them anymore. I gotta make my own way."

"How you making a way ... hustling, drinking, smoking, who knows what else? C'mon man."

"You still too young to understand, lil' brother," Gerald replied. At this point, Gerald's friends quickly lost interest in the conversation, and turned away to occupy themselves with other business. Gerald suddenly became very intrigued with the games that had started up again on the courts.

"I understand perfectly!" Tavaris said in determination. "I understand that I want my brother back. I want the person that taught me to catch a football. The dude that taught me to respect people that can't do the things I can do." Tavaris looked into his brother's eyes, searching for a glimmer of hope. Gerald just looked away. "What about that person that used to read the Bible to me every night?"

"C'mon, T. That was a long time ago," Gerald countered.

"You remember that poem I wrote you when I was five?"

"You know I'll never forget it."

Tavaris raised his eyebrows expectantly at his brother. Gerald sighed dramatically but said, "Big brother, big brother, I'll be there till the end. I'll always love you, you are my best friend." His eyes softened as he said it, and Tavaris saw his glimmer of hope.

"Ain't nothing changed G. I love you, man."

"I love you too, lil' brother," Gerald replied, blinking more than usual. He held out his arms to Tavaris who was already on his way in for a hug. They embraced each other and Tavaris rested his head on his big brother's shoulder for a second. He could almost pretend they were kids again, and they'd be able to hang out and play video games before bed.

"Meet me at the hospital tonight?" Tavaris asked, as he released the hug. "For me, if nobody else?"

Gerald sighed again but said, "Okay. I'll be there baby bro." Tavaris' face broke into the happiest smile and he slapped his brother's hand, and gave him another man-hug.

"All right!" he said. "I know I can always count on you."

Gerald grinned and shook his head, waving his little brother off.

Smoke, right on cue, chirped, "Yo, all that backing fools down got me *starving* T. You wanna grab some burritos?"

"Sounds great!" Tavaris agreed and smiled again at his brother. Gerald held his index finger and thumb up like a play gun, and pointed it Tavaris, who nodded. He and his buddy walked to their car and Smoke climbed into the driver's seat, jabbering about how lucky Tavaris was, that his big brother saved his life.

Smoke wheeled out of the parking lot, and headed to the neighborhood Taco Bell. He decided to take the back roads as he figured correctly that traffic would already be starting to back up on the main roads. Tavaris absently spun his basketball on his finger, while Smoke sang along with his latest R&B download from iTunes, apparently deep in thought. Suddenly he said, "T, we need to have a serious conversation."

"About what?" Tavaris replied, surprised at his friend's tone.

"About what? About the court!? Man, you could've got us killed out there."

"Boy, please! I fear no man," Tavaris clicked his tongue.

"I fear no man? I fear no man! Okay, mister badass... so... that means you told your dad you been seeing that party girl, Keisha, right?"

"What! I'd fight G-man 10 times before I tell my dad that," Tavaris said in mock horror. They both erupted in laughter.

"I fear no man," Smoke shook his head. They chuckled again for another moment.

"I kinda feel bad about that now they both laid up in the hospital," Tavaris said, looking out of the window. Smoke kept his eyes straight ahead, not knowing what to say for moment. "I feel ya, T."

***

Down a narrow side lane, a green Ford F350 barreled along while, behind the wheel, its middle-aged driver cursed into his cell phone, "I told you Sally-Beth, this divorce is not going to happen. I don't want to hear another word about it, until we've talked things out completely!"

His face reddened as an angry female voice squawked out of the earpiece.

"Hello? Hello..."

"GAAAWD- AARRGGHH!" The man yelled, as he whacked the steering wheel with the heel of his hand. He looked at his phone as he approached the intersection, tapping the last called number with his thumb. As the call dialed, he held it up to his ear.

"We're sorry. The customer you are trying to reach is not available. Please try again la-"

The man punched the red phone button with his finger, ending the call. He gritted his teeth and looked down, opening his texting app, and began to thumb a message.

***

Tavaris and his buddy, bounced in their seats, to the smooth bass line and flawless vocals of the latest hip-hop track downloaded on Smoke's phone.

Smoke looked over at his friend and said seriously, "Man, I'm telling ya...one day homey. I'm gonna be a star. I know I got what it takes."

"Oh, I know you do homes! You gonna get your big break singing the national anthem at one of my NFL games," Tavaris replied with his lightning fast wit.

"Oh, is that how it's gonna be?" Smoke feigned offense.

"That's how it be, son!"

"Okay, dat's cool! I'll take it," Smoke conceded with mock humility, and they both cackled loudly as they approached an intersection.

***

Seething, the man glanced at his phone every five seconds, already imagining responses for his wife's reply. "Only a damned woman knows how to shred a man's heart in pieces," he grumbled to himself as he wiped away a tear. He was angry at himself for caring, and angrier still that he couldn't control his emotions. He snatched up the phone as he saw a message come in. His heart sank as rage built up in his chest.

"LEAVE ME ALONE OR I'LL GET A RESTRAINING ORDER!"
He swore again as he punched his finger into the reply box, and smashed out a response. He cursed himself for allowing another tear to run down his cheek. He glanced up to check he was still in his lane, but didn't register the two-way stop he was approaching. Through traffic wasn't required to stop.

***

Tavaris flipped his basketball up and down, and bobbed his head to the music. Smoke was adding ridiculously cool harmonies to the melody, and simultaneously tapped along with the bass line. Tavaris shook his head at his friend's talent, and for a moment, could see the future where he truly was a superstar. "Man, if you were only good looking, you could be so famous!" Tavaris teased.

"Aw dude, you know I'm the pretty one. It wouldn't be fair if I worked out as much as you homey," Smoke jabbed back.

"Haha... working out more wouldn't help you dude! The girls all wear heels. You gonna have to eat more green beans to grow some."

"Aw we hittin' below the belt now?" Smoke replied. "I have honeys you don't even know about T!"

Tavaris laughed, hung over the front passenger seat to look in the back. "Where these honeys hiding?" he snickered, rifling through Smoke's stuff.

***

The F350 approached the stop sign at around fifty miles an hour. The driver's eyes were red with tears and rage and fear. He'd swerved back onto the road twice, drifting onto the rumble strip of the shoulder while he typed. He told himself he didn't even care if he flipped into the ditch; that would teach her to appreciate him. He blinked his eyes as he continued typing his reply that if his wife left, he would never allow her back in his house again. He knew it wouldn't work but he had nothing but his pride left to save. He was still looking down as he hurtled through the stop sign.

***

Smoke threw his head back laughing. "Yo you won't find 'em hiding back there bro, they all over town!"
"Yo man, did your mama give you a bag of clothes to take to Goodwill or what dude? This car is a mess" Tavaris prodded relentlessly as he stretched over, pretending to look right under his seat. Smoke was laughing hysterically while he looked at the back seat.
"Hey...is this my watch you borrowed like six months ago?" Tavaris held up an expensive-looking diver's watch.
"Oh...oh hey yeah man...sorry I meant to give that back to you a while back. I thought I'd lost it." Smoke replied sheepishly.
"Maaan, that's not cool homes. This watch is my lucky charm for the ladies..."

"Well, it's been working for me, T!" Smoke erupted in an impish laugh.

"Heeeck no!" Tavaris protested, putting the watch on his arm, then continuing to rifle through Smoke's clothes.

"Hey T, get outta there..." Smoke exclaimed looking into the back seat. "There's nothing else you nee-"

The F350 slammed into the passenger side of the car, ripping halfway through the frame, as glass and shrapnel exploded into the air. The truck lurched crazily off to the right, almost rolling, as the car screeched sideways in a terrible, twisting heap of metal. It spun wildly off the road, and dug violently into the ditch, bouncing to a jarring stop. The driver of the F350 sat behind his deflating airbag in shock, the deformed car coming into view through the hissing, rising steam from the truck's gnarled hood. He saw what looked like one man hanging backwards over the front seat, and the driver slumped out of his window. Both remained motionless.

11

COLLAPSING FRAMEWORK

The officer had only been on the force for six months, and had only had to deliver news like this twice before so he thoroughly dreaded the conversation to follow. Not only did he consider himself severely undertrained for it, but this case was highly unusual. Being the first responder to the scene of the wreck, however, meant that he had to deal with it. He considered himself a real man, able to handle dangerous situations, tough foot chases and even aggressive suspects who had no problem taking a swing or a shot at the police, but this was far more of a challenge, and there was simply no way around it.

He paused for a moment sighing deeply, then took a step toward the doorway and knocked.

"Come in!" a deep, friendly voice called from around the corner. The trooper took a step into the room, and caught the surprised attention of a woman in the left hospital bed. She had a bandage around her head, but was sitting upright. *Mrs. Church*, he thought to himself. He walked into the room, and saw, who had to be, Reverend Church lying on the bed closest to the door. He did not look well, and that made the trooper's stomach flip with anxiety.

"Reverend and Mrs. Church?" he asked, his voice cracking a little.

"Yes. What is this about?" the Reverend asked, struggling up onto his pillows.

"Sir... and ma'am... I'm afraid there is no easy way to tell you this..." he paused and swallowed. *Never pause! he* chastised himself silently. *Just say it.* "I'm terribly sorry to bear the news that your son Tavaris has been involved in a car wreck.... a uhh... fatal car wreck."

"What?" Mrs. Church said, sitting forward in the bed. "What do you mean? Fatal? Fatal to who?" Her eyes flooded with panic.

"Tavaris did not survive the wreck Mrs. Church. I'm truly sorry for your loss." The officer waited.

The air hung with terror and trepidation as the trooper's eyes locked onto Reverend Church's.

"NOOOOOO!" Reverend Church erupted in something between a groan and roar.

"No, it can't be. There is a mistake! Tell me it's a mistake!" Reverend Church howled. When the trooper froze, the giant man threw his face into his hands and cried out again.

"GOOOOD! NOOOOOOOO! This can't be happening!" Sandra Church became hysterical, and began hyperventilating and shaking her hands in front of her body, as if she could shake off the horrifying reality. "No no no no no...that can't be right!" she jabbered. "Tavaris was just here a few hours ago. He would be at the park, playing basketball. Smoke was with him... they drove together. It can't be right... he's my baby boy... my precious baby boy..." Her voice broke into a whine and she started sobbing at the realization of what must have happened.

"Officer..." she begged. "Tell me it may be a mistake."

The trooper cleared his throat again, and became visibly pained. "I'm sorry ma'am, but the boy had his driver's license on his person."

"Nooo," she whined and threw the bed covers off herself. "I have to go see. It isn't Tavaris, you'll see! It's not him, I just know it." The trooper was panicking, and glanced over at Reverend Church for help but he still had his face buried in hands, sobbing.

Mrs. Church proceeded to get out of the bed, and at this point the doctor and nurses who had been waiting at the door, rushed in and gently restrained her. The trooper stepped forward awkwardly, wondering if he should try to help, or if he would make it worse. He decided he would be making it worse, and stepped back, waiting to see if and when the couple might want to hear any more of details. Even worse, he had to find someone to identify the body. Even though it was likely a formality, it was necessary.

After a minute or two, the doctor and nurses managed to get Reverend Church lying back on his pillows. He was still covering his face and crying over and over, "God, no! God? It can't be. Why GOD, WHY?"

Mrs. Church was not so easily pacified and insisted on going over to her husband's bed. Instead of allowing her to get out of her bed, the nurses dropped the left arm of her bed, and wheeled it over next to her husband's, dropping the right side of his, so they could be together.

"We're so sorry for your loss Reverend and Mrs. Church," the doctor said quietly. "Please for the moment, for your own health and safety, remain in your beds. Reverend Church, your I.V is still attached, and Mrs. Church, we're still not sure the surgery has not affected your balance."

Mrs. Church was now leaning over and buried her face in her husband's chest. He put his arm around her, and together they wept, oblivious to the outside world.

"We're going to be right outside if you need anything at all," the doctor continued. "I might suggest a tranquilizer to help a little during this difficult time." With that, he nodded to the nurses, who left the room with moist eyes.

"Perhaps ask if they need any information, and then you might leave them to grieve," he whispered to the obviously inexperienced trooper. The trooper nodded, clearly thankful for the advice. He waited for a few seconds, then pulled a business card out of his wallet.

"Reverend and Mrs. Church, I want to give you time to grieve but if you have any questions, you can ask me now, or I'm going to leave my card with you, and you can call me any time during the workday."

The couple continued sobbing so he placed the card on the stand at the end of the end of Reverend Church's bed and left. On his way out, he gave another card to the doctor, just in case.

As the trooper walked out the double doors, he saw the doctor speaking to a man who was identifying himself as clergy and an acquaintance of the Churches.

"My name is Jeffrey Lee. I can help, I promise. I'm a friend of the Church's, not to mention a certified church counselor." The man, who appeared to have heard this news for the first time himself, was clearly shaken up.

He must be on other business, the doctor thought to himself. The doctor paused for a moment, then nodded and allowed him to enter.

Jeffrey Lee walked up to the couple, who were still groaning and weeping, and simply stood next to Reverend Church's bedside, clasped his hand between his own, and bowed his head.

***

Bernice's one-bedroom apartment was in an older neighborhood, but she had searched for the best location her meager salary at a fast-food joint could afford. She had enough money to get a better place, as she worked double shifts at least three times a week, but instead it was spent on the latest line of jeans, makeup and jewelry. This apparently left very little time to keep the place tidy. Taco Bell wrappers and leftovers were strewn over the coffee table, and rumpled clothes lay about the living room. That didn't seem to faze a very drunk Gerald, who despite her protests and shoves, wouldn't stop pawing at her.

"C'mon baby... you know I've only got eyes for you!" Gerald slurred, as he fumbled with his metal Altoid mint box, eventually victorious in extracting one, only to drop it on the carpet and start the whole process over again. "Gerald I told you, I am not going to let you bring me down anymore." Bernice stood with her arms crossed, staring in frustration at his endless attempt to open the mints. "All you want is a booty call when none of your other chicks want you." He kept fumbling with his mint box and after she couldn't take it any longer she snatched the box from him, took one out, and put it in his hand. Gerald responded by grinning and flopping his arm around her, groping at her. "Get OFF me Gerald!" she yelled, shrimping away from him again. "God! What don't you understand about 'No!'?" "Aw you confusing me baby!" he said in mock surprise. "C'mon... you know you love it," he grinned idiotically. "No Gerald. Not anymore. I don't love it, and don't want no part of it until you prove to me you've changed." His face turned dark. "What you want some money?" He staggered slightly as he dug his hand into his pocket, and pulled out a healthy roll of notes. He peeled off a hundred dollar bill and flicked it in her face.

"I don't want your dirty money Gerald," she said slapping his hand.

"Aww.... look at you all high and mighty. I know you want Mr. Franklin over here... you want me to pay? Huh? Is that what you wanna be to me?" His face was full of aggression and contempt.

"Get your stupid ass outta here," Bernice spat. "I knew I shouldn't have let you in."

"Yeah, so why did you?" he argued, grabbing her arm.

"That's a damned good question! LET GO OF ME!" she yelled, as she jerked her arm away. Gerald's face was bitter as he staggered after her, but she pushed him backward as hard as she could and he tumbled over the coffee table, sprawling onto the floor.

"Aw see now you got me hella mad..." he muttered to himself as he tried to push himself up to his knees. Bernice darted around the other side of the coffee table toward the door, a look of fear crossing her face. As she did, Gerald's phone lit up and rang on the coffee table. Bernice snatched it up and examined the number. It didn't come up as a contact, but few of the numbers on Gerald's phone did. He simply knew those numbers by heart.

"Yo, if that's Little Ricky tell that fool I'm dry today," Gerald slurred. "He gonna have to swing by Sugar himself."

"This better not be one of your hos!" Bernice snapped, and answered the phone.

"Thought you didn't care..." Gerald muttered to himself, grinning and somehow managing to get to one knee.

"This is Bernice, who is this?"

A male voice squawked on the other end.

"Yeah he's here but he's completely drunk and probably high on God knows what. I've been trying to get him out of here for ten minutes but he won't go. Who am I speaking to?"

Bernice listened as Gerald began a new quest to dig his mint box out of his pocket. He didn't notice her eyes widen as he wobbled to his feet, but decided to abandon the mint challenge. Instead he took the opportunity to slide behind Bernice and kiss her on the shoulder. She covered her hand with her mouth, oblivious to Gerald's advances.

"WHAT? Oh dear Lord Jesus, are you sure?"

The voice squawked on the other end of the phone and Bernice became aware of Gerald touching her. She shrugged away. "Oh my God. Yes... yes I'll tell him. Okay. Goodbye."

"Tell me what baby? That you can't resist me?" Gerald said playfully, shuffling toward her for one last try.

Bernice grabbed both of his arms tightly and said, "Gerald! Look at me...LOOK AT ME!"

He frowned and tried to pull away from her grip, but she moved her head into his view again, forcing him to make eye contact.

"Gerald, that was your brother-in-law. It's Tavaris..." Her eyes glistened, and she choked up.

"What's Tavaris angel? Come on... give me some sugar..."

"Gerald!" she said insistently. "Tavaris was in a wreck. A big truck ran a stop sign.... He... he didn't make it."

Somewhere in the fog of Gerald's altered state, reality tried to slap him hard in the face. He frowned again and stared at her, still swaying slightly and trying to focus.

"What'd you say?"

"Honey I'm so sorry..." Bernice stepped toward him, and put her arms around him. "He didn't make it."

"Wait, wait, wait...you messin' with me! That's cruel girl. T's my baby brother... ain't nothing happen to him. He got a bright future ahead of him...he's fine."

"I'm so sorry..." Bernice could only repeat, choking through tears. "I'm... I'm so sorry Gerald."

"You for real?" he asked, cold hard truth sobering him fast. "T was in a wreck?"

"Yes baby..."

"Naw man... T's my baby brother... I just saw him at the park. He's my baby bro..."

Gerald's eyes filled with tears but he kept denying the news. Suddenly his knees gave way and he crumpled to the floor, falling through Bernice's arms.

Startled, she cried out, and then lowered herself wrapping her arms around him.

"He's my baby brother...I was there for him today...he's my baby bro..."

Gerald wept like an abandoned lamb, rocking back and forth as the life-changing news bore down upon him.

"It should've been me..." he wept. "It should've been me..."

12

FALLOUT

Jeffery had served in ministry long enough to know that in these situations, saying nothing at all is worth more than anything you could offer. The crushing silence, however, was difficult to resist, but he knew that any single sentence uttered in the midst of such intense grief would, more often than not, come out as shallow and insincere. So Jeffery simply stood next to the hospital bed, with a bowed head and a hand on Reverend Church's shoulder, while the man and his wife wept for the plight of their youngest son.

After his legs and feet and arm had become numb for many minutes, Jeffery slowly patted Reverend Church on the shoulder and walked to a chair, where he sat and began to pray silently. If he believed in coincidence, he would say his arrival at the time of the news of Tavaris' untimely passing certainly qualified. He had come to visit the Churches, and weigh up the Reverend's condition to see if he could share with him, what he wanted to. As these things sometimes happen though, he had arrived about thirty seconds after the police officer and was about as shocked as the Churches, to hear the news from the hospital corridor. He was thankful he was there, as he was sure his presence was somewhat comforting to the couple. At least they weren't entirely alone in those initial moments, but he knew he couldn't share the news he needed to. And he knew time was of the essence.

After a long while, Reverend and Mrs. Church's sobs ebbed, and they fell vacantly silent. The two of them remained in each other's embrace for some time, then Reverend Church sighed as if releasing his last reserve of hope.

"Why?"

Jeffery flinched at the sudden question, his head jerking up. "I'm sorry Pastor, what did you say?"

Reverend Church paused, staring into the distance. Just as the silence became uncomfortable he said softly, "Why my son?"

Lee understood the question. It was one of the oldest, and most common in grief. He knew the Reverend meant *Why did God allow this to happen? The disease and money issues I can handle. Why my son?* He knew the prescribed answer by heart, but strangely in this situation it didn't really make sense to him. So he replied honestly, as was his policy.

"I'm so sorry Pastor, I have no earthly idea."

Reverend Church nodded slowly, his face grey and empty.

"At the very least Pastor Church," he added softly. "We know Tavaris is in glory with our King right now." It was the only hopeless thing Jeffery knew to be absolutely true, without sounding like a meaningless platitude.

Reverend Church remained silent and staring.

"How could this happen?" Mrs. Church said softly. "We serve so faithfully. What about the angels protecting him?"

Jeffery had been in many situations where people had questioned God, but he had never been trained to counsel one of the most prominent pastor couples in the region. If he had to be perfectly honest, Jeffery had a few questions of his own.

"My precious friends," Jeffery said softly. "God will see you through this. I'm sure we can agree, He didn't cause this tragedy."

Reverend Church only sighed, and his wife buried her head into his shoulder, beginning to sob softly again.

"Tavaris always spoke of how much he loved and respected you Jeff," Reverend Church offered quietly. "He said you always took time with him in Kids Church and Sunday School, since he was a young man. He said your tutoring in math and economics helped him remain on the football team."

Jeffery just nodded a quiet thanks, but suddenly his emotions were getting the better of him too. The shock of it all, and the sight of this precious family in pain, brought a fresh wash of grief, and Jeffery bowed his head to hide his own tears.

After about fifteen minutes, one of the nurses quietly walked back into the room with a tray carrying two little cups of pills.

"Reverend and Mrs. Church, I have some calming aids we think will really help you through this time." There was no response from the couple, so Jeffery just nodded for the nurse to put the tray down, and motioned that he would ask them later.

The nurse put the tray down but announced, "I'll have to check some vitals on both patients now." The use of the clinical term *patients* indicated she wasn't going to take no for an answer, so Jeffery stepped aside, allowing her to attach some sort of machine to Reverend Church's arm. After a minute, the nurse turned it off and frowning, typed some notes into the attached keyboard.

She next went over to Mrs. Church's side and performed the same routine. She then said, "Mrs. Church, I'm afraid I'm going to have to insist you take this medication. It's a simple tranquilizer, but is absolutely necessary as your heart rate is severely elevated, which could endanger you since you've just undergone a cranial procedure, and your blood pressure simply cannot spike." Mrs. Church was about to protest, when a quiet nod from Jeffery made her relent. "It can't hurt Sandra," he said kindly. She swallowed the pills and turned back to stare at the sheets, her face curled up in anguish.

Another soft knock at the door made Jeffery and the nurse look up. Standing in the doorway was Dexter practically holding up his wife, Jewel. The moment she saw her parents, she wailed and collapsed into her husband's arms. Dexter struggled to hold her up, and Jeffery jumped forward to help. They carried Jewel over to her mom's side of the bed, while Jeffery pulled his chair up for her. Jewel instead, stabilized herself and leaned over her mom's bedrail and wept in her mother's arms. Mrs. Church held her daughter's head, and began weeping again. The moment was so emotional, it was difficult for the rest of the group to maintain their composure.

"How could this happen? How could God let this happen to my baby brother? He is such a good boy." Jewel sobbed. Everyone instantly became silent again, and Reverend Church reverted to his thousand yard stare.

During his tenure in ministry, Jeffery had seen many things. Things he wished he could forget. But he had never seen anything quite like this. A prominent pastor, afflicted with a mysterious illness, under scrutiny for financial fraud - which Lee didn't believe for a second. Next his wife falling ill with a malignant tumor and now the man's *good* son tragically passing away. Lee quietly shook his head at the absurdity of it all. Indeed, he had several questions of his own, because he knew the scriptures. He knew the right answers, but in times like this, it took tremendous faith to hold on to the assurance that God would make all things turn out for good for those involved in the situation.

> *Though the fig tree does not bud*
> * and there are no grapes on the vines,*
> *though the olive crop fails*
> * and the fields produce no food,*
> *though there are no sheep in the pen*
> * and no cattle in the stalls,*
> *yet I will rejoice in the Lord,*
> * I will be joyful in God my Savior.*
> *The Sovereign Lord is my strength;*
> * he makes my feet like the feet of a deer,*
> * he enables me to tread on the heights.*

Jeffery knew the verse by heart. In fact, he had quoted it to himself just the day before. He shook his head at a sudden thought that popped up. *Imagine trying to rejoice right now? How would one even begin to try to do that?* He concluded he had no idea, and some mysteries were best left to the Lord. He looked up to Dexter who caught his glance, and blinked and shook his head slightly as if to mirror the man's thoughts. *I don't know the answer,* he seemed to convey. He put his arm around Dexter and whispered "You okay man?"

Dexter nodded, but you could see the agony in his face. He was desperately trying to be strong for his wife, but he loved Tavaris like a little brother. The shock of it all had hit him hard. He was clearly thankful that someone was asking about him though, and he could let his guard down for a second. The two men looked up as yet another soft knock was heard at the door. Reverend Church's three companions were standing there with grim faces, but

Reverend Williams mouthed "Can we come in?" to Jeffery. He nodded, and he and Dexter moved over a little, making some room.

Jeffery pondered the fact that Reverend Williams, Bishop Davis and Pastor Baker always seemed to show up as a group. He admired the three men, and was glad they were there. Sort of. *They should know what to say,* he thought to himself. Each man, with somber expressions, gave Jeffery a firm handshake as they made their way to the head of the bed. In a sudden, swirling moment he mentally stepped back from himself and wondered if this was all really happening. He simply couldn't believe Tavaris, whom he had always believed would take over the church from his dad, was actually dead. It was enough to rock one's existential framework. Everything they taught and believed as a church seemed to be rattled by this one lone and very final occurrence. He supposed he was more shaken by the fact that Reverend Church's typical "I got this," demeanor had disappeared. What was left truly troubled him.

The three Christian leaders stood at the Church's bedsides, and simply prayed quietly. Reverend Church, who had remained relatively strong until now, began crying again, as Reverend Williams held his hand and Pastor Baker patted his shin over the bed covers. Perhaps it was the dashed hope that Tavaris would someday become like the four of them; a minister in his own right, stately and anointed like his three friends, full of wisdom and knowledge. Perhaps it was just the overwhelming nature of all that had come against him, but Reverend Church found new reserves of tears. He wept and wept and wept.

It almost became too much, even for Jeffery, who was stoic by nature but seeing so many people close to him, mourning so bitterly, he decided he needed a breath of fresh air. He went outside, and prayed for God to comfort his friends. Yet even Jeffery began to wonder what the purpose of this all was.

13

THE DARKNESS

Unseen to the naked eye, but more real than his own flesh, a shadow drifted like wisps and tails from within Reverend Black. Wherever he walked, something unnatural, dark and malignant emanated from within his being, its eerie tendrils trailing behind him, curling like dark vapor. The man had long been increasingly aware of the presence that inhabited him...that drove him to the ends of its own purpose, yet he became comfortable with this. He had in fact, accepted it and reasoned it as helping him in his mission. The presence served his own desires, which of course, was how the entity came to dwell within him.

There was a time when Reverend Black's spirit belonged wholly to God, and he had operated in God's power, will and purpose for his life. Reverend Black, however, had naively left certain areas of his life unchecked for many years. Areas that at first appeared benign, but were clearly outlined in the Word of God as critical to one's ongoing walk with God. Despite cautions from various friends, ministers and colleagues, ministry slowly became a god to him, an escape. As all deception creeps in, his desires were about ninety percent pure. Yet for the remaining ten percent of that dream, if he were honest, Reverend Black would admit it was his own, personal desire to have a successful international ministry, supported financially by a large, faithful home mega church, full of devoted believers-in him. His plan was to woo and foster more than a few millionaires, spiritually nurtured by him, and in turn, they would continually "bless" his ministry.

As time went on, the alarm bells and warnings increased along the way. Deacons, elders and friends requested personal, loving meetings in which they tried their best to approach these concerns for Reverend Black. They said he was beginning to neglect his young wife for the ministry, and focusing perhaps on marketing, more than feeding the flock. Also the teachings were becoming increasingly focused on money.

"Teaching on giving, and sowing and reaping," they each tried to explain, "...is not in itself a bad thing, nor unscriptural. But it was only a *part* of what the full gospel was about." At first, he would always agree but never changed course.

They explained, "God would give us what we needed, when we needed it, *if* we were diligent to walk in His will." Reverend Black, considered their words, but always weighed their objections against his own lofty goals for the church. He decided he would consider their advice, but would not allow these slower moving, old men to derail the vision he convinced himself the Lord had given him.

It was at this time, the enemy struck the hardest. At first, several lower ranking demons were assigned to distract the prayer warriors in the church. Their strategy was to sidetrack these few disconnected members who knew they had an anointing from God to intercede for their church, yet during that time, were somehow never able to come together as a group and meet regularly.

Individually they were attacked, one with unforeseen problems at work, another with illness in the family, a third with two cars breaking down and general financial stress. With the prayer shields down, a group of malicious and determined specialists focused on Reverend Black and his wife. One devil worked endlessly to create delusions of grandeur and obsessive goals for the Reverend's ministry. Another, specializing in vanity and pride, whispered to Mrs. Black of how much greater value she was than what she was currently receiving. She had far too much worth to be ignored. It whispered she was wasting her beauty and musical talents serving tirelessly and thanklessly in her husband's self-glorifying church.

At first Mrs. Black knew to resist the thoughts, and pushed them aside. Yet she sadly lacked the knowledge to *speak* the written Word of God to these thoughts, unaware of their origin. She believed they were simply her own, exhausted mind. Over and over and over the relentless special agent wore her down. As Reverend Black, spent longer hours at his church office, the devil whispered to Mrs. Black that her husband was perhaps seeing someone else. This thought she failed to resist. It made sense to her, and it made her exceptionally angry.

Mrs. Black accepted the suspicion, began to mull it over, and one day decided to check her husband's email, and phone call history. She saw a few unrecognized numbers, and began googling them, becoming more and more obsessed. Any number she didn't recognize, she circled and called anonymously to hear who was on the other end. One day, after calling many numbers, hiding her own with *67, she heard a woman's voice. *She sounds* *young and beautiful,* a voice whispered. Mrs. Black believed it was her own. She was now fully convinced her husband was having an affair. Within weeks, she was confiding in the worship leader; a young, single and highly charismatic young man. Unknown to her, another demon, specifically skilled in the arts of lust and seduction, had been working on this young man for some time.

The news of the affair, and resulting church split entirely blindsided Reverend Black. His wife demanded he move out. She unleashed a torrent of rage at him, and said he spent so much time at the church, he might as well just sleep on his office couch. She also accused him of having his own affair, even though she couldn't prove it. Surprisingly, at this point, Reverend Black was the closest he'd ever been to getting his focus back to his Lord. He knew something had been wrong, and he broke down in tears, asking the Lord where he had failed. While angels of light fought to get through to protect Reverend Black, he began to succumb to the enemy's lies. The wicked spirit whispered "*You have been serving God so diligently. It was all for His kingdom... how could a good and loving God allow this to happen, while you worked tirelessly to build His church?* "

Sadly, Reverend Black had ignored the gentle warning voice of the Holy Spirit for far too long. Somewhere in the depths of his heart, he knew this was a pivotal, gravely dangerous moment...a do-or-die decision. But he had little strength to fight against the compound attacks, as he had been out of practice for years, no longer praying deeply, nor drawing on the strength of the Holy Spirit. Jealousy, rage and rabid unforgiveness took root in Reverend Black's heart.

As he couldn't, or didn't want to hear anything from Heaven, he swore he would have his vengeance. He vowed to create the largest, most successful ministry America had ever seen, and remarry a Christian supermodel. Then he would teach on national television how, even though people fail us, God will always bring something better. As he swore these goals to himself, the Holy Spirit reminded him that his purpose was the Great Commission, to lead people to Christ. Reverend Black's countenance darkened, as he said out loud, "If Jesus can let this happen, I want no part of Him, nor His ministry. I'll do it my way!" The evil spirit, crouching, waiting...slithered inside Reverend Black's being, and took up residence.

As Reverend Black was making his fateful decision, his wife was praying a last ditch prayer of her own. Many in the church had reviled her, and viciously turned against her and her lover. She felt ashamed, dirty and desperately wondered how it had all gone so horribly wrong. The worship leader had since left the church, and instead of repenting and seeking restoration, spoke to the owners of an outlet mall. He wanted to use a personal loan to rent a storefront, and start his own fellowship.

He hadn't returned her calls in several days, so Mrs. Black prayed one last time, asking God to forgive her. "Lord, If You can only turn my husband's heart back to me," she prayed, "and You help him make an effort to spend time with me, I promise I will humbly beg his forgiveness for my unfaithfulness, and take him back into the house."
The next morning, a sheriff knocked on Mrs. Black's door and delivered notarized divorce papers. As she opened the envelope, her tears blurred the lengthy pages where Reverend Black's attorney stated he would be providing zero alimony, in light of her betraying their marriage vows. Phase one of the enemy's plan was complete.

***

"Sims, I'm not going to tell you again. Just follow the plan, and everything will be perfectly fine," Reverend Black paced back and forth, his anger rising.

The voice of his deacon squawked a response on the other end.

"Listen, we simply cannot keep this cash on hand any more, and I'll be damned if the government is going to steal half of it."

The phone squawked again.

"The last thing Sugar wants is for me to *sic* Stone and his goons on their entire operation. Just chill. You are fine Sims. Sugar knows how much is in the cases. We know how much is in the cases. No problem. Just make sure the money gets on the plane, and we're golden. Sugar's boy will do the rest once they get to the islands."

The phone squawked one more short burst, and then the men said goodbye and hung up. Reverend Black muttered a quiet curse and threw the prepaid burner phone into his desk drawer.

Deacon Sims climbed out of his car, and walked around to the popped trunk. He opened it, and stared at the two travel-sized cases laying there. It was hard to believe so much money was contained in such small cases. Sure many of the bills were singles, and five dollars, but it was still a giant load of cash. Enough that he would be set, if he bolted with it...he wondered for a second what would happen if he simply took off. He shivered suddenly, and shrugged off the thought. There was something very unsettling about Reverend Black when he was enraged, and he didn't want to find out more about it. Not to mention Sugar and his crew of monsters.

He knew what he was doing was possibly wrong, and highly illegal, but by the same token he had been persuaded by Reverend Black that over a year of cash from the church's offerings would be better served to the ministry's purposes tax-free, in a carefully crafted, not-for-profit shell organization in the Cayman Islands. Deacon Sims knew very well that churches don't pay taxes on their donations, however, the grand and pretty ingenious schemes of Reverend Black's stock market trading would require that the church would, in fact, need to cough up a good chunk of dues to Uncle Sam. This transfer to the Cayman account however, would enable, through a web of concealed cash infusions, a Bible-based restaurant, Christian music-label and other business schemes to not only operate at a loss on paper (writing off even more taxes.) They would also guarantee rewarding those who spent time tirelessly working on these ventures.

"Give to Caesar what is Caesar's, and to God what is God's," Reverend Black would chant when Deacon Sims first questioned if it was all ethical. The way he explained it, the cash was still going to ministry purposes, only much more would be able to be utilized for the good work of the gospel. Deacon Sims never felt completely comfortable with the reasoning, but when Reverend Black wrote down a number, reflecting his first year's cash rewards for faithful service, Deacon Sims couldn't say no.

He sighed, hefted the two cases out of the trunk, and gazed at the ridiculously swollen muscles of the larger-than-life men leaning against the side of two Cadillacs. Next to the cars, a Cessna had its door open and staircase dropped. He reluctantly headed over to the plane.
"Yo, Sims... you got somethin' for yo' Sugar daddy?!" the leader of the group called out. The man was at least six-foot-four, two hundred-and-eighty pounds plus of pure muscle, and wore a permanent snarl.

"You sure ain't my daddy Sugar," Sims replied testily. He hated these men, and wished he could have nothing to do with them.

"Ooh? The lil' mouse got a squeaky lil' voice!" Sugar jeered, standing up straight. "You got anything more to say mouse?" Sugar's men stood at attention, as their leader stepped forward, looming over Deacon Sims.

"Look man, I'm just trying to give you the packages, and be on my way, okay?" Deacon Sims averted his eyes nervously.

"The packages?" Sugar laughed, turning to his men. "He think he in some Ice Cube gangsta movie!" Sugar cackled. His men chuckled with him. Deacon Sims just stood there in humiliation.

"You mean THE MONEY?" Sugar barked. "The eight hundred and seventy five thousand dollars you and your pastor are hussling outta yo' faithful church members?" He paused for effect. "Man, that's cold! Even Sugar don't mess wit' hustlin' churches. Y'all got a special place in hell, fer real."

"We're not hustling them okay. We're still using the money for church projects," Deacon Sims protested weakly.

"Oh okay playa," Sugar laughed, looking back with wide eyes at his men, who cracked up again with him.

"Look, here's the money. Just call Reverend Church and confirm, okay?"

"How I know it's all there?" Sugar asked, his face becoming dead serious. Deacon Sims instantly looked panicked.

"It's all there! I swear it. Count it!"

Sugar's demeanor changed back instantly, and he laughed and laughed. "Ahaha this fool nearly peed on hisself." The men laughed again, dutifully. "Yo, it better all be there. If it ain't you got real problems."

Sugar snatched up the two cases as if they were empty, and motioned with his head for Deacon Sims to leave. "Bye!"

"I need you to call Reverend Church and confirm, Sugar." Sugar smiled down at him, and slowly reached for his hip, which boasted a custom leather holster, and what appeared to be the handle of a gigantic chrome Desert Eagle .50 caliber pistol. Deacon Sims' heart skipped a beat, and his eyes frantically darted from the gun to Sugar's eyes. In a split second he contemplated running, but knew he'd never cover the ground to his car in time.

Sugar slid his hand to his pocket, pulled out a phone and doubled over laughing. "Ahahahaaa... yo, y'all see his face? Ah, I'm dying..." he guffawed. "He thought he was done gonna see his Jesus today, right here on the runway." The goons enjoyed a hearty chuckle again too. Sims just stood there, looking traumatized and wishing nothing more than to get out of there.

"Yo, Rev. I got the cases," Sugar boomed into the phone. "I'll hit you up when your cut is cleared on the other side" Reverend Black's voice squawked on the other end, and Sugar replied "Cool."

"For real now... bye lil' mousey!" Sugar waved off Deacon Sims. He nodded as confidently as he could, and turned and walked away, praying silently that he wouldn't hear a pop and feel a stinging pain in his back.

He made it to his car uneventfully, and got in. "That's it, after my first payment, I am out. I cannot do this one more time," he said to himself.

Deacon Sims started his car but when he looked up what he saw turned his blood ice cold. Sugar and his goons were running behind their two Cadillacs, guns drawn, facing the terminal. He watched the scene play out in slow motion and with morbid curiosity he became totally confused. He was jerked back into reality by the sound of automatic gunfire erupting.

"Oh my God!" he shrieked, as he dove behind his dash. "Oh my god, oh my god, oh god!" he cried, fumbling with the gears. He waited for the bullets to come thudding into his car, as he heard tires screech and then sirens wail. Finally his car slammed into gear and the engine roared forward.

Deacon Sims peeped over the dash as the car hurtled toward the gate at least six black suburbans racing up to the plane. One of them slid in front of the plane's wheels, and one behind, blocking its path. The others were flanking Sugar and his men, returning their fire. Deacon Sims screamed and kept his head low in case of stray bullets, but guided the car toward the private airstrip's exit. He felt a surge of hope as the gates came into view, and then his heart dropped, as he saw a trooper's car next to the entrance. He slowed down, praying the officers hadn't seen him racing away from the runway. He tried to drive as normally as possible.

As he approached the gate, a trooper stepped out into the road, with one hand up, and the other on his holster. Deacon Sims panicked, his mind racing between trying to discuss with the trooper and fake getting away from the shootout, or flooring it through the checkpoint and risking death. The officer must have sensed his mental dilemma, because he unclipped his gun and drew it. *What are you doing? Just stop!* Deacon Sims' mind screamed, as he rolled up to the checkpoint. He braked quickly and slowed the car, but the trooper was already jumpy.

"STOP YOUR VEHICLE NOW!" the trooper shouted, his gun at half-mast.

Deacon Sims braked the car to a sudden stop, and raised his hands in submission. "Whoa!" he mouthed to the cop.

The trooper, now had the attention of his colleagues nearby, who were also approaching the vehicle, guns drawn.

Deacon Sims slowly reached for the window's power button, and rolled it down. "Officer, I'm just trying to get away from that craziness! What is going on?" he asked innocently. Deacon Sims wisely kept his hands in full view on the steering wheel.

"Step out of the vehicle sir!" the trooper commanded.

"Whoa! I heard what sounded like gunfire back there, and it freaked me out. If I was panicked I apologize, I'm just trying to get away from the danger."

"Sir do as I say and step out of the vehicle, NOW! Open the car door from the outside."

Deacon Sims sighed, and shook his head but complied, slowly opening the outer door handle. He stepped out of the car, and said, "Can I just talk to you a minute? I'm pretty traumatized here. Where is your supervisor?"

"Turn around and place your hands on the top of the car," the trooper barked. By this point, the others had run up too, guns drawn, wanting a piece of the action. Two of them grabbed Deacon Sims' arms, and wrenched them up behind him. One of them slapped a pair of cuffs on the church leader.

"What on Earth is going on?" he shrieked, as the two troopers pulled him up off the car.

"One moment sir. We're taking precautions," the trooper held up a finger to silence the man, and then pressed the button on his radio.

"Be advised, we have detained one African-African male, attempting to leave the area driving a..." the trooper walked around to the back of the car. "...maroon Chevy Impala." He then rattled off the license plate number.

"Can you confirm or deny involvement."

Deacon Sims nearly had a heart attack. His vision narrowed, and he began hyperventilating. The trooper waited for seemed like an eternity, and then the radio crackled.

"Be advised, involvement is confirmed. Place the subject under arrest. Repeat, involvement is confirmed."

Deacon Sims legs buckled beneath him, and the two troopers braced under his weight. They lowered him to the ground, where he sank to his knees, and heaved as though he was about to throw up.

"Sir, you are being arrested on the suspicion of involvement with an organized criminal enterprise, and conspiracy to evade income taxes and launder money. You have the right to remain silent. Anything you say can and will be used against you in a court of law..."

The trooper rattled off the rest of the Miranda statement as Deacon Sims began sobbing uncontrollably and crying out desperately to God. The troopers hauled him to his feet and dragged him to the patrol car. They opened the door, told him to watch his head and pushed him into the back. Deacon Sims collapsed his head between his knees and wept like an infant.

14

HOPE DEFERRED

Sandra Church was oblivious to the world. At the urging of her son-in-law, and more than one nurse, she had swallowed two horse-pills that had made her temporarily comatose. As the giddy euphoria began to set in, she'd reflected out loud with a sigh, "The brightest stars really do burn out the fastest..."

Her tone, more than what she said, was discomforting to the four men in the room.

"I suppose God knows best..." she breathed dreamily. Her eyes fluttered, then closed. "...still... I can't believe God would kill my baby boy.... but why isn't he here anymore.... why...?"

She sighed again, and fell into a slow, steady rhythm of breath. Her chest rising and falling, she lay snuggled into her pillows; a picture of seeming serenity. Dexter had taken Jewel to the cafeteria, forcing her to eat something, while Jeffery and the three friends of Reverend Church, remained in the room.

Apostle Baker cleared his throat, and stared at the floor. His two companions exchanged an uneasy glance, and then looked at their afflicted friend staring vacantly out of the window from his hospital bed.

Bishop Davis spoke first. "Theo..." the words jarred the silence, and he flinched at the sound of his own voice. It was the first time any of them had spoken in over an hour. Reverend Church appeared unaware.

"Theo... how you holdin' up brother?" Bishop Davis began. He shifted on his feet nervously. "I can't imagine what you're going through, but we just want you to know we're here if you need us." The words sounded strange, even to himself. In one breath it was as if he was asking his friend to hurry up and feel better. As if this mighty, Godly man's vulnerability was unbearable to them. The next breath sounded like an empty platitude. He decided he needed to hear something from his friend though.

"Theo... you gotta talk to us man. Bottling it up ain't healthy."

After a few moments Reverend Church turned slowly and gazed at his friend, with a frown. Just as it became awkward, he spoke, "How am I holding up?" His eyes seemed to burn holes through Bishop Davis. "I'm not." The Bishop shifted his weight to his other foot, and scratched his head.

"I'm not holding up Jim." Reverend Church held his gaze for a few moments longer, and then turned to stare out the window again.

"You know what I wish?" He squinted his eyes, as if picturing an unhappy dream.

"I wish I could place my grief on a scale. I wish I could quantify it somehow, so I could see just how much anguish God thinks I can bear."

"Aw now Theo..." Bishop Davis began, gently trying to reason with him.

"The Lord treats me as an enemy... making me a spectacle... I cringe to utter any of my family's names because they may be next."

"Buddy..." Apostle Baker said softly. He was going to say more, but Reverend Church continued.

"I don't want anything. I don't want a ministry. I don't want a home. I don't even want food. I hate it all. I wish God would give me what I long for..."

All three men stared at the floor, unsure of what to say.

"I wish it pleased God to totally crush me. Then He would turn His attention from me, and just cut me off."

His friends looked up. "Oh man...Theo please don't speak like that my friend," Reverend Williams cautioned. Jeffery frowned at the entire scene but remained silent.

"Then at least I would have some comfort," Reverend Church ignored his friend. "In my anguish, I would be able to take pride, because I haven't hidden the words of God. I have spoken them boldly, and done my best to raise my family...my church."

"Hey now, you're not thinking straight my friend. Words are powerful buddy, please don't say things like that," Reverend Williams chided again.

"I have no strength left," Reverend Church said, looking over at his sleeping wife. "I can't even hope. What is my end, that I should hope to keep living? Why? What's the point? There is no justice... any time, any place, God can bring me into judgment for being ultimately sinful. So I wish I could just die instead."

"Oh, hey now, hold up a second my friend," Bishop Davis gently chided. Reverend Church turned to look at him. "How can you say things like that brother? What if your congregation hears you? Do you really believe God isn't just? Do you think anything happens without a reason? If He chooses to take someone, He must have a very good reason."

Bishop Davis, paused for a moment, and considered his next words. He decided to speak them, anyway, "I hate to say it Theo, but we all know Tavaris wasn't a complete saint. If the good Lord chose to take him, He had a good reason."

Reverend Church's eyes widened, and a fire ignited inside them. He looked over at Reverend Williams who only offered an apathetic shrug of agreement. But Bishop Davis decided he wasn't done yet.

"If you truly sought God, and maybe even fasted and prayed as we should in times like this, if you were without fault, and sin, wouldn't God heal you, and all this could have been averted? Yet at the first real challenge you've faced, you say you want to die, and claim God is unjust? I'm sorry my friend, but I can't allow you to speak like that. Even at this terrible time of mourning."

Reverend Church stared at his friend as though he was insane. "Wow, you would think a man suffering, would be shown a little kindness by his friends."

"Theo, you're talking crazy pal. You wouldn't forgive me later on if I let you challenge God that way."

"Listen! Even if I completely abandoned my fear of God, and left the ministry and walked away from it all in anger, one would expect you to be a little compassionate. Instead you religiously judge me, not even twenty-four hours after my boy has died?"

Bishop Davis was about to protest, when Apostle Baker held up his hand, allowing Reverend Church to finish his thoughts.

"You guys have dealt deceitfully with me. It's almost as though you were waiting for me to fail. Tell me, have you ever once heard a scandal about me? *Anything* that has a shred of credibility? Have I accepted bribes? Flirted with my assistants? Or even ask you guys for help at any time? No. But I have helped each of you."

The Reverend was now fuming, and looked each man in the eyes. Then he continued, "So please, teach me, and I'll be quiet and listen. Show me where I'm wrong? You overwhelm the afflicted, and undermine your friend. Now look at me... each of you look at me. Would I lie to your face? Tell me if I'm lying? Am I speaking any injustice? Or do I have the right to question the justice in all of this? Do I have the right to ask to die?"

Reverend Church's three friends couldn't answer him, and Jeffery didn't say a word. Even though Bishop Davis thought he had something to say, he considered it carefully before speaking again. He wanted to say he was just trying to help his friend. That even lying in a hospital bed, and losing your son didn't give you the right to heresy; challenging God. True he'd never been through anything near as wretched, but he knew he would always maintain his devout respect for God in that circumstance. He prayed he never would have to find out for sure though.

***

"STANLEY SIMS," the guard called loudly, and the deacon jumped from the steel bed. He ran to the door and put his face up to one of the four reinforced glass slits.

"Yes! That's me," he called back anxiously, trying to sound as cooperative as possible.

"You have a visitor. Stand away from the door, and put your hands against the wall."

Deacon Sims was nonplussed, but complied quickly. He had been treated roughly since his arrival at the *Mecklenburg Central County Jail*, and although he was distraught, Deacon

Sims had been expecting his lawyer and was memorizing a long mental list of names and badge numbers to report. Two guards entered the room and wrenched his arms behind his back, then cuffed him. He cried out in protest, but it seemed to amuse them.

"C'mon Mr. Sims, it ain't that bad," the burly guard with a bowl cut, drawled.

"What's your full name sir?" he asked the guard indignantly.

"Aw... why you gonna tattletale on me?" the guard snickered. His friend laughed with him. "C'mon, git boy..." the oversized man gave him a push.

They led him into a room without windows, and seated him at a cold, metal table. One guard uncuffed one of his hands, then told him to place both his hands on the table. He did so, and the guard looped the free cuff around a metal bar on the table, and cuffed his other hand.

"Don't give him nothin'. Don't take nothin' from him. Don't discuss nothin' about the facility. You got ten minutes to talk, and only talk. I'll be in and tell you when you got one minute left," the oaf said smugly, and then lumbered out of the room with his compatriot.

Deacon Sims sat and looked around the room for a few minutes, expecting the door to open any second. He waited for five minutes, ten minutes, fifteen. Finally as he was becoming frantic, the door opened, and the oaf lumbered back in, and held the door open for the visitor.

"Don't give him nothin'. Don't take nothin' from him. Don't discuss nothin' about the facility. You got ten minutes to talk, and only talk. I'll be in to tell you when you got one minute left," he parroted, then waddled out and left the two men alone.

"Uncle Jeff? What the heck man? I'm waiting for my lawyer."

"Yeah, I don't know that your lawyer is going to be here any time soon buddy," Jeffery said, eyeing the cuffs sympathetically.

"What are you talking about?" Deacon Sims snapped, fear flooding his face.

"Your mama told me she called Reverend Black, and he said he was trying to figure out the money for the good lawyer he uses, but it would take some time. His exact words were to 'pray and wait on the Lord.'"

Deacon Sims was paralyzed with terror.

"Now, don't freak out nephew, I'm tryin' to work something out for you, but it's not with that sneaky, no-good rat lawyer Reverend Black kisses up to. Actually I think you want to steer clear of anything further to do with ol' Reverend Black, wouldn't you agree?"

"Why, what are you talking about? I don't know anything man. I don't even know why I'm in here." Deacon Sims' poker face was terrible.

"Really?" Lee said impatiently. "We're gonna play this game?"

Jeffery's mouth puckered up obstinately.

"Okay man... lots of luck," Jeffery said, pushing his chair out, and stood up to leave. "How am I going to explain this to your mom?"

"Wait, wait..." Deacon Sims said, anxiously waving Jeffery to sit back down, as his cuffs clanked against the table. Jeffrey Lee just raised his eyebrows.

"Just WAIT... okay." Deacon Sims was visibly on the edge of cracking. It pained his uncle to see him sitting there in that orange jumpsuit, chained to a table like a violent offender, but at the same time he was glad to see the smug grin Sims had worn the week before, was gone entirely. His smirk when his own uncle had been wrongfully terminated, came as a surprise.

Lee sat back and down. "You ready to talk?"

"Talk about what? Listen man, you don't know what's going on here."

"Oh, I think I know more than you think," Lee said thoughtfully. Sims' face registered surprise.

"What are you talking about?"

"Gosh man, I honestly figured you a little sharper. I figured Black would be sharper too, hmmm," Jeffery lost himself in thought for a second.

"Uncle Jeff?"

"Oh sorry," he said, returning to the conversation. "Dude, haven't you realized, I knew those accounting books inside and out. And I knew the computer systems too." He waited for a response, but his nephew wasn't forthcoming. He shook his head and cut to the chase, "You don't think know I'd know when someone installs VPN software on the server. And software used to wire money to and from banks?"

Deacon Sims' eyes grew wide, and he looked around as if the walls had ears.

"Uncle Jeff!" he scolded in a forced whisper. "Keep your voice down. You have no idea what you're talking about!"

"I really think I do," Jeffery replied matter-of-factly.

"No man, you don't realize *who* you're talking about. There are some heavy players in this game!"

"Oh I know. You mean ol' Sugar? He's in another solitary cell, probably not far from yours. I'll bet they're keeping you both in lockup so he or one of his boys doesn't get tempted to silence a potential songbird. If you know what I mean," he winked at Deacon Sims. Dismay returned to the deacon's eyes. "Oh yeah...," at that point Jeffery did lower his voice. "And our pal Sergeant Stone. I'll bet he has all kinds of connections here in corrections?"

Sims was now visibly terrified, and it was more than his uncle could bear.

"Listen, I *may* have a way out for you, but you're going to have to cooperate, okay? I need you to tell me everything. How you did it, where the final accounts are, and most importantly, how I can get evidence of all this."

Sims could hardly believe his ears. "Listen man, I have no idea how you know so much, but I don't want any part of this anymore. I cannot tell you anything though, or I am clearly a dead man. You just said it yourself. I can't do it Unc!" Sims was approaching hysteria so Lee spoke softly to calm him down.

"Shhhh... listen. You've messed up bad okay? Real bad." Jeffery took a moment to make sure that registered with his nephew. He nodded and kept listening. "I have a way out for you, but you have to listen to me. If you don't follow what I say, you can get us both killed. Now I've accepted the situation I'm in. The situation *you* and your boss put me in. Are you ready to accept your situation, and work with me?" Sims thought for a moment and saw the flash of frustration on his uncle's face, and quickly conceded, "Yes, yes... I'll help you," he whispered hoarsely. "What are you offering though? How are going to help me?"

"I'm going to front you the money for a *real* lawyer. A godly woman who has the respect of every criminal judge in the city. When you get out of here, and we recover *Holy Light's* money, you're going to pay me back. But you're going to have to be tough! I'll arrange for you to remain in solitary confinement, eat all your meals in there, and I'm going to ensure only certain guards have access to you. In fact, it's already in the works *if* you cooperate."

Sims stared at his uncle as if he'd been a secret special ops agent the entire time. "Man, how're you going to get all that done? You're just a deacon at a church? Who do you know?"

"I'm glad you acknowledge I'm still a deacon. And don't you worry how I'm getting it done; just trust me."

"Oh I'm not doing a single thing until you tell me how you're gonna pull this off," Sims' stubbornness returned. "I'm serious! I'll take my chances with Sugar and his goons before betting on my white collar deacon uncle."

Lee weighed him up carefully, and came to the conclusion that his dumb nephew was serious. He wondered if he should just walk out, or if it would hurt to share some details. One thing was pretty sure, without the encryption keys, even if he took the cops to the server, and showed them what he knew, they'd likely never get any real evidence on Reverend Black.

"You know that lawyer who all these judges love and respect?" he asked coolly.

"Yeah..."

"Well, she's my cousin, on my dad's side. And she's already pulled the strings so the guards on Stone's payroll aren't feeding you rat poison tonight."

Sims thought about that for a second, then shook his head, "Whatever man! You're blowing smoke..."

Lee rubbed his head in frustration. *This kid's even dumber than I thought.* "Sims, have you ever thought about why I'm doing this? How I know all of this, and why I'm trying to help you?"

The only answer Lee received was a sullen look of confusion.

"I'm doing it because for one, I love *New Day Church,* and I love *Holy Light Church.* They're both close to my heart, and so are the people who actually serve God in both of 'em. Second, I love God and I hate to see corrupt men try to rob

Him. Third...my sister, your mom, is heartbroken right now. Don't make it worse for her, okay?"

"Okay so..?" Sims replied. "How're you gonna protect me in here?"

Lee shook his head again, "Your guards have already been switched. In approximately thirty... seven seconds," Lee looked at his watch, "....a guard is going to come in and announce we have one minute left. It will not be that guard who was only slightly less bright than you. Thanks to my cousin - your new lawyer - it will be a new, upstanding Christian guard. Now when he comes in, you're going to have to decide really quickly if you're going to cooperate, because after that you only have one minute to tell me what I need to know to save your life."

Sims knew Lee was telling the truth but stubbornness had always been his weakness. He waited out the thirty-seven seconds. The door opened, and a middle-aged, stocky man opened the door and nodded to Jeffery with a near-imperceptible smile.

"Jeffery, you have one minute left with your friend sir," he announced, and promptly closed the door.

Sims now looked at his uncle in awe.

"You'd better spit out some details as quick as you can buddy, or ol' *Deliverance* is gonna be back to give you something extra in your dinner tonight."

"The PGP encryption keys are on the sixteen gig USB drive in Black's top left office desk drawer. He doesn't suspect anyone of knowing, so he's pretty lax with them. If you get those, you got all the details and history you need from the server. Rev is planning to do a few more wires."

"The alarms codes for the church have changed. What's the master code?"

"I only know my code!"

"What's your code Sims?" Lee said impatiently.

Sims appeared terrified again, but weighed the option of the burly guard sprinkling some d-Con rat poison on his dinner, and answered quickly. "Five eight seven four."

"Thank you! Jennifer will be in to see you."

"Who's Jennifer?" Sims said.

"My cousin..."

"Oh right... hey Uncle Jeff, you can jimmy the lock on his drawer with a pocket knife. Just push the blade down onto the lock and twist it to the left, while pulling the drawer out."

Lee shook his head with half a grin. *That sneaky li'l rascal's tricks are actually going to come in handy,* he thought as he walked to the door. Right on cue, the guard opened the door again, as Lee stepped out to leave.

"Oh Sims..."

"Yeah?"

"Don't accept any visitors besides me, or Jennifer Lee, okay?"

Sims nodded vigorously.

***

The cell phone buzzed loudly from inside the drawer as Reverend Black jogged over to the desk. He flipped the phone open just before it went to voicemail.

"Yes?"

"Sims just had a visitor."

"Really? And who might that have been?"

"Take a wild guess..."

"Don't play games with me Stone."

"Jeffrey Lee."

"You're kidding!"

"You know I don't kid."

Reverend Black pondered that for a moment.

"Okay, I guess the idiot has done it to himself. Have your boys take care of it."

"Well, there's a hitch. Seems Lee is trickier than we thought. Some hotshot chick lawyer somehow rigged an order from Judge O'Leary to replace Sims' guards. Plus they're keeping him in solitary. I can't touch him for at least a few days."

"Yes you can. Make it happen."

"Listen Rev, you don't understand..."

"I understand perfectly. Now you know we're in this together, and if you think for a second I don't have a plan B, C and D, you've underestimated who you're dealing with. Now I'm definitely not threatening you, but I know you'll find a way to take care of our mutual problem."

"Man, who do you think I am?"

"I think you're the one and only Sergeant Stone."

The line was silent for a few seconds, then the sergeant chuckled, "Well, I guess I am... okay, let me see what I can do."

The Reverend hung up the phone and smiled. He opened his office drawer and tossed the burner in. He stared at the phone thoughtfully for a few seconds. He slowly reached back in, picked the phone up, and placed it in his jacket pocket. Then he reached back in the drawer, scooped up his three USB drives, and dropped them into his pocket as well. Then he closed the drawer and left.

15

COLLAPSING FRAMEWORK

Jewel stared out of the window from her unmade bed, watching the clouds drift aimlessly on the late Friday afternoon. She wished she could cry. She wished she could feel anything other than this numbness that had set in, but even wishing felt pointless. Jewel had mentally explored every possible solution for the questions she had, and had arrived at nothing. Her Bible lay on her nightstand, unopened for days, but Jewel had been praying. Not necessarily in a devout, penitent way; more in a rock-bottom, raw, question kind-of-way.

"Why are these things happening God?" she'd asked gravely.

"I've been faithful to you, and I can't fall pregnant. My brother, one of the best kids in town was killed in a violent car wreck. My parents are both seriously ill. Where are you God?"

Jewel strained to sense a leading of the Holy Spirit, a sense of what to do, but heard nothing. That was the maddening part. She picked up her Bible, flipping through it randomly, looking for some answer but she'd only landed on pages that appeared completely unrelated.

Usually her mom would talk through these things with her, but her mom wasn't here. *She may never be again,* Jewel thought to herself, her tears welling up at the thought.

She heard the front door open, and slowly looked over at the staircase landing through her open bedroom door. She couldn't even feel anything when Dexter had to leave early on a Friday morning to go over some project plans. *Perhaps he'll have some news to cut through this fog*, she thought, searching for any glimmer of hope.

Dexter poked his head in the bedroom door, "Hi babe, how're you holding up?" He held his arm behind his back, hiding something.

Jewel smiled weakly at him, "I'm okay I guess. How was your day at work?"

"Boring. I got you something though." He produced a huge bouquet of roses, and walked over to kiss his wife on the forehead.

Jewel smiled sadly and sniffed the flowers. "They're beautiful. Thank you my love."

"Have you done anything today?" Dexter asked, cringing as the potentially insensitive words left his mouth. "I mean, you know, have you eaten anything, or had a shower? You may feel better."

Jewel shook her head, and turned to look back out the window.

"Hey honey, do you want me to make you a bowl of cereal or something? Or I could run out and grab you something quick? I hate to say but I have to head out for a bit again, but I can grab you something real quick before I go."

Jewel looked back at her husband with narrowed eyes. "What? Where do you have to go?"

Dexter sighed, "I'm so sorry babe. Larry asked me to meet him at Old Chicago's to go over some of the new stuff we're lighting up on Monday. I couldn't really say no. I won't be super-long though, I swear."

Jewel stared at her husband in disbelief. "Are you serious?"

Dexter frowned, but didn't say a word.

"Dexter, how can they ask you to work on a Friday night when your brother-in-law has just passed away, and your in-laws are both in the hospital. I really need you right now. You've already been at work all day."

"Honey, they know, it's just that I've taken off so much time already this week to be there for you and your folks, I just have to play a little catch up. I won't be long, okay?"

"I can't believe you're serious. What if we had Tavaris' visitation tonight?" Jewel said, pushing herself up straight in the bed.

"Aw babe, but his visitation is *not* tonight. I'm doing my best here."

"For all I care, that job can be damned," Jewel snapped bitterly. "They should give you at least a week off considering the circumstances."

"Oh come on Jewel!" Dexter replied in frustration. "You know I need this job. For both of us. It's just a couple of extra hours."

"Oh so now it's a couple of hours? I thought it wouldn't be long. Dexter, you've worked over sixty hours a week, for the past year, at least." Jewel replied, her voice rising. "They owe you at the very least, some time off to be with your wife, even if *you* aren't grieving!"

Jewel never wanted to fight with her husband, but in a strange way it was a relief feeling anything, even if it was pure, white-hot anger.

"That's just unfair Jewel, I don't even know what to say to that. You know this has hit me just as hard, and I'm dealing with it in my own way, but I'm trying to hold everything together too okay?"

Jewel just shook her head.

"I'm only going to be away for a couple of hours at most. I've been there for you all week," Dexter said indignantly.

"That's what you said this morning, and now you're going again! You're unbelievable Dexter. And you haven't been there for me all week. You've been to the hospital with me twice. TWICE DEXTER!" Jewel yelled. Her eyes were aflame. Then they cooled, and she returned to a perfect calm. "Fine. Just go."

"Aw what, you're gonna give me the silent treatment now?" Dexter asked in frustration.

"Dexter, if you know what's good for you, you'll leave right now. And take this cheap bribe with you." She picked up the roses and tossed them at him.

Dexter fumbled for the flowers, and shook his head, "There's just no talking to you sometimes. Look I'm sorry okay. I'll be back in a flash, and all will be well."

Jewel turned away from him. He sighed and left.

***

Jeffery breathed in deeply, as he sat in his car. He wore black jeans, black sneakers, and a black, long-sleeved shirt. On his lap lay a pair of blue latex gloves. He didn't think he'd be this nervous, but as he sat in his car, praying for wisdom and protection, he knew he had to try to find some shred of evidence to expose Reverend Black, once and for all. He had considered calling the police, but who knew how far Sergeant Stone's tentacles reached. Plus, if he called in an anonymous tip, and nothing was found on the servers, or in the offices, Reverend Black would erase every track of every trail. He had to find something conclusive, and then call. The VPN keys would be gold, if he could get them. Without those keys, even with the VPN software on the server, it would be near impossible to trace the funds.

Here goes nothing, he thought and stepped out of his car. He'd parked a couple of streets behind the church and had chosen the spot for the dense tree-line on the sidewalk. They created dark shadows almost all the way to the church building, concealing him pretty well. Lee suddenly felt guilty for sneaking around in the dark. He wasn't even experienced at this sort of thing, he had simply thought it through as carefully as possible. If the situation got too hot, he'd have to abort, but that was the last thing he wanted to do. But he had to try.

He strolled through the shadows, his soft-soled Chuck Taylors not making a sound. As he reached the open-planned parking lot of the church, his heart beat faster. *This is it.* He looked around cautiously, and then stepped from the shadows into the bright parking lot lights. The side door was perhaps fifty paces across open ground. He had previously decided to casually walk this distance; if he ran, it would look furtive to anyone who might see him. He already looked suspicious in all-black, but it was worth more to him to be able to slip into the shadows.

He walked calmly, but alert to every sound. A dog barked, and he flinched. It was nothing though. *I've walked across this parking lot a thousand times, and here I feel like a criminal,* he mused to himself. *What you're about to do is actually criminal,* a voice whispered in his ear. His stomach dropped, but he shrugged it off. He was only halfway through the parking lot, and it felt like he'd already walked a mile. *Those lights are so bright!* he thought. *I guess it really is a good deterrent.* Suddenly, he froze. The lights in the offices were on, and he heard a faint noise coming from inside the building. *Aw shoot man, just my luck.* He wanted to scream. The cleaning crew typically cleaned every night except Friday and Monday nights. *Why are they here tonight?* he screamed in his mind.

As he got closer, he saw the two cleaning vans outside the side door, and could hear the festive sounds of mariachi music playing inside. Suddenly he paused, a thought occurring to him. *Hmmm, that would be a bold move, but it could work.* He had his latex gloves crumpled up in one hand, ready to whip them out to punch in the alarm code, but he slowly tucked them into his jeans pocket. *What are the odds they know I've been let go?* he thought. Jeffery knew the cleaners weren't given a list of hired and fired staff. It was just something no-one ever thought of. It had never been necessary.

The side door was held open with a small wooden wedge. The church's neighborhood was safe enough, and the cleaning crew had to go back and forth to get supplies from the vans, so they simply left the door ajar. He opened the door with his knuckle and poked his head inside. No-one was there. He stepped inside the church, and looked down the hallway. He could hear the boom box squawking happy trumpets and guitars all the way down near reception. Another wild thought occurred to him, and he simply turned and walked toward Reverend Black's office. Not really sure if it was a good idea or not, he decided to just go into the office and see what he could find. One of the cleaning crew would probably see him, but it would be like any other night he'd worked late. Yeah, the slight exception would be that he was in Reverend Black's office, wearing all black but would they really care? Besides, he knew all of the long-timers by first name. Heck, he even knew their kid's names, smiling at the cute pictures on the crew's phones. He always made a point to know the people who worked behind the scenes, even though the cleaners spoke only in broken English. These people who were invisible to most, and were usually ignored, but that was not Jeffery's way. He took the time to chat with them in his own broken Spanish, laughing as he flubbed the words, but clearly made the point: *you're human, and valuable to us.*

Jeffery always invited each of his new friends to church, and had even arranged for a free visit to a local clinic for Maria's little boy, Jorge. She conveyed the baby had experienced a severe bout of what sounded like croup cough. He arranged for free antibiotics through the church's connections as well. He smiled sadly as he thought he may never hang out with them again. *Still though*, he thought to himself. *It would be better right now if they didn't see me.*

He swiftly walked to Reverend Black's office, and jiggled the handle. It was locked. He looked behind him, and then pulled out a Starbucks rewards card he had prepped in his back pocket. He shook his head, as he realized again he actually possessed the skill set of a deviant. *How did it come to this?* he complained to himself. He pushed the door handle slightly, revealing a small gap between the jamb, and the handle, then slipped the rounded corner of the card right in line with where the curved back of the spring-loaded locking mechanism would be. After a jiggle or two, the curved side of the lock's bolt gave way to the card, sliding back as the door popped open silently. Lee stepped inside quickly and closed the door behind him. It was all a little more exhilaration than he cared for. He reached into his pocket, pulled out his phone, and hit the button for the *Lamp* app. Bright, white light flooded the room. He walked over to Reverend Black's desk, clicked on his lamp, and turned his phone off. Jeffrey Lee's heart was pounding.

He pulled on the top left office drawer. It was predictably locked. He pulled a pocket knife out of his jeans, and flipped open the blade. *Push the blade down, and twist to the left*, he muttered, while performing the maneuver. He pulled on the drawer and it popped open. Lee shook his head, smiling at his devious nephew. He wished Stanley didn't know these sorts of tricks, but right now he was really glad he did.

Jeffery flipped his phone light on again, and peered inside the drawer. All he saw was a few pens, a worn *Moleskine* notebook and a few random items like bulldog binder clips and a cell phone charger. *No USB thumb drives!* Lee's heart sank. *Man! What now?* An icy chill ran over him, as he wondered whether Sims had set him up. *He didn't know when I would come though,* he thought to himself. *Still, they could be watching me from somewhere.* He was starting to get paranoid, and forced himself to think objectively. As he pondered whether he should leave he picked up the notebook, and opened it. Inside were pages and pages of notes. Reverend's Black's handwriting. It was a journal of sorts, but that's not what interested him the most. In the center of the notebook lay a photo. Jeffrey Lee's eyes widened as he realized who was in the picture. Standing between a smiling Reverend Black and an obviously proud Reverend Church, was Gerald Church, the good Reverend's eldest son. The young man was dressed in a graduation cap and gown and the trio were in front of the prestigious *Southern Baptist Theological Seminary*. Jeffery stared at the photo for a few long moments wondering why Reverend Black kept this picture of Gerald. He knew the families had been close, and he knew Gerald had confided in Reverend Black for some time, years ago, but he wondered if they were still in such close contact. Gerald's downward spiral suddenly made sense, if it were true. He

suddenly had a strong, overwhelming urge to find Gerald;
an urge he knew from experience to be from the Holy Spirit.

Jeffery jumped as a door slammed in the next room.
Next a key slid into the office's lock and he panicked,
lunging for the switch on the desk lamp. He clicked the light
off and slid under the desk as the door swung open. It was
still dark, so he pulled the leather chair as close to the desk
as he could. The light overhead flipped on and he heard one
of the cleaners wheel their squeaky vacuum into the room.
Why the heck did you hide? He yelled at himself silently.
Now what if they find you?

Jeffery heard the cleaner plug the vacuum into the wall
as he saw the desk drawer laying wide open. He grimaced
as he slowly reached up, and tried to slide it closed. He
prayed it wouldn't squeak. The vacuum roared to life, and
he quietly slid the drawer closed. The cleaner stopped in her
tracks. Lee froze. *Oh Lord, oh God, I'm busted.* The cleaner
yelled something in Spanish and he almost jumped out of
his skin. *Oh well, time to come clean,* he thought as he
dropped his head. He began making his slow exit from
under the desk, hands raised when he heard another voice
yell something from down the hall in Spanish. He paused.
Now this person (whom he could have sworn was Maria,)
yelled something back. This time he caught the end of what
she said. "Something something... *he terminado.*"

Whew, I'm not done, Jeffery thought to himself.
She's talking to her friend! The vacuum shut down, and
Jeffery remained dead still. Maria's friend yelled something
that this time, he did catch, "Está bien, vamos a volver más
tarde." *It's ok, we'll come back in a bit.* Lee held his breath.
He heard the lady set the vacuum down, then waited a few,
long agonizing minutes as he heard them lock the side door,
and one of the van's engines roared to life. *They must be
taking a lunch break.* Finally, after waiting to make sure the

place was silent, Jeffery crawled out from under the desk and leaned both hands on the desk, and heaved a sigh of relief.

Jeffery pulled opened the notebook, and stared at the photo again. He flipped to the back of the book and saw pages of what looked to be a list of supplies. He flipped back to front of the book, and read one of the first pages:

> *"Today I got that feeling again. As if I was not myself. Things happen around me that I can't explain. I feel like the opposite of an angel."*

Lee paused and frowned. *Whoa,* he thought. Then he flipped the page.

> *"I'm so, so tired. It's been an exhausting day. I feel like I'm being invaded by something. I got so angry at Vanessa, I smashed a glass and cut myself today. Lord help me."*

Lee paused again, and tried to absorb what he just read. His mind was racing. *No way,* he thought to himself, considering the worst case scenario. He flipped to the back of the book, and read more.

> *"I received more insight into the vision for the church during meditation today. We are going to be richer and more powerful than any church before in history. We are going to take this city by storm, and spread our message in every street. The first phase was revealed to me in full today. I am to invest in the stock markets, especially biotech, and alternate energy."*

Lee slammed the notebook closed. He couldn't believe his eyes. He snapped back to his task, and absently fumbled around the drawer, searching for a hidden panel of some kind, but eventually he had to admit there were no thumb drives. After debating himself for a second, he pocketed the notebook, then he closed the drawer, flipping the lock back up with his pocket knife. He experienced a crushing sense of defeat as he realized he was at a loss to prove how the wire transfers were made, without those encryption keys. He took one last glance around the office and made his way out, thinking about something that was just as important as finding those thumb drives, *Buddy, you have got to find Gerald.*

16

THE EVIL THAT IS TO COME

"Have a seat," Sergeant Stone smiled, nodding toward the empty spot. The corrections officer pulled out the chair, flipped it around, and sat down resting his arms on the chair back. Both men wore civilian clothes, but the shaved, faded crew-cuts loudly proclaimed the men worked in law enforcement. The McDonalds that Sergeant Stone had selected for the meeting was located in *Rock Hill*, a small town a little south of Charlotte. He figured the likelihood of snoops who knew either of the men would be reduced outside the big city. "How's your wife doing Ted?" Sergeant Stone asked, sounding sincere.

The man shook his head slightly, "As well as can be expected, I guess. It's a day-to-day struggle." He looked down at the table, momentarily betraying his pain.

"She needs a kidney right?" Sergeant Stone asked with exaggerated compassion.

"Yeah... but there's no way that's gonna happen."

"Your state health insurance doesn't cover the procedure?" Sergeant Stone asked, already knowing the answer.

"Sure, but the deductibles will be between five and ten grand. Even up to twenty. I can maybe scrape together two or three from family, but that amount is out of the question."

"Ted, what if it wasn't out of the question?" Stone asked, his face full of concern.

Ted looked up quizzically.

"We've taken care of some 'business' before together right?" Sergeant Stone made air quotes with his fingers around the word "business." Ted nodded.

"We both know those sick bastards were guilty of what they did to that little girl, and they deserved exactly what they got."

"They sure did," Ted grunted, keeping his eyes fixed on Sergeant Stone.

"Well, we have a similar sort of situation in block six right now."

"A molester?" Ted asked, sitting up straight, his face instantly darkening.

"Well, he's booked on money laundering and potential connections with drug runners, but there's more to the story. See he works for a church, and uh...let's just say I have it on good authority there are several impressionable kids in the youth group, that he's...well, left an impression on."

Ted shook his head, and clenched his jaw.

"He's a slippery character too. With a good lawyer. Word is he's gonna walk." Sergeant Stone timed the line perfectly, and watched as it took effect. Ted tried to conceal his eagerness to bring justice to the sicko, but it was written too clearly on his face.

"How does that help my wife?" he asked, snapping back to the business end of their talk.

"Great question. Let's just say a person affected by this dude's uh...indiscretions, has offered a sum right around what you need for your deductibles. This someone wants to ensure the lowlife gets some true justice."

"Ten grand?"

Sergeant Stone knew better than to answer verbally, so he just nodded slowly.

"Okay, I'm curious. What's the plan?"

"That's the good part. You're friends with Wilkinson and Jones right?"

"Yeah," Ted nodded.

"Have lunch with the two of them. Find a way to discretely squirt a few drops in their OJ, or milk or whatever - it's tasteless - and they'll both become violently ill for at least twenty-four hours."

"Then what?"

"Then... I'll arrange for you to pick up their shift watching this guy's cell. We'll be short staffed at that point so it'll just be you. He'll have a visitor, and on the way to visitation, right between blocks two and three - you know the corridor the cameras don't cover?"

Ted nodded.

"Well, he's gonna shank you in the arm with this." Sergeant Stone handed over a crudely made steel blade with cloth tape wrapped tightly around the shaft for grip.

"He's gonna actually shank me?" Ted frowned

"Yeah, not deeply, and just in the arm or shoulder, but it has to be believable. After cutting you, you're going to shoot him multiple times, until he ceases being a threat."

"Whew..." Ted whistled. "That's heavy duty man. We just broke a few bones the last time."

Sergeant Stone just stared at him blankly. "If you don't think you can handle it, I know at least one other operator who'll settle for less cash. You're just a little smarter, so you're my first pick."

"Whoa, okay, hold the reins. I didn't say I wasn't going to do it, it's just-you sure this guy's guilty.

"Guilty as sin. I can introduce you to a kid," Sergeant Stone bluffed.

Ted nodded his head thoughtfully. "It's going to have to be timed perfectly."

"Well, that's why I don't want to give it to a jackass." Stone smiled.

"Okay Sarge... you sure this guy's a creep though?"

"Ten grand is positive he's a pure scumbag."

"What's his name?"

"Sims. Deacon Sims."

***

Around nine o'clock on Saturday morning, Jeffery parked his 2007 Toyota Camry in the multi-level parking garage of the *Carolinas Medical Center*. He locked his car with the remote, and headed for the hospital walkway. As he walked, intent eyes watched him from an unmarked police car on the other side of the parking level. He didn't know it but the car had discretely been tailing him since his house. The driver picked up a cheap phone from the passenger seat, and dialed a number from memory.

"Yes?" asked the voice on the other end.

"You sure you want to proceed with Lee?"

"Of course. I'm not a double-minded man."

"Listen, contrary to what you might think, I don't order this stuff from Amazon. If you change your mind, I can't be riding around with this package in my trunk."

"Just do it!"

"Alright then. Consider it done."

"What's the word on Sims?"

"I just spoke to my operator. Sims is the walking dead."

"Good. Let me know when you've done Lee's car."

"Ten-four."

Sergeant Stone hung up, started his cruiser and pulled into an empty space only two spots from Lee's car. He smiled that Lee had parked facing a concrete wall. *He even left me a bit of leg room in front,* Stone grinned to himself as he slipped a pair of lambskin gloves over his hands. He left his cruiser running, but popped the trunk, and walked to the back of the car. From the trunk, he pulled out a long *Slim Jim.* Leaving the trunk slightly open, he casually walked over to the Camry, and inspected the dash for a blinking telltale alarm light. He saw none, and could see no stickers on the windows, so he looked around to make sure no-one was about to walk nearby. Effortlessly he slipped the *Slim Jim* between the driver side window and the rubber seal, slowly moving the tool around various rods in the door, until the lock knob wiggled. He then gently popped the locking rod up, unlocking the door.

Too easy, he grinned to himself. He opened the door, ready to briskly walk back to his running car if an alarm sounded. None came. He leaned in, popped the hood, and walked back to his cruiser. He looked around again, to make sure Lee wasn't returning. He had given the man the customary three minutes, to avoid his return in case he forgot something in his car. He figured Lee would be at least ten minutes visiting the Churches, and would likely stay for thirty minutes or more. Stone would complete this task in two.

He looked around once more, his pulse quickening. He then lifted the carpet cover for the spare tire, and pulled

out a brown paper bag in the rough shape of a small brick.
He walked over to the Camry, took out his phone and hit his
Lamp app. He lifted the hood and shone the light into the
back of the engine compartment, and grunting, wiggling
and lifting a few hoses, he placed the package in a neat,
natural compartment in the engine. Sergeant Stone took
one last look at the package to make sure it was secure.
Satisfied, he turned the light off on his phone. The package
wasn't very visible, but that didn't really matter. What he
had planned would happen long before Lee next checked
his oil. Sergeant Stone dropped the hood, walked to the
driver side door and locked it. He then ambled back to his
car, shut the trunk, and got in. *Goodbye Lee,* he chuckled to
himself.

***

As Jeffery walked down the hospital corridor, he felt
his pocket to be sure he had the photograph with him.
Some called it a hunch, others an intuition; Jeffery believed
it was the leading of the Holy Spirit. When he had seen the
photograph of Theo Church, Gerald Church and Reverend
Black standing together on the campus of Southern
Seminary, a prompting, strong and undeniable stirred in
Lee's heart. For some reason he just knew he had to find
Gerald.

Jeffery walked up to the Church's hospital room,
and poked his head in the door. Reverend Church was still
sleeping soundly, but Sandra was awake. His heart dropped
each time he saw this elegant woman of God sitting in that
hospital bed, her head wrapped in bandages, and her face
getting more drawn each day. Despite a deep exhaustion in
her eyes, there was a still a small sparkle.

"Jeffrey!" she smiled softly. "Come in. Theo is still asleep; he had a rough night, but I doubt he'll stir."

"Did you get some rest, Sandra," Jeffery smiled back, trying to hide his concern over her apparent worsening condition.

"Yes, but those drugs made me hazy. Would you care for some snacks? We have at least three fruit and snack baskets over on that table." she asked.

Jeffery shook his head, "No, but thank you. I had a bite on the way over." He marveled at Sandra Church's unquenchable concern for others, despite her grief, and poor health. *The Churches are truly remarkable people,* he thought to himself.

"How are you guys holding?" he asked sincerely.

Sandra lowered her eyes a little. "We're trying to stand in faith," she said quietly. "In the natural, the doctors can't figure out what's up with Theo. They believe it's some kind of auto-immune deficiency, but when you filter the smoke they blow, it sounds like they have no honest idea. "

Jeffery nodded soberly. There was nothing really to say, except the truth. "I'm praying for you guys every day.

"Thanks Jeffrey. We really appreciate it."

Jeffery reached into his pocket, and pulled out the photo, staring at it for a brief second. "Sandra, can I ask you a personal question?"

She was slightly taken aback, but nodded with a curious frown. "Sure. How personal though?"

"It's about your family." He handed the photo to her. "What can you tell me about this picture?"

Sandra took the photograph, and immediately her expression changed. She looked up at Jeffrey Lee. "Where did you get this?"

"Would you trust me if I said I'll tell you later?"

She stared at him for a moment, then said "Sure Jeffrey. You know I trust you like my own kin."

"Thanks. Believe me, I'm looking into something that may help you guys."

"Okay," she said, still unsure of what to think. "What do you want to know about this picture?"

"I knew Reverend Black was a lecturer at Southern Seminary, a few years before he took the position at *New Day*," Jeffery explained. "I knew he knew Gerald, but are they still close?"

Sandra sighed. "Yes, when Gerald got out of high school, he attended Southern. He wanted nothing more than to pursue ministry. Probably more on the evangelist and outreach side of things, but he was completely on fire for God."

Jeffery nodded. "I remember."

"Yeah... Reverend Black was one of Gerald's mentors at Seminary. Gerald seemed drawn to him, and we always felt it may be good for him to have another Christian mentor to confide in, other than his dad."

"Hmmm... how close are he and Gerald now?" Jeffery asked.

"I don't know. I hope they aren't close considering some of the things I've been hearing about how Reverend Black has handled his divorce."

Jeffery nodded soberly.

"I think we all know Gerald is pretty lost right, Jeffrey" Sandra sighed. "Something happened to him along the way. He left here clean cut and respectful. Came back on drugs, running the streets, disrespectful. Even his dad can't get through to him. I would understand though, if Reverend Black still keeps his door open for Gerald. He's the only one who ever came close to reasoning with the boy."

Jeffery shook his head at Sandra's statement, hoping Gerald wasn't in close contact with Reverend Black, but something told him his fears were true.

"What?" she asked.

"Oh, hmm. Well nothing," Jeffery stammered. "Say, do you know where Gerald is now?"

"Your guess is as good as mine. We haven't seen him in days." This pained Sandra Church to say, and Jeffery felt bad about asking her these questions.

"At Seminary, or since, did you ever notice anything strange?" he asked.

"About who, Gerald?"

"No, Reverend Black."

"Like what?" Sandra asked, beginning to realize the object of Jeffrey Lee's concern.

"Like anything? C'mon Sandra, it's me Jeff. You can talk to me."

"Are you sure you should be discussing your pastor with me though, Jeffrey? This is pretty unlike you."

"He's not my pastor any longer, Sandra." Jeffrey admitted. "He fired me."

"What?" Sandra asked in amazement.

"Yeah... I don't really want to say too much, but I will explain everything later. I promise."

Sandra became a little distressed, and that was the last thing Jeffery wanted. He tried to reassure her.

"Seriously, it's all good. Please don't sweat it, and I can't tell you yet, how this affects you guys, but I really need to know anything you can tell me about Reverend Black. And any way I might be able to get hold of Gerald."

Sandra Church stared at the man for a long few seconds, her mouth turning up into a distressed frown.

"Okay," she said at last. "Well, when we first met Reverend Black he was really kind, and knew his scriptures like nobody's business." she paused for a moment, as if figuring out how to say what she felt. "But you know all the stuff that went down with his wife?"

Jeffery nodded.

"We always thought it might have been good for him to step down for a while, even on paid sabbatical, while they tried to reconcile. He was pretty angry though, and wouldn't listen to us. After that, he was still nice and kind to Gerald, but in a different sort of way."

"A different way? Such as?"

Sandra searched again for the right words.

"Well...it was like he was trying too hard. Almost like he was a different person. I guess that kind of experience would change anyone a little."

"Hmmm," Jeffery said, thinking about this revelation. "Is that all there was to it?"

"Well, Theo and I noticed something odd about the man, but never really discussed it too much. I didn't think anymore about it, but I could sense Theo felt something different."

"What you mean?"

"Theo became very uneasy around Reverend Black, and actually suggested Gerald not see him any longer. Gerald of course, took that as a sign to spend even more time with the man."

"Wow," Jeffery said, shaking his head. "Anything else?"

"Around that time, Theo began praying for hours and hours. Theo has always prayed, but a few times, I would hear him in the study praying for protection, and to be prepared for the evil that is to come."

"Really?" Jeffery said, in surprise. Sandra Church nodded. "Whew. Well, thank you Sandra," he began, then he remembered the main reason he came over. "Oh, do you have any clue where I might find Gerald?"

Sandra Church shook her head. "I really don't Jeffrey. Your best bet is his girlfriend - I guess that's what you could call her."

"Okay, do you have her number?"

"Sure." Sandra groaned a little as she leaned over to her bedside table, to grab her phone. Jeffery stepped forward to help her, but she had already reached it. "Her name is Bernice."

His hand dove into his pocket to get his phone out to save the number. Sandra read it off, as he punched it into his phone.

He put his phone back in his pocket, and sighed. "Thank you Sandra." She smiled and nodded to him. "You'd better get some rest. We all need you guys."

"Deacon?" she asked quickly.

"Yes?" He turned back to her.

"What is this really all about?"

Jeffery gazed past her for a moment. "The evil that is to come," he said softly. "I believe it's already here."

17

DELIVER US

Corrections Officer Wilkinson, and Corrections Officer Jones were doubled over on their hands and knees, just outside the cell door, groaning and fighting their gag reflexes.

"We need replacements *NOW*!" Officer Wilkinson spluttered into the radio. He sensed something weird was going on, but he was entirely preoccupied with the violent churning in his gut. Officer Jones couldn't restrain himself anymore, and heaved uncontrollably, expelling his lunch in the cell block corridor. Loud protests from the inmates echoed through the block, and soon some began banging on their cell doors, while others peered curiously out of their window slits.

In record time, Officer Ted Moore responded, and radioed for two gurneys. "I've got two officers down with what looks like some sort of stomach bug, in cell block six," he explained. He tried to comfort his two buddies, who appeared to only be getting worse. He then yelled at the top of his voice, warning the inmates that some time in the "hole" was in their near future if they didn't shut up. The noise quieted down to a few murmurs and off-color comments.

In a few minutes the gurneys arrived, and two medical staff loaded the men onto the stretchers and began checking vitals. "Strange..." the older medic said. "No fever."

"Huh!" Officer Moore said quizzically, taking a slight step back from them with just the right amount of theatrics. "Well I'll hold the fort down here, and you guys get them boys taken care of."

"Okay," the older medic said, as he nodded to Officer Moore. "I'll let you know what we discover, since you were in direct proximity."

"Thanks," Officer Moore replied with mock chagrin. The medics wheeled the two men off, as they writhed and groaned in agony.

Dang Sarge, what the heck did I put in their sodas?" Ted whispered to himself. He walked over to Deacon Sims' cell and nodded to him with a crooked smile. Deacon Sims had been observing the scene right outside his cell with curiosity, but he stepped back involuntarily. Suddenly a shiver ran down his spine.

***

Reverend Church lay in his hospital bed feeling strangely paralyzed. He turned his head slowly and saw Sandra sleeping a few feet away from him. She did not look peaceful, her face creased in a frown, her chest rising and falling in shallow succession. The lights in the hospital seemed dimmer than usual, and the sky outside was grey and windy. Suddenly the lights flickered a little, dimmed then brightened. Vaguely Reverend Church seemed to remember praying for his son, Gerald, but everything seemed so surreal. His lips kept muttering though, "Father protect my son. Let him not stray too far my Lord. He was raised in your path, and You promised me he'll return."

Reverend Church's ears pricked up as he heard footsteps walking down the corridor. Then he realized there were no other sounds in the hospital; no chatter of nurses going about their daily business, not even the distinct hum of the fluorescent lights. It was entirely silent; except for the footsteps that grew closer and louder.

"Hello?" Reverend Church said loudly, and looked over at Sandra again, secretly wishing she'd wake up. Undisturbed her chest continued rising and falling, rising and falling. The footsteps grew louder, until they were right outside the door. A strange, desperate fear gripped the Reverend for some reason.

"HELLO?"

"Hello Theo," a cold, yet familiar voice boomed from behind the door. Reverend Church strained to see the face of the shadowy figure that stepped out from the corridor, into the room.

"Harvey?"

"Ah you do remember your old friends?" the voice spoke.

"What are you doing here?" Reverend Church propped himself up on his pillows, suddenly feeling vulnerable.

"The question is... what are YOU doing here, Theo?"

From the shadows of the corridor, Reverend Harvey Black stepped into the light of the hospital room. His eyes were dark, his brow furrowed and he wore an ominous grin. Over Reverend Black's shoulder hung a leather satchel that appeared to carry something heavy.

"Pray all you want for that wayward boy of yours. He's never coming back," the man chuckled.

"Harvey! I reject those words in Jesus' name! Why would you say something like that?" Reverend Church replied in shock.

"Aah, your faith is still solid?" Reverend Black jeered. "I wonder how Tavaris' faith is doing? 'He'll not dash his foot against a stone?'"

Reverend Black's eyes widened in horror at the man's mocking of scripture, and felt a sting of pain as the question touched a nerve in his heart. *How could Harvey know my deepest question for the Lord?* He wondered.

"Reverend Theodore Church!" His tormenter announced suddenly, standing upright.

Reverend Church's tongue was paralyzed with fear.

"You have been weighed on the scales and you have been found wanting!" Reverend Black put his hand over the satchel flap, and opened it slowly.

"There are new players in this game, but the same rules apply. You are obsolete Theodore Church. We will not fail this time!"

The usage of the word "we" chilled Reverend Church to the bone.

"Theodore Church you are dismissed from this life! You will NOT rest in peace."

Reverend Church wanted to scream as the man slipped the bag off his shoulder, but his vocal chords were frozen.

Reverend Black held open the lip of the leather satchel and clutched the bottom, walking slowly toward the hospital bed.

Something dark and malevolent writhed and curled inside the bag. Reverend Church tried desperately to move but his entire body remained paralyzed in terror. Reverend Black stepped forward and with one, quick motion flung the contents of the satchel at Reverend Church's chest. Three giant serpents flipped and twisted angrily through the air, landing on Reverend Church's torso and legs, hissing and spitting.

The largest was black as night with a fleck of gold in its shiny scales; its head raised up angrily hissing at the Reverend's face. A fat yellow snake coiled then flipped in fury as it wormed its way up his chest. A long, green snake landed on his legs but wasted no time slithering rapidly up his body until it reached the Reverend's face. With sickening menace it struck first, sinking its fangs deep into the Reverend's cheek and nose.

The Reverend screamed in pain and terror, as the black and yellow snakes followed the green serpent's lead. Over and over they struck hard, ripping into his chin, then his eyes and forehead. Reverend Church emitted a sickening howl as he clawed at the hideous creatures latching onto his face. His wails pierced the empty hospital halls, and only Reverend Black's sinister laughter could be heard, rising maniacally above the sounds of terror, creating a bizarre symphony of evil and horror and death.

***

"Reverend Church! Reverend CHURCH! Wake up, it's only a dream." The nurse struggled frantically to restrain the great man as he thrashed around in his bed. His I.V tube whipped around his bed, as the needle in his arm began to leak blood. Sandra was halfway out of bed to help the nurse when Reverend Church awoke and stared, terrified at the nurse who was holding his hands, trying to stop him from clawing at his own face. He was still panting furiously as his wife put a gentle hand on his arm and said,
"It's okay honey. It's just a dream. A wicked, wicked dream by the sound of it. But you're okay. Whatever it was, the devil is a liar. God has it all in control."

18

DEAD EYES

The call went to voicemail again, and while Jeffery didn't want to leave another message he was beginning to panic. He hung up and threw his phone on the desk. He'd called four times now, and was starting to believe the Churches might just lose another son. Suddenly his cell phone lit up and vibrated furiously on the desk. He jumped forward and slid the screen icon to the right.

"This is Jeffery."

"Yeah Jeffrey Lee, you the one blowing up my phone?" The woman's voice sounded exhausted and annoyed.

"Bernice? Please forgive me it's urgent..."

"How you get my number?"

"From Mrs. Church. Gerald's mother."

"Listen Jeffrey Lee, I'm real sorry for all Gerald been through but I can't deal with him no more. I ain't talked to him since we got news of Tavaris..."

"Bernice, did you listen to my voicemail?"

"Naw man, you woke me blowing up my line."

"Bernice, I really need to find Gerald. He could be in serious danger."

"Aw he live in serious danger Jeffrey Lee. Don't you know that?"

"Bernice, I'm serious. Gerald is mixed up with some heavy duty characters, who I believe may be manipulating him. "

"Manipulating him? How?"

"Well, slinging their gear, but also emotionally."

"Well he always emotionally wrecked anyways. I tried to help him yet again, after poor little Tavaris died, but Gerald turned mean on me as he always do."

"Bernice, please I need to find him. You don't want his life on your hands do you?"

The line went silent as Bernice wrestled with this notion.

"Maaan, I just want to be done with him. I can't help you."

"Bernice, please, both of his parents are in hospital, and they just lost Tavaris. They cannot lose him. You can be done with him after I find him. I truly believe I can help Gerald, but if anything happens to him when all I needed to do was find him, you know your conscience will haunt you forever."

Bernice groaned. She was conflicted and Jeffery knew from years of experience, to just wait and let the Holy Spirit do His work. Finally she responded.

"Fine, I'll try to help you, but I have no idea where he is."

"Thank you Bernice! Do you have any idea where he might be?"

"I really don't know! Probably somewhere smokin' up or drankin."

"Bernice, I understand you're frustrated, but I really need to find him. I need your help and there's not much time. Could I beg you to ride with me and we'll search for him. You'll know who to talk to, and where he might be. I'll be shooting in the dark if I go on my own."

"Aw man, Jeffery you really getting ready to get on my nerves."

"I'm sorry Bernice. I wish we weren't in this situation either, but perhaps God can turn it around into something good? But please, just help me this one time."

Bernice sighed again, and then said, "Okay Mr. Jeffrey Lee. C'mon by my ratty apartment and we'll go hunting for someone I don't care about."

"Thank you Bernice! You are an angel," Jeffery said in relief.

"I don't know 'bout all that but here's my address. Best hustle before I change my mind."

She gave Jeffery her address and apartment number, and he ran out to his car, roared the engine to life, and took off.

A way down the road, an unmarked police cruiser was parked. An officer started the engine, and slowly pulled out, maintaining a good distance behind Jeffrey Lee's Honda. The officer picked up his cell phone and dialed a number.

"What's up?" a voice squawked on the other end.

"Lee is on the move. Seems in a hurry. You want me to go ahead now?"

The other party had thoughtful pause, then said, "He was in a hurry?"

"Yeah, he's lighting it up outta here. Having trouble actually talking and following him so if you could let me know pronto, that would be great."

"Follow him for now and keep me posted. I'll call the Reverend and see if he wants to hit him now or see what he's up to."

"Copy that."

***

Reverend Black flipped his office's giant wall-mounted T.V on just as he always did, whenever he walked into the room in the morning. The markets were closed on a Saturday, but that didn't mean news and speculation ceased. He walked toward his desk, removed his jacket then paused. Something was wrong. He cocked his head and gazed at his leather chair. It was situated just slightly off center in the empty space under the desk. His eyes darted around the desktop, then rested on the top left desk drawer. It was opened an eighth of an inch from the desk.

Reverend Black gritted his teeth and stepped over to the drawer. He slowly pulled on the handle and it stopped on the lock. He pulled his keys out of his pocket, slid the drawer key into the slot, and turned the lock. The drawer opened and he peered at the items. Everything had been moved around. His eyes grew dark, his jaw clenched and his hand began to tremor. He shuffled the items around, eventually picking up pens and papers and business cards and throwing them on the desk. His Moleskine notebook was missing. He leaned forward with both hands on the desk and bowed his head.

"I'm going to kill that son of a..." he whispered to himself. "And I'm going to laugh as I watch the light leave his eyes."

His cell phone vibrated in his pocket. He pulled it out and looked at the number, then slid his thumb across the phone.

"Great timing," he said.

"Huh?" Sergeant Stone's voice croaked on the other end.

"What do you want Stone?" he said, his foul tone betraying his mood.

"Whoa, I thought your highness might be interested to know Lee is heading somewhere like hell on wheels."

"Don't get smart with me Stone. Remember who pays the bills in this equation."

"Aw don't get your panties in a bunch Reverend. I told Brooks to follow him instead of proceeding with plan A."

"Well you get a gold star for that," Reverend Black replied acidly. "Turns out we need to keep this fool on a string just a little bit longer. He's figuring to be squirmier than I imagined."

"Oh? How's that?"

"Seems he got into my office somehow. Took a piece of very personal property."

"What? Wow? That's bold. I didn't think he had it in him. You sure it was Lee?"

"Oh it's Lee alright. Call it a sixth sense."

Sergeant Stone wanted to say something, but cleared his throat nervously instead. He knew all about Reverend's Black's sixth sense, and quite frankly, it unnerved him.

"Well..." he stuttered. "I guess Brooks can pick him up if you want."

"No... let him go. He's going to find Gerald Church... and when the time is right, I want you to nail both of 'em."

***

The trip from Jeffery's house slowly turned from suburbia to modern office parks, to quaint gentrified neighborhoods to downtown industrial complexes. On the outskirts of the industrial district, was Bernice's apartment building. Laundry hung over various balconies, and a tween girl and a boy sat on the steps of the entrance. A second boy pedaled his BMX around in circles while arguing with his buddy on the steps. Jeffery made sure he'd locked the car, then squeezed by the kids, and ran upstairs. He knocked on the door and heard the clacking of heels walking on hardwood floors. The door flung open and before him stood a young lady, probably in her mid-twenties who could be really pretty if she wanted to. She wore a tight leopard skin jacket, black leggings and hot pink stilettos. She chewed gum like it was cud.

"Well hello Mr. Jeffrey Lee!" she smirked. "You didn't tell me you were cute."

Jeffery coughed, and extended his hand. "Nice to meet you," he said too formally.

Bernice chuckled and accepted his handshake with a raised eyebrow. "*Very* nice to meet you too."

"Uh...you ready to go?" Jeffery mumbled.

"Honey, I was born ready." Bernice seemed to be enjoying herself.

"Well alright then, let's go find Gerald."

Bernice grinned to herself again, and shook her head as she locked her door.

"Aww Bernice got herself an uptown man!" the BMX boy yelled as Jeffery held the passenger door open for her.

"You hush and get on your way ya little hood rat," Bernice yelled back with a giggle.

Jeffery frowned and walked around to the driver side, climbing into the car. "Where's that kid's mom?" he asked with concern.

"Who Lil' T?" she asked rhetorically. "His momma's probably high at her peddler if you wanna know the cold truth."

The words made Jeffery flinch. "Mm mmm," he said shaking his head. "Man, someone needs to start an outreach down here."

"An outreach?" Bernice squawked. "Ain't nobody gonna respond to no outreach down here. Can't nobody help most of these folk."

"Jesus can help anybody," Jeffery said with assurance. "And everybody," he said with a gentle look at Bernice.

She glanced up at him like a guilty kid.

"So you really think you can help Gerald?" she asked softly.

"Well, I believe Jesus can help him, if Gerald will let Him. But I really think that if we don't find him, he's a marked man."

"Marked man? By who?"

"A really bad dude. Worse than even these crack slingers out here."

"He not in trouble with his suppliers?"

"No. This guy's a-well let's just say he's a wolf in shepherd's clothing."

Bernice frowned and shook her head. She remained quiet as Jeffrey started the car, and they pulled off.

After weaving their way through old mills, shipping warehouses and an array of other factories still clinging to their building deeds of yesteryear, they drove across the railroad tracks. At one time Jeffery supposed the area could have been a pleasant subdivision. He pictured families taking evening walks and children playing outside the neighborhood corner store. Now steel bars and grates covered every store window, garbage and litter was strewn about the streets, and almost every house had peeling paint and boards or sheets in the windows.

"We getting close?" he asked.

"Yeah, that's the Foxy Lady right up there where that white car is pulling out."

Jeffery squinted his eyes and saw a flashing red and yellow sign, guiding the patrons in, even though it was midday. He parked a few cars down the street from the entrance and asked, "This is where Gerald hangs out?"

Bernice shrugged, "Guess he got a thing for Foxy Ladies?"

Outside the club a huge man sat on a stool, completely preoccupied with his phone. Jeffery got the photograph out of his pocket and walked over to the bouncer. The man didn't look up as Jeffery approached, so after standing in front of him for a second, he cleared his throat and asked, "Say brother, have you seen this dude?"

The man slowly raised his bowling-ball head and furrowed his brow. Jeffery held up the photo. "Is he inside?"

The behemoth shook his head slowly without saying a word, then returned to playing a game on his phone.

Frustrated, Jeffery turned to leave.

"Who's askin'?" the man growled, still transfixed on his phone.

"Honestly? I'm a friend and member at his dad's church," Jeffery pleaded. "He may be in serious danger."

The man tapped his phone.

"WONDERFUL!" the game congratulated him for a successful score.

"Try the *Dew Drop Inn*, over on Forty-Sixth and Market. That where he like to slang and light up."

Jeffrey Lee, surprised by the sudden compliance just stood there for a moment. The bouncer just kept tapping his phone.

"Uh thanks man. I really appreciate it."

The giant just nodded, his eyes still locked onto his phone. Jeffery turned and walked back to the car.

"One more thing homey," the man called out without looking up.

"Yeah?" Jeffery turned back to him, standing in the middle of the street.

"You may wanna lose the Five-O in the blue Crown Vic before you drop in."

Jeffery stood there confused for a few seconds. Then he looked down the street and noticed a blue Crown Victoria with the telltale silver spotlight on the driver-side window, about six cars back from his. The stocky man behind the wheel quickly averted his gaze, and pretended to fiddle with something in the console. Amazed, Jeffery walked back to his car and got in.

"The *Dew Drop Inn?*" he announced to Bernice.

"Oh lawd," she rolled her eyes in disgust. "I didn't think he was hitting that dump up again. Guess I shoulda known."

"I'm assuming it's not a five-star bed and breakfast?" Jeffery asked.

"Oh you can get a bed and you get breakfast. Any kinda breakfast you want, as long as you cookin' it up yourself and bring your own needles or pipes."

"Whew," Jeffery whistled as he started the engine. "God help that boy."

"Mm hmm," Bernice agreed.

"By the way, did you know we were being tailed?"

"What? By who?" Bernice whirled around.

"Not exactly sure but I have a hunch."

Jeffery started his car, and slowly pulled out of his spot. He passed the giant bouncer on the stool. The man looked up and gave Jeffery the slightest wink and a nod. All Jeffery could do was nod back and smile in surprise. He looked back in his rearview mirror to see if the Crown Vic was going to follow. His stomach knotted when it pulled out, and began driving down the road after him. Suddenly he saw the giant bouncer get up off his chair and hobble out into the middle of the street. Then the man fell to one knee clutching his chest. The Crown Victoria screeched to halt, trying in vain to swerve around him. He heard the police siren bleep and the car's horn give a few short blasts. The colossal man just toppled over and lay sprawled out in front of the car. Bernice whirled around and said "What the..." She looked at Jeffrey Lee. "What was that all about?"

"I guess guardian angels come in all shapes and sizes!" he grinned, as he floored it and turned on the next street.

They soon left that neighborhood behind, and as they approached the *Dew Drop Inn*, Jeffery knew which building it was from two blocks away. Several people with dazed expressions were perched on the curb or sprawled on the pavement, and two young men, both wearing stained wife-beaters lazily shadow-boxed in the street.

"My Lord..." Jeffery whispered to himself.

"Oh you didn't know it was this bad? Why you think I want nothin' to do with this cat no more?" Bernice quipped.

"Let's just go see if he's here." Jeffery said, as he pulled into an empty spot across the street. He bowed his head momentarily and said softly, "I pray God's angels are encamped around Gerald and our car in Jesus' name." Bernice grinned, as if his prayer was futile in this place. They walked up to the steps of the entrance as the curb-squatters turned their dreary gazes toward the strangers.

"Oooweee girl!" one of the shadow-boxers hollered, ignoring his buddy's bobbing and weaving. "That's what I'm talkin' about!"

"Aw you couldn't afford that even if you had a job, fool," his buddy chirped as he landed a jab to the stomach.

"Hey now... she's a lady," Jeffery interjected, facing the inherent danger of searching for Gerald in his treacherous stomping grounds.

"She don't look like no lady!" the first kid challenged.

"You better believe I'm a lady you strung out little chump."

"Yo, you best watch yo' mouth ho!" the kid snapped angrily. "What you doing down here anyway?"

"You heard of G-Dub?" Bernice demanded.

"Let's just go inside," Jeffery whispered, but Bernice shrugged him off, her eyes on fire.

"You ain't no honey of G-Dub's," he replied, but his confidence was visibly dented.

"You wanna go ask him yo'self if you can call his main girl a ho?" she yelled, stepping up to the kid, and pointing in his face. His sparring partner backed away slowly. "Let's go ask him," she shouted. "He inside ain't he?"

"Yo, I didn't mean no disrespect girl. I was just throwin' you a compliment 'til you turned on me."

"Yeah... you fulla respect ain'tchoo?" she yelled. "That's what I thought. All your smoke blowin' away now."

The kid just twisted his mouth up, but looked away. The dazed observers were about five percent more alert from this interaction but could still only track the duo with lifeless eyes, as they walked into the building.

Bernice and Jeffery walked up to the reception area where a greasy-looking man in his mid-sixties sat on a barstool reading a newspaper, and smoking a cigarette.

"Ten dollar for thirty minute. Fifteen for hour," he said, trilling his R's in a broken Russian accent.

"We're not here for a room," Jeffery explained. "We're here for him." He held up the photo.

The man's expression said he recognized Gerald's picture but ne shook his head firmly, "Nyet."

"Listen, we know he's here. We don't want no trouble," Bernice explained. "He in real trouble."

"Nyet. No can do," the man replied stubbornly. "His people more dangerous."

"Please listen," Jeffery begged. "His brother has just died, and the guy is emotionally unstable. I believe he may be suicidal."

That got the Russian's attention, but he still shook his head. "No can do."

"Listen up," Bernice said, the fire returning to her eyes. "Think about it this way, that boy O.Ds in one of your rooms and we tell a news crew that we tried to prevent it and you wouldn't help, you're gonna be taking a lot more heat than his crew will bring down on you!"

Jeffery stood there speechless as the man grimaced at Bernice. Suddenly he slipped off his barstool, and said "Come." He turned, and walked down the hall. Jeffery raised his eyebrows at Bernice as if to say *Wow! Not bad,* and she just smiled at him.

The three of them climbed a flight of stairs to the second floor, and walked up to a room three doors down. "This one," he pointed at the door, then turned to leave. "Wait!" Jeffery said as he knocked.

"Nyet," the man said, scurrying to the staircase. "Don't say who show you room!"

"Just wait!" Jeffery held up his hand, imploring the man. The Russian stopped at the landing of the staircase. Jeffery knocked again.

"Gerald!" Bernice called loudly. "Gerald open the door! It's me." There was no sound from the room, not even a scuffle. Bernice banged loudly on the door again. "GERALD! OPEN THE DOOR!"

"Wait, wait!" the Russian called, waving her to stop. "You disturb everyone." He shuffled over to the door, and produced a key out of his pocket as Bernice stepped aside. "You say door was open, da?"

"Da!" Bernice agreed, and allowed the man to unlock the door. "Thank you!" She gave him a few seconds to shuffle back to the stairs then opened the door and the two of them stepped inside.

Bernice screamed.

Spread out flat on the bed, wearing only jeans, Gerald lay motionless, staring at the ceiling with dead eyes. On the rickety table next to the bed, a lighter stood upright, with a bent spoon laying next to it. Wrapped loosely around

Gerald's left arm was his leather belt, and out of a vein in his elbow joint hung a needle and syringe.

19

GREATER THINGS THAN THESE

Reverend Black's clenched fists rested on his leather desktop. He leaned forward in his chair, his eyes glaring intently at nothing. Anyone's first guess about where his thoughts were, would undeniably conclude in murder. His cell phone vibrated.

"Yes."

"I just received an interesting call from a dispatcher at the station."

"And what was that?"

"One Gerald Theodore Church was just admitted to The Carolinas ER." The caller paused to beg the question.

"Dammit Stone, if you don't just tell me what you called about so help me..."

"Chill Reverend Black. Let's not forget that your insurance plan is presently incarcerated for money laundering."

Reverend Black snorted. "Again, you really think I don't have backup plans for my backup plans?"

Sergeant Stone chuckled. "Aw honey, let's not fight!"
Reverend Black exhaled and clenched his jaw, trying to
control his temper.

"Assumed heroin overdose. Our boy, the honorable Jeffery
called it in. Along with a Bernice Young? Junkie girlfriend
maybe? Of Gerald's that is."

"Is he alive?"

"No idea."

"You think your knuckle dragger buddy can handle it this
time if you put him on watching Lee's car again, at the
hospital?"

"Hey man, I don't know how Lee does it, but he's the
luckiest man alive. Everyone's luck eventually runs out
though." Sergeant Stone replied bitterly.

"I'm going to the hospital. Tell your gorilla not to
acknowledge me if we cross paths."

Sergeant Stone just hung up. Reverend Black shook his
head, got up and grabbed his jacket.

He walked past reception, and told the front desk "I have to
make an emergency hospital visit. I'll probably be out all
afternoon. Cancel all my appointments please."

"But sir... you've rescheduled the Barium Springs Children's
Home twice..."

"CANCEL ALL MY APPOINTMENTS!" Reverend Black shouted
at his assistant. He turned away from the shocked lady, and
walked out of the front door without so much as a glance
back at her.

***

"Hey... what you doin' babe?" Dexter opened the
bedroom door slowly. His wife was sitting cross-legged on
the bed with an open study Bible, and a pen resting in the
middle of the pages.

Jewel looked up with tired eyes, but seemed more at peace. "Praying, and finding promises in the Word."

"Oh," Dexter said. Even though Jewel never lauded it over him, he had never been as knowledgeable as her in matters of scripture. "What kind of promises?"

"Good ones," she smiled at him, and traced the words on the page with her finger:

> "Because he has set his love upon Me, therefore I will deliver him;
> I will set him on high, because he has known My name.
> He shall call upon Me, and I will answer him;
> I will be with him in trouble;
> I will deliver him and honor him.
> With long life I will satisfy him,
> And show him My salvation."

"Wow. That's your mom and dad right? God promises they'll live long?"

Jewel nodded, still smiling.

"What scripture is that? Like what book and verse?" Dexter didn't want to appear ignorant but he was intrigued. He'd never really grasped the concept of claiming God's promises in action before.

"Psalm ninety-one. Verses...fourteen, fifteen and sixteen," she replied looking down at the page.

Dexter nodded, impressed. "Any other good ones?"

"Tons. My favorite is first Peter two twenty-four... by Jesus stripes we *were* healed." The apostle Peter is actually echoing from Isaiah fifty-three verse five which says:

> 'But He was wounded for our transgressions,
> He was bruised for our iniquities;
> The chastisement for our peace was upon Him,
> And by His stripes we are healed.'

In Peter's letter though, he says we *were* healed. Past tense. We just have to believe it."

"Wooow! That's pretty cool babe. Why've you never taught any Bible studies, or anything?"

"Aw, I don't know?" she smiled, massaging her own neck. "Gerald was supposed to be the preacher, then Tavaris was next in line I guess."

"That doesn't exclude you!" Dexter protested. Jewel just smiled lovingly at her husband, but held out her hand to him.

He shuffled over to the bed, and took her hand, and sat behind her, wrapping his wife in his arms. "I love you so much Jewel Church McAlister. You give me so much strength."

"Oh honey," she smiled, and lay her head back on his shoulder. "God is good. I just know that. This trial has to be for a purpose. My parents are some of the most godly people on the planet."

"That's the truth," he replied.

Dexter kept his wife in his arms, but leaned his head to the side and said, "You know honey, I've really been thinking."

"About what?"

"It doesn't matter if we don't have a child naturally. I love you and will always love you. Heck, we could adopt, and change some little baby's entire life."

Jewel turned around and looked at him with hopeful, puppy-dog eyes. "Really?"

He smiled and caressed her face gently. "Really. And, you are totally right."

"About what?" she said softly.

"I put too much faith in medicine when it's obvious I should be putting more faith in God."

"Dexter, it feels so good to hear you say that."

"Maybe we can even find some promises for a baby, and start looking into adoption at the same time? Hedge our bets?" He chuckled.

Jewel swooned. "I love you Dexter McAlister. Man of God."

"Hehe," he chuckled. "Wow, I've never heard that before."

"Hey if Gideon can do it, anyone can."

"Gideon?" he asked with a frown.

"Never mind. I'll explain another time," Jewel grinned sweetly, and threw her arms around her husband. He returned her squeeze, and kissed her on the forehead.

"But do me a favor okay?" Jewel asked.

"Okay. Anything."

"Could you not be alone with Miss Fertility at any time?"

Dexter stifled a giggle at the term, and said, "Uhh okay, sure. It may be tough when we have to meet but you know I would never do anything inappropriate babe. You're the only girl in the world for me."

"I know my love. It's not you I'm worried about. That girl needs Jesus, and until she finds Him, just cover your behind. If you have to meet, meet in a glass office, or with the door open, or with another colleague present."

Dexter was still surprised, but he sensed wisdom and not jealousy in his wife's words. He nodded, "You got it my love."

Jewel smiling, embraced her husband and gave him a passionate kiss.

***

The heart monitor bleeped in constant rhythm, providing an unusual comfort to Jeffery as it proclaimed Gerald's life remained in him. Typically, non-medical staff were not allowed in ICU but the doctor had made an exception in Jeffrey Lee's case. Gerald had been stable while

Jeffrey and Bernice rode with him in the ambulance, and Jeffrey held his hand, praying. The *Naloxone* administered to Gerald to mitigate the effects of the heroin had increased his heart rate, but he remained unconscious. When he was rushed into ICU, without Jeffrey and Bernice, his vital signs began to drop. The doctors quickly called them back in, and while Jeffrey prayed fervently at his bedside, Gerald began to stabilize once again.

"Miss Bernice Young?" a police officer asked quietly, but firmly from the doorway.

She turned around and looked at him with slight attitude, but didn't say anything.

"Ma'am, could I speak to you for a moment please?"

"My boyfriend's in critical condition, and you want to speak to me?" she flared up.

"Whoa, whoa," the doctor interjected quickly. "Please let's remain calm for Gerald's sake."

"Bernice, it's okay. I've got this covered, go ahead," Jeffery assured her. "You've done nothing wrong. My statement will corroborate with yours. Obviously just be honest."

Bernice cast a glance back at the officer, then turned to Gerald, "You come through baby. You come through and we'll go to church together and we'll be happy. We'll get our lives straight, and be happy. You just pull through Gerald!" She leaned over and kissed him, becoming a little emotional at the end, and the heart monitor blipped a little faster.

"Okay, he's in good hands Miss Bernice," the doctor said, putting himself between her and the comatose Gerald. She looked back at Gerald as she walked to the officer. He gave her a polite smile, and held the door open for her.

Suddenly Gerald's vital signs began going haywire. His heartbeat began blipping crazily, and his blood pressure monitor spiked.

"Code Blue!" the doctor yelled, and the two nurses scurried around frantically.

"Sir, move back to the edge of the room immediately!" a nurse instructed. Jeffery released Gerald's hand, and retreated in panic.

"Oh Lord Jesus, do not let this young man die!" he begged.

"Rose, clear that airway, and begin CPR! Jane get those paddles ready," the doctor instructed.

Rose propped Gerald's contorting head back, and placed a firm rubber mask over his face. She held Gerald's nose closed, and began pumping air into his lungs with the attached rubber ball. His chest rose and fell, but his heart monitor was still going crazy. Jeffrey noticed Gerald's hand was now contorted too, clenching at something invisible. Suddenly his heart rate dropped to a near flat-line.

"Get those paddles primed!" the doctor squawked.

Rose was now applying chest compressions in a timed sequence. Gerald's heart remained at barely a single beat every four or five seconds. Jane applied a clear gel to the two handles, and rubbed them together, evening the gel out. Suddenly the machine made a high-pitched zinging noise and a green light flickered on the one handle.

"Clear!" Jane said.

The doctor took the paddles, and placed them on Gerald's bare chest. He depressed the shock button and Gerald's torso jolted up violently, and fell to the bed again. His vitals normalized a little then, dropped again.

Without instruction, Jane moved in, held Gerald's nose, and applied the rubber mask again. There was no change. The frantic bleeping was maddening and Jeffery prayed furiously from the corner of the room.

"Don't you give up Gerald!" the doctor said firmly. "You've come this far. Don't you let go!"

Gerald's heart beat was now barely a blip on the monitor and his hand was slowly releasing its gnarled pose.

After what seemed like an eternity, the doctor hit him with the paddles again. Gerald's heart blipped crazily for a moment, and even Jane paused anxiously to see if he was coming back.

BEEEEEEEEEEEEP. The monitor flat-lined.

"Oh my Lord," Jeffrey whispered placing his hands on his head. "No, no, no, no! This cannot happen. Lord they won't recover. An entire family will be wiped out. Jesus help us!" Jeffery prayed fervently.

"Get him back!" the doctor barked. Jane applied CPR steadily, while Rose prepared a syringe full of a clear liquid. Once Jane was done, the doctor took the paddles again, and shocked Gerald's chest. Aside from the electrical spike of the paddles, Gerald's heart remained flat-lined.

"Adrenaline," the doctor ordered and Rose stepped forward, handing it over. The doctor inserted it into Gerald's arm, and Jane resumed CPR. Nothing. Not even a blip. Rose began preparing another syringe.

Jeffrey was in a full panic as Jane completed two more cycles of CPR. The doctor gave him another shot of adrenaline. Still nothing. A glance from the doctor to Jane made Jeffrey Lee's stomach sink.

"Get those paddles ready one more time," the doctor ordered. Rose applied a fresh covering of gel. "Stand clear!" the doctor ordered, then jolted Gerald again. His torso jumped, but the heart monitor quickly returned to flat-line.

"Check everything," the doctor ordered, and the two nurses went over every piece of equipment that was attached to Gerald, and checked his IV and pulse. Jane shook her head. "Resume CPR," the doctor said wearily, and Jane dutifully complied. Nothing changed.

After several minutes of CPR, and another jump from the paddles, the doctor wearily handed them back to Rose. He cast a quick, apologetic glance to Jeffrey Lee.

"I have to call it. Time of death..." He looked at his watch. "Two-eleven p.m."

Jeffery couldn't move. He stood staring at Gerald's lifeless body, the entire scene feeling like a dream. A nightmare. He knew the boy's parents wouldn't recover if they found out they'd lost another son. He didn't notice the doctor walk over to him, and he jumped when the doctor gently laid a hand on his shoulder.

"I'm so sorry sir. We did everything we could."

The words ignited something in Jeffrey Lee's heart. "What did you say?"

The doctor, a little fazed, cleared his throat and said, "I'm terribly sorry sir. There was nothing more we could do."

"No that's not what you said. What did you say exactly?"

"I said...we did everything we could?" the doctor replied, wondering if Jeffery was having a traumatic psychological episode.

Something welled up inside Jeffery, and he felt his spirit charging up like those paddles.

"That's right. You've done everything *you* could. But with God all things are possible."

The doctor glanced nervously at Jane, who acknowledged him only with her eyes and began walking toward the door.

"Mr. Lee, why don't you sit down for a minute?" the doctor waved to a wooden chair in the corner.

Jeffery ignored him, and stepped toward Gerald.

"Sir...Mr. Lee, I'm afraid I'm going to have to insist."

Jeffery was almost to Gerald's bedside, when he turned and looked the doctor right in the eyes. His piercing gaze of determination made the doctor flinch and freeze.

"Only believe!" was all Jeffery said.

He turned back to Gerald, and lay both hands on his torso, praying loudly, "Father, I come before your throne room of grace boldly today. You said in your Word, we would heal the sick and raise the dead. You know this young man needs another chance. His parent's need him, his family needs him. Father I plead for your mercy! In the mighty name of Jesus' Christ, GERALD I COMMAND YOUR SPIRIT TO RETURN TO THIS BODY!"

The words poured out of Jeffrey Lee's mouth, but it didn't feel like himself praying. It was if the Holy Spirit, in all His purity and truth had risen up inside Jeffery and had spoken through him.

"RIGHT NOW! GERALD, COME BACK TO LIFE!"

Nothing happened for a second but Jeffery kept his hands on him. Instantly Gerald jerked upright and uttered a blood-curdling scream, as he began thrashing around crazily. The IV flicked wildly around the bed, as Gerald flailed his arms screaming, "GET THEM OFF ME, GET THEM OFF ME! HELP ME!" Jeffery's heart surged with joy, but his veins turned to ice at the young man's screams. He grabbed Gerald's wrists instinctively with his powerful hands, and restrained him as the doctor and nurses came running up to help.

After a few seconds of struggle Gerald realized he was in a hospital theater room, and began to calm down, but was panting furiously. Jeffery noticed the heart monitor beeping loudly and consistently again.

"Gerald, you are at the Carolina's Medical center," the doctor said quickly. "You are safe, and in good hands. You overdosed on heroin, but you're okay. Please try to remain calm while we check your vitals."

Gerald looked over at Jeffery with wide eyes. "You called me back. You called me back!"

Jeffery was grinning like Cheshire cat, and nodding. He knew the implications of what had just happened, and it was medically documented.

"I repent of my sins!" Gerald cried. "I repent before Heaven and Earth, before God and Man, and I submit to Jesus Christ as my Lord and savior again!" That got Jeffrey Lee's attention. He didn't have to ask what he was sure had happened to Gerald.

"Jesus I accept you, save me from my sins," he cried. "I make you my Lord right now. Forgive me Lord, and save me. Save me Lord God, please!"

The young man began sobbing and Jeffery leaned forward and put his arms around him. Gerald fell into his shoulder and sobbed like an infant.

"He's forgiven you son. Just receive it. You're a new creature and your life is sealed with Him for eternity just by your confession. Be at peace Gerald. He's given you a second chance."

"My God!" Gerald cried in a muffled voice. "It's real. It's all real."

"I know son. It sure is, but you're safe now. No one can snatch you out of His hands. Just relax. You're safe."

Perplexed, the doctor and nurses waited nervously. They'd seen a lot in the ER but had never seen anything quite like what they were witnessing. Jeffery slowly took Gerald's head in his hands and said, "Lie back for a second. Let them do their job real quick. We know you're okay, but let them check you for the record."

Gerald slowly lay back but kept clutching Jeffrey Lee's hand. The doctor and nurses walked up to the bed and performed their checks in complete silence. When they were done the doctor said, "Gerald, you're a miracle my friend. You had been flat-lined for several minutes."

Gerald shook his head, "It felt like years."

***

Reverend Black pulled his great touring sedan into a parking space near the emergency rooms. He had seen Jeffrey Lee's car, and who he believed to be Sergeant Stone's clown watching it very conspicuously. He shook his head as he walked into the hospital.

"I'm here to see Gerald Church," he asked the receptionist with the perfect mixture of worry and warmth.

"Gerald Church..." she repeated as she typed the name into her computer. She raised her eyebrows when she found the admission record, but then resumed her poker face and asked, "Are you a friend or family?"

"Family," Reverend Black lied with a warm smile.

"Okay, please sign in and have a seat. We'll let you know when you can go back and be with the rest of his family."

"Is he...is he okay?" Reverend Black faked perfect fear in his voice.

"I'll let the doctor speak with you Mr., er, Reverend Black."

"Ok, thank you." He knew better than to push his luck, he took a seat and waited.

In a few minutes, the one-way door to the emergency theater opened, and Jeffery stormed out.

"You got some nerve you know that?" he said walking straight over to Reverend Black, looming over him.

Reverend Black's eyes changed to a cold, hard grey and he stood up, face to face with Jeffery. "You're gonna tell them to let me back there and see Gerald."

"You'll never get near him again."

"You wanna bet?"

"I'll bet my life on it."

Reverend Black smirked and held his stare. "That's *exactly* what you're betting Lee. And you're gonna lose that bet."

"Are you threatening me?" Jeffery said loudly.

"I don't make threats buddy. I give guarantees."

"Black, after what I just saw, there is no way you can scare me. Where did you go wrong man? How did you get so corrupted?" Jeffery shook his head, but kept his eyes fixed on Reverend Black's.

"That's bold coming from a thief who breaks and enters."

"I guess I'll ask for forgiveness. I still have your secrets." Reverend Black's eyes darkened and he nodded slowly, "You have exactly one hour to get that back to me. Otherwise my guarantee goes into effect."

"Oooh..." Jeffery gave a fake shiver. "You can't scare me Black. You ain't no Reverend anymore, and greater is He that is in me, than he that is in you."

Reverend Black began laughing. At first it was a low, sinister rumble, then it kept getting louder and louder until it was evil roar. His eyes were still transfixed on Jeffrey Lee's, as his chest bounced up and down, laughing maniacally. Without warning, he turned away from Jeffery and headed for the exit.

"ONE HOUR!" he called out before he left, and kept laughing. As he reached the lot, Reverend Black pulled his burner phone out and hit a speed dial number.

"Yo!" came the response.

"The second this fool Lee drives off this hospital lot, I want you to hit him."

"Oookay. My man will have to tell me when he's leaving."

"I don't care what happens, I want YOU to be here. Don't screw this up or we both go down. I don't think he knows what he has, or we'd both be in a world of hurt, but he's not going to find out either."

"I'll take care of it!"

"You'd better," Reverend Black said abruptly and hung up.

As Reverend Black left, Jeffery turned to the receptionist whose eyes were raised in disbelief.

"That was creepy!" she announced.

Jeffery rolled his eyes and shook his head. "You have no idea. If that man so much as sets foot in this building again, can you have him arrested on the spot?"

"Only if he's committed a crime."

"Well you just heard him threaten my life repeatedly, and he tried to impersonate family. Surely that's enough to at least get him off the premises if he comes back."

The woman nodded, and picked up a phone presumably to call security. As she did, Lee's phone rang in his pocket. He pulled the phone out, and saw it was his cousin, Deacon Sim's attorney. He sighed before he answered. Hopefully she had some good news.

"Hey!" he greeted her.

"No, I'm not with them right now. What is it?"

Her voice squawked on the other end, then all the color drained from Jeffrey Lee's face. He stood motionless for several long seconds. Her voice squawked again.

"Oh no. How could that happen?" was all he could say. She repeated her message again, and Deacon Lee lifted his eyes to view the afternoon sun out of the window.

"You sure?" It was rhetorical. He felt like he was stalling the inevitability of dealing with what his cousin had just told him. She squawked through the earpiece again.

"Okay, has anyone called his mom?" he responded.

"Man, if the cops already told her, one or both of us needs to go and be with her."

Jeffrey's cousin's voice squawked on the other end.

"Okay, I really appreciate that cuz. I'm going to head over as soon as I can. If you can believe it, I have some other emergencies at the hospital I'm helping with. I believe it's all actually related, but I'll explain more in person."

He listened to his cousin again, and his eyes changed to a look of sheer exhaustion.

"I don't want to think about pressing charges now. Obviously the prison is at fault, or my little nephew wouldn't be dead right now. They're obviously lying. Saying Stanley Sims would attack a prison guard is like saying Ghandi carried an AK47 around with him. It just wouldn't happen. They couldn't protect him even when they knew he was a target!"

Jeffery's eyes now welled up with tears, but he just kept staring out of the window.

Her voice squawked a little more, then he said in a choked voice, "Okay, I'm gonna jump off. Pray for me cuz. And pray for his mom too."

20

INSULT TO INJURY

"**B**rother Lee, I just received a text message from Reverend Black." Reverend Church held his phone up with a frown. "He says you told the hospital staff to refuse admittance for him to come back and see *Gerald*? Gerald is here? In the hospital?"

Reverend Williams, Bishop Davis, Apostle Baker and Sandra all swung their heads to look at Jeffrey.

"What?" Sandra exclaimed.

Jeffrey stared at the ground for several moments, considering his response. He knew Reverend Black's primary intention was to sow discord, and add to the Churches stress, and he regretted not having anticipated this move.

"Yes," he replied honestly. "Gerald is here Reverend and Mrs. Church. He had an incident, but although he is shaken up, he is stable and will be perfectly fine. I didn't want to concern you with this news until you felt better." Jeffery wondered whether or not to tell them about Gerald's very convincing rededication to Christ. He nearly did, but decided he would have to explain the overdose and that was the last thing he wanted to do.

"What happened? When was he admitted?" Sandra tried to yell, then groaned and clutched her head.

"Mrs. Church, please don't be alarmed. Gerald is perfectly well. Honestly, he's better than ever, please trust me, but if you don't mind, I'll let the doctors explain what happened as I'm not really qualified to present the details."

It was the truth, but he was obviously skirting the issue. He simply didn't want to stress them out.

"Jeffrey, tell me right now what happened. I demand it." Reverend Church, even from his sickbed, retained an air of authority, and sheer scariness that removed the options for Jeffrey Lee.

"Gerald overdosed," he said frankly. "On heroin. He is okay though. He's in recovery, is eating something as we speak, and amazingly, there appears to be no traces of the drug in his body. Gerald is adamant it is the first time he tried it, and it was only due to grief from his brother's passing. I believe him completely."

All five of the others stared in disbelief.

"Oh my God!" Sandra finally erupted in a wail, "My baby! Heroin? God how could this happen right now? How much more can we take? Why is God doing this to us?"

"Mrs. Church, please...Gerald is perfectly well and I think he's had a really good scare. I actually believe this may have been exactly what he needed to turn his life around. There are often blessings in disguise."

Jeffery considered telling her of Gerald's near death experience, and subsequent rededication to Christ, but that would mean telling her about, well, Gerald's near death experience and several minutes of flat lining. Jeffery wasn't a violent man by any definition of the word, but in that moment he wished he could have strangled Reverend Black.

"Oh don't preach to me about blessings in disguise!" Sandra cried. "My only other son nearly dies, and that's a blessing? We're laying up here in the hospital, and who knows if we're even going to make it out and that's a BLESSING? Give me a break! How could I forgive God for this?"

"Sandra, please, this isn't good for your health," Apostle Baker chided.

"No, she's right Toby," Reverend Church interjected. "How much more can one family take? This is getting even beyond my faith levels. Whatever happened to the promises in Deuteronomy 28 when we walk righteously? Or the Psalm *The steps of a righteous man are ordered by the Lord?*"

Reverend Church's face had darkened. "I've served God my entire life, and I've hung on strong but if I lose another child, I don't know if I could ever hold my faith."

His words hung in the air like a dark cloud.

"Theo! Please! Mind your words!" Apostle Baker rebuked sternly. "I've been silent for much of yours and our friend's discussions, and I know you are going through a horrendously difficult time but as your lifelong friend I have to say enough is enough! What God chooses to do is His business! He is entirely self-sufficient, and you know very well he needs nothing from us, least of all our alleged righteousness."

Reverend Williams and Bishop Davis nodded their heads in unison, but Reverend Church only rolled his eyes, knowing that Apostle Baker was just getting started.

The muscular man cracked his neck, then continued, "Theo you claim to be righteous, but that very claim is arrogant before God. I'm sorry to say I can't listen to your rants any longer. How dare you say you can't hold your faith. You act as though God were deserving of forgiveness. You, my friend, are in fact guilty of very great wickedness."

Jeffery shook his head, and couldn't believe what was happening right now. He had popped in for a brief minute to check on the Churches before he left to deliver incredibly tragic news to his sister. Now he was caught in the middle of this argument. He was beginning to get annoyed.

"God is not punishing you because you fear Him, Theo," Apostle Baker continued. It is because of your tremendous sin that I've just witnessed." His words seemed to have no effect on Reverend Church, who stared blankly, waiting for his friend's tirade to be done. Sandra looked as though she was ready to get up out of that bed and attack Apostle Baker.

"I don't know what else you might have done for God to bring this upon you. Maybe you lent money to someone and demanded some necessity of theirs as deposit? You know God speaks against that. You give publicly but I don't know, maybe you were too busy one day and kicked up your heels at a beggar on the street, denying him food and water? I know you control a lot of land and resources. Maybe it's gone to your head? Do you think those resources only belong to the powerful and privileged? Any number of these offenses may be why you're surrounded by snares and these terrors keep springing themselves upon you. There is no judgment without a sin Theo, and I think you've proven there is more to this story than everyone knows."

Reverend Williams and Bishop Davis were still nodding gravely, but remained silent to this point.

"Theo, as your friend, a wise rebuke is better than a deceitful placation. You appear to be valuing wickedness, and you believe God won't see it. I urge you to repent, and these disasters will stop. You know what you have in your heart. I know the outside often looks good but search your heart. There must be something in there that is offending God. Something you know is true. Return to God and He will bless you, and answer your prayers, and then who knows? Maybe you can even begin saving others again someday."

When Reverend Church was satisfied his so-called friend was done, he replied, "Tobias, with all due respect, you and your two friends speak like Pharisees who sit in an ivory tower valuing only judgment and punishment, while never descending to experience the plight of the suffering. If I could stand in front of God right now, with Him as my judge, I would ask Him to judge my actions for the past twenty years and see if He could find any major sin of which you speak. The truth is the heavens feel like brass. God is nowhere to be found right now, and it just keeps getting worse. It is *not* because of my sin, and I have not left God's paths. I have treasured God's Word, but God's dealings with me have me utterly terrified. I don't compromise like our corrupt Reverend Black." He cast a meaningful glance at Jeffrey. "

Oh yes, I know exactly who Reverend Black is, and I've been praying for him for years. But I don't trust him as far as I'd like to sometimes throw him. Men like him wear the cloth, yet sin with arrogance. They have left the faith, and do no good works. They are selfish, and drain people under the guise of leadership. They oppress the poor in their congregations, compelling them to support their lavish lifestyles, yet they don't lift a finger to help those people. Yet God doesn't seem to hear the people's cry, nor punish these wicked men. I ask you right now James, or any of you for that matter, to show me where my sin is. Interrogate my wife right here, and ask her, before God, if I am guilty of hypocrisy."

"Theo, I don't think you understand what we're saying," Bishop Davis said, chewing one of his fingernails. "Can anyone really be righteous before God? Even the prophet Isaiah said our righteousness is as filthy rags before

Him. God is almighty. He created this vast universe, and can destroy our planet with the flick of a finger. We are worms and maggots in comparison to God and His majesty. How can you be pure before God?" Bishop Davis' chubby cheeks dimpled as he offered a weakly patronizing smile. Jeffery wanted nothing more than to leave, but at this point, he had to hear the response. He didn't want to burden the Churches with his personal problems. He wanted to leave and be with his sister. But he wasn't sure what Reverend Church's friends would say next, so he hung out for a bit just listening.

"Brother," Reverend Church began with a sigh. "I'm sorry but your advice is completely worthless. In fact, none of you have helped me in the least. Do you think I am someone with no experience? No knowledge? Do you think I'm one of your congregation who hasn't been studying the Word for decades? I don't say this arrogantly, but I'll one up each of you guys in knowledge of God's omnipotence: He's Lord over the dead and the living. He's God over all of creation and the spiritual realm. In fact, none of us can even come close to understanding the true greatness of His power. What's more is even though God has removed justice for me and my family, I still claim that I don't speak wickedly. I am innocent, and I know there is no hope for those who have turned aside to wickedness."

Reverend Church paused, and Apostle Baker tried to speak again but Reverend Church held up his hand to silence him. "Wait Toby. You've had your say," he said firmly. "Let me teach you about wickedness. The wicked may seem to get away with it for a while, but he never does. The difference between justice upon the wicked, and the trial of a righteous man is the wicked man's destruction comes swiftly and suddenly. You can bet your bottom dollar the wicked will get what is coming to him, in this life or the next. I have had a blessed life when God watched over me and prospered me, and for that I am extremely grateful. But now, it appears I am the focus of mockery by envious men. I have to wonder if God saw how I wept for the suffering, and sick and those afflicted by tragedy before. In fact, I am willing to accept punishment if I have operated deceitfully in ministry, or any area, or if I have committed adultery, or mistreated my staff or neglected the poor in our communities, the widows, the many fatherless children. I have taken care of every one I could. If I trusted in and lusted after money, or went to fortune tellers, or any other weird form of false religion, or if I turned away any strangers or homeless people, then I would accept my punishment. If I tried to hide any small, daily sins then I would embrace what God is doing. But now I lay in this hospital boldly asking God to show me what my sin is. To show me what I have done to deserve this. This is my last defense to you all, on the topic. May God judge me as He sees fit, but I am confident I have walked as righteously as I could before Him. And you know what? I still fear God, and I'll still walk as righteously as I can before Him. I don't understand why justice is absent, and wicked men seem to get away with their wickedness, but I will still avoid evil at all costs."

Jeffery sighed, and broke the silence first.

"Reverend Church, again I am so sorry you're going through these trials. I have to leave to take care of some personal business, but I wanted to stop in and let you know I'll be back later tonight. If you need anything, you have my number. Gerald is okay, and I will bring him by as soon as they release him from observation. Please, you and Mrs. Church try to get your rest."

"Thank you Jeffrey," Reverend Church said with a nod. I don't think we need anything but I'll let you know.

With that, Jeffery gave a nod to the other three men, and offered a feeble smile to Mrs. Church, then left the building. A tear ran down his cheek, as he considered the task that lay ahead. He hoped above all else his nephew had repented and rededicated his life to God in that prison cell. He silently prayed for his precious sister, who he knew was about to have the worst evening of her life.

21

NO WEAPON FORMED AGAINST US

"Oh my Lord!" Jewel cried, covering her mouth. "Is he okay? I'm coming down there right now!"

"Honey, please try not to stress," Sandra said shakily. "We've called the ICU and spoken to the doctor. Gerald is still being held for observation but the doctor says he's very blessed to be alive, but he's okay."

"Oh my God..." Jewel frowned. "I'll be there as soon as I can."

Her mother said goodbye and they hung up just as Dexter walked into the room buttoning the cuff on his shirt.

"We've gotta go to the hospital right now!" Jewel exclaimed. "Gerald overdosed."

"What?! Is he okay?" Dexter froze in his tracks.

"Mom says he's okay but they're keeping him under observation. Who knows what's going to happen next though!" Jewel replied bitterly.

"He's okay though right?"

Jewel blinked at him through wet, red eyes. She knew her husband well, but wanted to make sure she was hearing him correctly. "What?"

Dexter cleared his throat, "He's... he's okay right? He's stable?"

"What are you really asking Dexter?"

"Aw honey...I've had this meeting set up for weeks. It's the final phase of the project. You knew I had to meet my team today?" Jewel just stared at him. "Gerald is *always* in some mess," he continued, throwing his hands in the air.

"I can't believe you're saying this Dexter," Jewel replied in shock. She stood staring at him, little streams running down her cheeks but her face was blank.

"Aw Jewel, please... I've taken so much time off during this critical phase of the project already with you and your folks at the hospital. I'm starting to get concerned my bosses are noticing."

"Really? Like your sixty-to-eighty hours a week isn't enough?"

"Jewel..."

"What happened to putting more faith in God?" She asked pointedly.

"What's that supposed to mean?" Dexter shifted his weight nervously. Jewel had her father's holy fire in her eyes at that moment.

"Our conversation this morning? You said you were going to start putting more faith in God. Don't you think God can either change your job circumstances, or provide one where you don't have to sacrifice your family time?"

"Honey, of course I do. But right now if I lose this job, we're never going to be able to finish building that house."

"The house? Really, that's what you're concerned about?" Jewel cast him a knowing look that made Dexter both insecure then a little defiant. "My brother almost died and you're concerned about maybe losing your job because maybe thirty plus hours a week isn't enough?"

"I'm doing it for you Jewel. Okay fine, I'm leading this meeting but let me call them and say 'Sorry I can't make it. My wife's troubled brother is at it *again*."

Jewel's eyes narrowed but she appeared unmoved by Dexter's words. She just stepped closer to him, and sniffed his collar.

"Say Dex... is *Acqua di Gio* necessary to lead an after-hours meeting?"

Dexter screwed up his mouth in protest, but he had no response.

"I'm packing an overnight bag, and unless Gerald is discharged into my care, I'm staying at the hospital."

Jewel looked him square in the eyes before she spoke again, "Dexter you're on extremely dangerous ground of being led astray by the enemy. You're being really insensitive to your wife's needs right now, and I'll tell you God is not pleased with you. Take this as a word from the Lord; if you don't man up and start following Christ's example, there is only trouble ahead. Not any trouble I'll bring, but you're headed down the wrong path. You're my husband, and I love you, so I have to speak the truth. If you won't take the spiritual lead in our marriage, I have to by default. Whenever you're ready however, I am waiting for you to lead."

Dexter was visibly rocked. He looked confused as she kissed his cheek, then walked upstairs to pack her bags.

***

Jeffery stared blankly at the steam rising and curling from the stale cup of cafeteria coffee. His way was to reduce any given problem to a set of finite, manageable variables and from there, by deductive reasoning arrive at the most logical causes for any given scenario. He used this method time and again to predict events, outcomes and lasting effects. Jeffery had a technical mind with one unusual difference; he based much of his reasoning - what he believed to be concrete data - on his faith. It all began when he was a young man, seeking truth like so many others, and stumbling across a passage that would become the catalyst to an, as yet, unending treasure hunt. That passage was from the very first Psalm, in the very first verses:

> *1 Blessed is the man*
> *Who walks not in the counsel of the ungodly,*
> *   Nor stands in the path of sinners,*
> *   Nor sits in the seat of the scornful;*
> *2 But his delight is in the law of the Lord,*
> *   And in His law he meditates day and night.*
> *3 He shall be like a tree*
> *   Planted by the rivers of water,*
> *   That brings forth its fruit in its season,*
> *   Whose leaf also shall not wither;*
> *And whatever he does shall prosper.*

Jeffery had taken that verse at face value, and simply believed it. He determined in his heart to test it for three months, cutting ties with friends he knew were subtracting from his life, adding a daily prayer and Bible study routine, then charting weekly results. This was his personality, as much a part of him as his face or height or eye color. It was a time he desperately needed money, and had experienced a string of broken personal relationships. If the experiment produced no results, he would have, without a second thought, abandoned the notion of his parent's somewhat-mediocre faith. But after one month his life had turned around so drastically, as a result, he became the most effective type of believer, someone who puts into practice what the scriptures say, as opposed to only hearing it.

Very rarely did his method fail him, and he would always figure out why, but today, for some reason, it seemed as though Jeffrey's mind was trapped in an infinite loop. Over and over he stepped through the warning signs of Reverend Black's gradual but stubborn deviation from the truth, and the related scriptures about those who abandon the Lord's paths. He stepped through his faithfulness, the related scriptural promises and then his subsequent release from the church. He pondered Reverend's Church's faithful service to God, and how the good pastor's troubles were somehow related to what was going on with his own. But that *somehow* was slowly driving him crazy.

He knew Reverend Black was responsible for the embezzled funds from *Holy Light*. He knew envy and greed was a likely cause, and that he, being caught in the crossfire, coupled with his refusal to look the other way had resulted in his removal from the church. He even knew his nephew Stanley Sims had been murdered because he'd not heeded those first three verses in the Psalms. The poor kid had been seduced by the allure of illicit wealth, and when he'd become a liability, he was coldly removed from the equation. *How far the so-called Reverend had fallen.*

What gnawed at Jeffery most however, was the seeming coincidental tragedies and afflictions endured by the Church family. No-one outside of perhaps a clandestine government agency could orchestrate so many terrible attacks on one family. And what reason would any organization have to attack the Churches? No human organization would have reason at least. Jeffery had no doubt the Churches had been enduring severe spiritual attacks, he just couldn't figure out why. He'd listened to Reverend Church's three closest friends present their cases, and he'd remained silent. Their reasoning so far had not meshed with what he had personally proven from scripture.

Throughout this process, Jeffery had been waiting to hear something profound from the Reverend and his three alleged friends. As the days and ramblings wore on, however, he was rapidly growing tired of expecting wisdom from their mouths.

Jeffery's phone awoke suddenly on the table, loudly interrupting his thoughts. He looked at it for a few seconds then swiped the screen and held it to his ear.

"Hello?"

"Mr. Lee?"

"Yes."

"Doctor Lewis is satisfied that Gerald Church's vital signs are stable so he is ready to be discharged. As you know, considering his circumstances, it would be better if he was discharged into the care of a custodian. His sister has been to see him, but he is asking to be discharged into your care."

"Ok, I'll be right up."

He was exhausted but he stood up and a slight smile crossed his face. *At least something was going right.*

***

"I still think you should have seen your parents man," Jeffery said shaking his head, as he opened the car door for Gerald.

"I will Uncle Jeff, I will." Gerald had been soft spoken since his stint in the ER. Jeffery glanced at him as he walked around to the driver side of the car, a little surprised at his newly humble tone.

"Why didn't you just say hi so they don't worry?"

"I don't know, when I go back to my dad, I'm gonna go before him a hundred percent, if you know what I mean. I'm going to apologize for everything I've put the family through. I just don't feel prepared right now." Gerald was humble and sincere. "I mean, I'm ready... I just want to go to my dad totally cleaned up and all."

Jeffery nodded his head, acknowledging Gerald's words. He knew what the kid meant, and believed him.

"Hey listen, I have to swing by my sister's house for a bit. I hate to have to do this now, but I have to see her."

"Okay," Gerald shrugged. "Anything I can help with?"

"No man, not really. Well, you actually may know him. My nephew, Stanley Sims, died in police custody this morning? He's her only son."

"Deacon Sims? From *New Day*?" Gerald asked in horror.

"Yeah man. The authorities just notified her and my cousin is headed over to be with her at this time, but I have to go see her. I'm going to reassure her I'll take care of her, no matter what. Stanley was all she had."

Gerald put a compassionate hand on his older friend's shoulder. "How are you holdin' up Uncle Jay?"

Jeffrey bit back a tear, and nodded his head. "I'm okay man. I have to be....for now at least."

Gerald squeezed his shoulder, and Jeffrey just stared at the ground nodding desperately fighting his emotions.

On the far side of the parking lot, a plain clothes officer in an unmarked cruiser discretely picked up his cell phone and dialed a number.

"Yello?"

"Sarge, they're on the move."

"They? Who's with him?"

"The deacon and the kid."

"Perfect. Tail them and keep me posted so I can intercept. Stay close in case I need backup."

"You got it."

Jeffery started his car and after just a second it cut out. He frowned and turned the ignition again. This time the engine roared to life. Gerald closed his door and Jeffery pulled out of the parking spot, heading toward the hospital exit.

"So Gerald, I was in the hospital room when uh, you were revived. I believe you've made a change, but please understand I'm taking you into my home and there will be some rules you need to abide by."

Gerald nodded. He looked the man square in the eye and said, "I swear to you, you will have zero problems Uncle Jeff."

"Bernice, or any girls can't stay over, you know that right?"

"Uncle Jay, I can't express how grateful I am to both of you but Bernice and I are going to have a long conversation about our relationship. And she definitely won't be staying over anywhere with me."

Jeffery could tell he was serious. At the very least, he believed Gerald intended to follow through.

As they pulled onto the road the unmarked police cruiser slowly wheeled through the parking lot, staying just in sight of the Toyota Camry. Jeffery accelerated and the car spluttered for a second. He frowned as the car resumed speed.

"What's up?" Gerald inquired.

"Aw nothing, it was just idling a little high for some reason, and then just now it cut out a little."

Gerald raised an eyebrow but didn't say anything else. Jeffrey didn't seem too concerned.

They pulled up to a light, as the cruiser turned slowly out of the hospital parking lot.

"So Uncle Jay, let's be real for a minute," Gerald said, glancing over at his driver.

Jeffery looked over at him curiously, but nodded, "Sure... what's on your mind?"

"Bernice said you were pretty intent on finding me. Why were you looking for me?"

Jeffery took a deep breath, then exhaled thoughtfully. "You know Gerald, I've been asking myself that same question. To be honest, I found something that had me concerned about your relationship with Reverend Black."

"Reverend Black?" Gerald asked knowingly.

"Well, I can't discuss everything with you right now, but call it an intuition, I just knew I had to find you. It's related to recent events involving Reverend Black."

"You mean like Deacon Stan's death? Wait, aren't you also one of his deacons?"

"Was...I was one of his deacons."

"What do you mean was?"

"Gerald, I believe I discovered Reverend Black is embezzling money from *Holy Light*, and he fired me. My cousin Stan was involved, and it seems he's paid the ultimate price. He was killed at the prison by one of the guards."

"Oh my Lord!" Gerald exclaimed. "Stone!"

Jeffery nodded, and a steely cold set into his eyes. "So you're aware of Reverend Black's dealings?"

"Well, only a little. He says he maintains connections to 'reach' the hood, but I always knew better. Whoa, if this is true, Black is way outta control."

"Yeah buddy."

Gerald's eyebrows raised, but he was beyond putting anything past Reverend Black.

"I'll explain more as we go. You might actually be able to help," Jeffery said. He didn't want to involve Gerald, but he figured Gerald was already involved. Jeffery put the key in the ignition.

The car slowed as they approached a red light. Gerald wanted to say more, but before he could respond, the car misfired then jerked back into gear.

"Seems like your ride needs some tuning Uncle Jay!" Gerald chuckled.

Jeffery frowned at the dashboard, "That's so weird, it was driving smoothly this morning."

"Have you had an oil change, or had anything done to it?" Gerald asked. Jeffery shook his head.

"Maybe you drove it a little too hard or something rushing me to the ER? Hit a bump or something?"

"No, I don't recall anything like that." Both men stared at the rev counter as the car idled at around four thousand.

"So what happened with Reverend Black? How did he fire you?" Gerald asked, now intrigued.

"He just told me to get out, and offered me severance- a payoff for my silence."

"Hmm," Gerald said pondering his words. "That' messed up, but I think you're concerned for good reason."

"What do you mean?"

"Well, I've heard things you know, and I guess I've seen one or two things. I don't want to diss anyone but Reverend Black sure doesn't seem to be who I thought he was."

Jeffery certainly agreed.

About five hundred feet behind them, another cruiser pulled out from a side road, joining the car following them. It then it sped up and took the lead.

"Say, how severe was your uh, fallout with Reverend Black?" Gerald asked.

Jeffery paused for a second, and then replied, "Pretty severe. In fact he came to the hospital and tried to get in to see you and we had a little...incident. Why?"

"Really?" Gerald was now concerned. "Did he threaten you?"

The car misfired yet again.

"Yeah, you could say that," Jeffery replied.

Gerald frowned as he tried to connect a few dots in his mind. "Yo Uncle Jeff, did you see anyone unusual around your car while you were at the hospital?"

"What do you mean? Like who?"

"Anyone unusual? Perhaps lurking around your car."

"No, not around my car. Outside of Black."

"Hmm," Gerald replied thoughtfully. "Anyone else?"

"No. Well I guess I thought I saw Sergeant Stone earlier this morning, but I wasn't sure it was him, and if it was I figured he was at the hospital for police business."

"Wait, Stone was there?" Gerald replied visibly concern.

"Yeah, why?"

Suddenly a siren blooped behind them and Jeffery looked in the rear view mirror to see a police cruiser with flashing lights tailing them. Gerald whirled around to see the cruiser, as Jeffery began to slow down and pull to the road's shoulder.

"What? I wasn't speeding."

As the car slowed, it hesitated and misfired again. Instantly Gerald jerked the steering wheel to the right, pulling the car back into its lane.

"UNCLE JAY, DO NOT STOP FOR ANYTHING! We gotta outrun these guys."

"*What?*" Jeffery replied in shock. "What are you doing Gerald?"

The police cruiser's siren flipped on and it sped up to the Camry.

"Jay! Listen to me!" Gerald squawked. "If you stop we're both going to jail. They got something in your car. We gotta outrun this guy and get somewhere safe to check out your car! Trust me!"

"Trust you? What are you talking about man?"

"THAT'S SEARGENT STONE BEHIND US DUDE! They planted something in your car! Trust me, I've heard mad stories about this cop on the street, and we both know he's Reverend Black's honcho! DRIVE!"

Something inside Jeffery flipped and he slammed the pedal to the floor. The car spat loudly then surged forward. Immediately the cruiser lurched forward as well, as did the second car, now with its lights and siren also screaming.

"How far are we from your house? Where do you live?" Gerald demanded.

"I live way out near my church man, but I know someone who lives by the *Harris Teeter* on Plaza and Central."

"Ok, whatever you do don't get on 277, we gonna take the back roads! Hit a left now!" Gerald pointed to a side street. Jeffery braked hard and dragged the steering wheel to the left. The car dug into the road, but maneuvered the turn successfully. Behind them the two cruisers screeched to a near stop, then navigated the turn slowly, buying the Lee and Gerald a few seconds of lead.

"Turn right up here," Gerald ordered. Jeffery obeyed. The sirens were getting loud again.

"What are we going to do when we get to the house?" Jeffery asked.

"They got a garage?"

"They have a car port behind a gate."

"That'll have to do!" Gerald said. "But we gotta lose Stone, otherwise it's gonna get hairy."

"Dear Lord Jesus, protect us from this evil," Jeffery prayed as he floored it down the side street. "You said in your Word Lord, that you would deliver us from injustice and that no weapon formed against us will prosper. I pray you protect us, and keep us right now, in Jesus' mighty name."

"Amen," Gerald echoed, and nodded to Jeffrey Lee. Both men were doing their best not to freak out.

The police cruisers had gained ground, and were right back behind the Camry.

"Okay Uncle Jay, we're about to come up to Providence Road, but just before there is a little alley to the left. You need to brake hard and get into that alley. We don't want to be on main roads and we sure don't want to stop for no red lights."

The Camry sped along the side street and sure enough, as they approached Providence Road, Jeffery could see a tiny alley to the left. How he was going to fit the car in there at this speed he had no idea. He maintained his tremendous speed, with the two cruisers right on his tail, lights glaring and sirens blaring. Stone had to believe he was about to run the red light ahead, but about ten feet before the alley Jeffery slammed on the brakes, and swung the wheel hard to the left. The Camry swung around and the rear wheels screeched loudly across the asphalt. Sergeant Stone's cruiser flew past them, missing the Camry's tail by millimeters, while the right side of the Camry fishtailed into the alley wall. The rear quarter panel scraped deafeningly across the brick as the car corrected and sped off again. The second cruiser had enough time to screech to a stop, back up a little and then roar down the alley after them. Sergeant Stone swung a left onto the main road, and raced along parallel to the alley.

Stone dialed the other cop and put his phone on speaker.

"Man, this guy can drive!" the voice squawked through the phone.

"Stay on the phone, I'm running parallel to the alley, I'm going to pull ahead and cut him off at Charlottetown. If he turns off let me know."

"Shouldn't we call it in now? He's driving around like a lunatic?"

"Hell no. They're both going to resist *if* they survive this chase, and I want to teach 'em what the consequences of that are!"

"Gotcha."

"Ok, keep flooring it," Gerald said. "Bet you Stone is going to try to cut us off at Charlottetown... I guess we're going to have to hang a left on Torrence. It's not the next left, but the one after."

"Whew!" Jeffery said, as he wiped beads of sweat from his forehead. Never in his wildest dreams did he think when he woke up, that he'd be shredding his Camry up on a police chase that evening.

"Lord Jesus protect us," he whispered again.

"Okay this one coming up!" Gerald yelled, and Jeffery steadied himself to make the turn. As he slammed his foot onto the brake and began to swing the steering wheel to the left, three kids riding their BMXs appeared in view, all riding abreast on Torrence Avenue. There was no way he would miss them. Frantically he released the brake, swung the wheel straight again, and the Camry veered wildly back to the right, fishtailing crazily across the alley, but continuing along their original course. The cruiser behind them slowed a little, anticipating their loss of control, but somehow the Camry righted itself and continued speeding toward the main road.

"Holy....they nearly just took out a bunch of kids trying to hang a left on Torrence," the cop yelled into the phone. "Stone this is nuts!"

"Did they turn left?" Stone shouted.

"No, no, they're still headed toward Charlottetown. Are you in a position to intercept?"

"Almost, you just push 'em into me," Stone cackled.

"There's no escape for these dead men now."

The Camry raced toward the main road and Gerald began to panic, "Man, Stone's sure to be trying to head us off at Charlottetown!" he shouted. "We're outta options Jeffrey."

Jeffery kept his eyes locked on the road ahead as the cruiser pushed up close behind them. He kept his foot flat on the floorboard as the Camry roared toward the main road.

"Lord Jesus, protect us," he whispered again.

As they approached the intersection, he could hear the siren of the cruiser approaching from the right.

"Oh Lord Jesus!" Gerald shouted as he braced himself in the seat.

Sergeant Stone tore around the corner and was racing toward the side street to intercept them.

"How close are they?" he shouted into the phone.

"T-minus three seconds," the voice shouted back. Sergeant Stone grinned wickedly in anticipation. As his cruiser roared toward the side street, he veered into the lane of oncoming traffic, preparing to ram them as the car exited the alley. The Camry sped past garbage cans and metal staircases, flying toward the main road. It sounded like Stone's siren was right upon them.

"Ok, they're gonna exit the alley" Stone's honcho squawked. Stone bit down, leaned back in his seat, so as not to be hit in the face by the airbags, and gripped the wheel tightly at ten and two.

Suddenly, as he were an apparition, a homeless man in filthy, tattered rags stepped from the middle of the street into the path of the oncoming cruiser. Reactively, Stone swung wildly to the left to avoid the man as the

Camry rocketed out of the alley. Glued to its tail was the second cruiser, placing it squarely in the path of Stone's careening car. With a sickening crunch Stone's cruiser slammed into the other, smashing it into the corner of the alley wall. With a deafening impact, Stone's cruiser launched up over the roof of the other car in an explosion of glass and debris. It flipped halfway in the air, then crumpled into the concrete wall with a deafening crash. The inverted car swung violently as it hit the wall, and slid on its roof a few meters down the sidewalk until it came to a swaying stop. A bloody, uniformed arm lay limp out of the shattered driver's side window.

"OH MY LORD!" Gerald shouted. "DID YOU SEE THAT?"

"Oh dear Jesus, I can't take much more," Jeffery groaned. "Is that homeless guy okay?"

"Dude, that was INSANE! I know for sure Stone ain't okay!" Gerald yelled. "There's no way those guys survived that!"

"Father forgive me please," Jeffery prayed. "But thank you for protecting us."

"Forgive you? For what? They would have killed us if they had the chance Uncle Jay," Gerald said loudly.

"I know. I guess, I just hope they're okay."

"Yo, God just saved us man. That homeless dude was like an angel or something. God doesn't play when people are tryin' to harm his people."

Jeffery pondered Gerald's words as he raced toward their destination. He was sure he'd seen that homeless man at Reverend Church's celebration the Sunday before.

After zigzagging through back alleys just in case, the unlikely duo skidded in to Jeffrey's friend's driveway. He knew his buddy would likely be at a Saturday night church service, but if his friend objected to them parking there temporarily, he'd just beg for forgiveness. He turned off the car's lights but left it running as they coasted up to the tall, metal gate. Jeffery pulled up the parking brake, got out of the car and walked over to ring the doorbell just in case. There were lights on inside, but nobody answered. He walked up to the gate, lifted the latch, and pulled it to the right. It slid open.

He looked over at Gerald and nodded in relief. During the entire chase, he was secretly terrified the gates would be locked. But he swung them open, jumped in the Camry and pulled the car under the carport. Gerald closed the gates, as Jeffrey popped the hood.

"You really think they planted something?" he asked Gerald.

"Well unless your car has been misfiring and idling super high for a while, I think I know exactly where they put it too."

"Hmm, well I'm certainly intrigued."

Gerald popped open the hood, took out his phone and clicked on his flashlight app. He shone the light behind the engine, at a mass of snaking hoses. Behind the hoses, on a natural little shelf in the engine lay a square package tightly wrapped in what appeared to be brown paper, plastic wrap and tape.

"Whew," Gerald whistled as Jeffrey's eyes widened. Gerald reached back under the hoses, and extracted the package.

"About one-and-a-half kilos," he said, bouncing the package in his hand. "Ten to twenty years hard time baby! That's what we just avoided."

"Lord Jesus help us," Jeffery instantly turned pale. He steadied himself on the car.

"He just did," Gerald laughed. "You can drive like Luke Duke no problem, but you get queasy when you see the goods that would've put you away?" Gerald was a lot more at ease.

"They would have killed us in prison, Gerald."

"Yeah..." Gerald agreed soberly. "Good thing you can drive, and God was looking out for us!"

"You got a knife in the car?" he asked Jeffrey Lee.

"Huh? No, I mean what for? I have a screwdriver."

"A screwdriver will do," Gerald replied. Jeffery walked over to the passenger side and retrieved a flathead screwdriver out of the glove box and handed it to Gerald. Gerald looked around the yard, then walked over to an outside faucet, where a garden hose lay coiled up neatly. He put the package under his arm, turned on the hose, and carried it to a storm drain on the edge of the property. Jeffery walked after him, and watched as Gerald lay the running hose on the ground, then took the package and ripped a hole down the middle of the plastic with the screwdriver. A fine puff of white powder rose from the package, as Gerald continued ripping open the plastic. When the hole was large enough, he turned the package inside out, emptying the contents into the storm drain. Then he lifted the garden hose, and washed the powder away, and rinsed out the plastic. He threw it down the drain as well, and washed his hands off.

"Man, I hate littering like that but I think it's best if that wrapping gets as far away from us as possible," he grinned at Jeffrey.

"I think it's okay just this one time," his friend managed a smile.

"Wow man... what was that? Cocaine?" Jeffery asked.

"Yup. Unless they were playing with some china-white heroin, but I doubt that."

"So are we clear?" Jeffery asked. "Should we look for any more stuff?"

"Nah, I doubt he'd want to risk planting two packages. Doesn't make sense," Gerald replied. "We're clear Uncle Jay. Besides, I don't think he's about to come looking for another package."

"Okay, well now we need to find out if we're wanted for running from the police."

"Yeah," Gerald agreed somberly as they walked back to the car. "I guess there is that."

Jeffery lifted the hood of the car, and was about to close it when Gerald stopped him.

"Oh hey man, one more thing," Gerald lifted the hood back up and propped it open again. He flicked on his phone flashlight, then leaned into the engine and pushed a rubber hose back onto a pipe, just above the little shelf where the package had been. "Your vacuum hose was loose," he grinned.

"Good thing Stone was an amateur or we wouldn't have known."

22

BEFORE THE DAWN

"We should probably bounce huh?" Gerald scanned around the outside of the Camry, while fishing in his pocket for the tin of Altoids. "Mint?" he offered the tin to Jeffrey, as he popped one in his mouth.

"No, no thanks." Jeffrey shook his head. "I'm thinking we need to go to the police station and report what happened."

"What?" Gerald squawked. "Why?"

"Gerald, we could go to jail for evading the police when they told us to pull over."

"Uncle Jay, I respect that, and doing the right thing is noble but what are we going to say? That Stone planted drugs in your car so we felt obliged to outrun him and his henchman, likely resulting in their *deaths*? We don't even have the drugs anymore to prove it!"

The older man was silent. He knew Gerald had a point, but it still didn't feel right. He had to admit he had no idea how to handle the situation.

"Yo, I think at the very least, we should pray about it. We didn't hear any other sirens and didn't see any other cop cars comin' down Providence. You know a whole squadron of 'em would be rainin' down on us if he radioed it in!"

Jeffery folded his arms as he leaned against the car and stared at the ground in thought. He slightly bobbed his head from side to side, as if silently weighing up various options. Then he looked up at Gerald, "Yeah, I guess you're right. But at some point, we have to notify the authorities."

"Okay, cool," Gerald nodded in relief. "But let's pray though. For real."

"Please do," Jeffery smiled.

"Father, we come to you in Jesus' name. First we thank you for delivering us out of the mouth of the lion. We cried out to you Lord, and you snatched us right out of the devil's jaws. I came mighty close to havin' to change my drawers with Jeffrey's drivin' Lord, but You guided him and we're alive."

Jeffery shook his bowed head.

"But Lord, we ask you now to just help us figure out a way to tell the police about what went down. We even pray Stone and his crony are okay Lord, if it be your will, and they're willing to repent. But please give us a clear way out of this mess, and protect us until we figure it all out. Amen."

"Amen," Jeffery agreed, looking up. Gerald grinned widely, as if to say, "Smooth prayer huh?"

"My driving is the reason you and *your drawers* are still in one piece buddy."

"Aww, Uncle Jay! I'm not dissing you," Gerald laughed as he threw his arm around Jeffery's neck. "I'll just say it's always the quiet ones that are the most *cray*!"

Jeffery stifled a chuckle, and shook Gerald off. That was all he could do without laughing, while Gerald smirked at him mischievously.

"Hey, we can say God can even use crazy skills that weren't developed for His glory huh?" Jeffrey mused.

"Oh, like knowin' where to look for that dirty *coco*?"

"Yeah Gerald. Thank God for your sharp sense, and knowing Stone had messed with my car."

"Aw, you know how I am," Gerald laughed as he puffed out his chest, and dusted his shoulder off.

"And thank God you're redeemed from all that right?"

"Oh yeah! I'm saved. Saved, sealed, delivered, free. I've seen the devil's house, and I don't ever want to see it again," Gerald said solemnly.

"Amen. Well still, thank God you knew where to look."

"Aw, it ain't hard when somethin's hiding in plain sight," Gerald shrugged.

Jeffery was in the process of nodding when an idea visibly flitted across his brain. "Wait, what did you say?"

Gerald looked up, surprised. "What? It ain't hard?"

"No, no, the rest?"

"When something's hiding in plain sight?"

Jeffery's eyes shone, and he ran over to Gerald and lifted him off his feet. "Gerald, you're a genius!" he cried, kissing him on the head.

"Hey, hey, yo, easy there Uncle Jay. People could be watching now," Gerald grinned nervously.

"You're still a genius! And God knows exactly what He's doing." Jeffery pulled his phone out of his pocket, and dialed a church member's number.

"Hello," crackled a high pitched voice.

"Hey Jen, it's me. Listen I don't have time to explain, but do you have Mary Willis' cell phone number?"

"Huh? What for Jeffrey? She hasn't been at church all week, you know!"

"Oh Lord," Jeffrey paused. "I gotta find her!" I think God just opened a door to get my nephew's killer."

***

The mighty oak trees swayed and rustled as the wind picked up outside *The Carolinas Medical Center*. Jewel leaned forward with both hands on the window sill, watching as a young family walked together. The dad snuck up behind his little girl and scooped her up, making her squeal in delight. He kissed her cheek as he propped her up against his hip, carrying her effortlessly with one arm. The little girl kissed her dad's cheek, then flung her arms around his neck and tucked her head into his shoulder, hiding from the wind. Even from the window Jewel could see the mom grinning widely at her husband and child. Jewel looked away with glistening eyes.

"You okay baby girl?" Sandra crooned from her hospital bed.

Jewel tried to wipe her eye discretely, "Sure mom."

"Just call him," her mother urged. "Don't let pride get the better of you angel."

"Ugh, it's not pride mom. I just don't want to cuss my husband out in front of my parents is all."

Her mother rolled her eyes, and picked up her book. Her head was still bandaged, but for the first time in a few days, she had a little energy. The effects of the radiation therapy were finally wearing off, and she was extremely grateful for that. Sandra was determined to read the first chapter of the inspiring new release by her favorite Christian author. As she settled in to the first paragraph a bubbly, young nurse came breezing into the room.

"Hello my darlings," she sang to Sandra and Reverend Church. Sandra gave a slight sigh but put her book down and looked up with a smile at the infectiously happy nurse. She clearly loved her job.

"Hi Mabel," Sandra Church sang back.

Reverend Church's chest and belly continued to rise and fall as he lay napping contently.

"You doing okay Miss Jewel?" Mabel asked.

"Me? Just okay, I guess," Jewel grunted.

"If any more of you want stay the night, we're going to have to get a bigger suite for the whole family." Mabel knew she could get away with a little jest as she flitted over to check Reverend Church's I.V.

"We'll be admitting my husband too if he doesn't get his act together," Jewel muttered under her breath.

Mabel must have heard her because she just mouthed a big "OH!" to Sandra with wide eyes and placed four dramatic fingers over her mouth. Sandra couldn't help but giggle.

As if summoned, Dexter popped his head in the door with a cheery, "Hey Mrs. C! Hey Babe. How's everyone doing?"

"Hi Dexter," Sandra widened her eyes at Jewel, who said nothing.

"How're you feeling Mrs. C?" Dexter inquired.

"I'm doing well thanks."

He leaned over and glanced at Reverend Church, realizing his father-in-law was still sleeping. He nodded a *hello* to the nurse, and then fidgeting with his phone asked, "Hey, uh, could you excuse Jewel and I for a moment?"

"Sure, son." Sandra nodded at Jewel, with more of a mother's command to go with her husband, than a grant of permission.

Jewel chewed her lip and gazed obstinately at her mother for a second.

"Jewel?" her mother said firmly. Her daughter relented and walked over to Dexter. Together they walked outside the hospital room.

"Uh oh," Mabel creased her brow, but said nothing more. Sandra smiled, but gave no reply and picked her book up again.

"Can we find one of those little private conference type rooms?" Dexter asked, looking up and down the hall.
"There's one three doors down on the right," Jewel grunted. Dexter followed her down the hall and into the room. "You didn't get my messages?"
"I got them," Jewel said coolly.
"Ok listen, I know you're mad but honey-"
"Dexter, please I don't want to hear one single 'but.'"Jewel cut him off. "If you're ready to talk about the real issues here, we can talk, otherwise-"
"Jewel, honey, now you let me talk!" Dexter said firmly but calmly. Startled, Jewel stopped talking.
"Baby, you know I love you so yeah, let's talk about some of our real issues." Dexter realized he actually had the floor so he inhaled, and began.
"For one, I really appreciate your Word knowledge, and your spiritual intuition but sometimes you wield it like a weapon."
Jewel was taken aback.
"What's more," Dexter continued. "I know your family is going through hell right now, and I'm here for you and for them, but honestly before all this craziness went down, you often put them before me. They're helping us out with a place to stay while we build our house, but I realized I've felt powerless to really be the spiritual head of our home. You know I respect your dad, but when you're under his roof we're technically under his spiritual authority, so it becomes very difficult for me to lead. I love you with all my heart Jewel, but I think sometimes, maybe subconsciously, you use the fact that you're anointed like your dad as a bit of a power trip. I'm not tryin' to slam you my love, but I

have to speak the truth because I want us to work through these things. "

Jewel had never heard her husband take a stand like this, but through the shock, something in her eyes said it resonated with her.

Dexter kept talking, "So here's what's going to happen, we're going to do whatever it takes to get your parents taken care of, and out of this hospital. If we need to take care of them at home for a while we will, but we are also going to start looking for an apartment. I don't care if it takes us another two years to build our house, I'm not going to lose this marriage."

Jewel blinked but kept listening.

"Next, we're *both* going to sign up for night Bible school classes. Yes, I want to learn the Word as well as you know it, and grow to higher levels spiritually but up until now, I have been more resentful than motivated. So that's gonna change."

Dexter took a deep breath, but his expression was still resolute.

"Lastly, I am going to stop working as much and spend more time with you. I need to repent to you, I simply haven't wanted to be around much lately, and that's not how a man is supposed to emulate Christ in his marriage. All the pressure of us trying to have a child, and living with your folks just became too much and I confess to you, I was using work as an escape. I ask you to forgive me."

He looked at his wife half-expectantly for a moment, but when he realized she was still dumbstruck, Dexter finished what he had to say. "We're gonna change all these other things then trust God for a child any way we can get one, work on our relationship and keep growing in the Lord. Now as my wife and equal in Christ, is there anything you disagree with or would like to add?" Dexter took a huge breath and braced himself for whatever came.

Jewel's eyes softened and she just looked lovingly at her husband for a long few seconds. Her mouth slowly turned up and her brow wrinkled as she held her arms out to Dexter.

"C'mere my love." He stepped forward, and she pulled him into herself. Dexter's steely expression slowly melted into one of relief, as he tightly embraced his wife.

"Thank you my darling," she whispered. "It's me that has to repent. I'm so sorry I made you feel inadequate."

She clung to her husband. "I know I'm full of fire sometimes, and I do need to learn to let you to lead. I never want to push you away. Please forgive me."

"It's already done my angel," he replied softly.

They held each other for a long, precious moment rocking back and forth as Jewel felt a sense of relief. Dexter stroked her head, and relished the moment; something had definitely changed. Something in the spiritual realm broke for them, and they both knew it as joy flooded their hearts.

"Hey!" Dexter pulled his face back from his wife's shoulder, and looked into her eyes with a tender smile. "Life gets rough, but we're always going to get through it, okay? Together. With Jesus."

Jewel's eyes sparkled as she bit her lips together.

"I love you Dexter!"

"I love you Jewel! You're my heart, girl!"

He pulled his wife into his chest again, and held her tight.

"It's always darkest before the dawn, my angel. And I have a feeling something good has to be on its way."

23

UNNATURAL STILLNESS

On Sunday morning, Reverend Church turned in his bed, groaned in pain and checked his phone for the time. *12:17 p.m.* He longed to be preaching in his precious, beautiful church. Reverend Church was pleased however, his friend Bishop Kenny Willis from Atlanta had made the drive Saturday night. He would minister at the main campus's three services, but Reverend Church still felt, as any good pastor would, his people needed him now more than ever. When Kenny had come to visit the night before, he'd prayed a powerful prayer that the Lord would soon bring this trial to an end, and Reverend Church and his wife had "Amened" loudly, feeling greatly encouraged.

He thought of Sandra, and what she was enduring right then and shook his head. It was difficult to not become bitter when he thought of her beautiful hair, now shaven, with gauze taped over the ugly wound.

Why won't you answer me Lord? he prayed quietly. He'd searched his Bible all week, had asked God numerous times to show him a sign, give him a word, anything. Reverend

Church desperately tried not to think about his precious boy, Tavaris, but it was futile. A deep sadness covered him like a heavy robe. His happy, energetic, beautiful boy was laying on an ice-cold slab in the morgue. He couldn't even bury his own son, because he was bedridden in this cursed hospital. He struggled furiously against the bitter thoughts.

A soft knock made him look up, and forget his grief for a moment. Standing at the door was his buddy. Although Jeffrey was a little younger, Reverend Church considered him a true friend; especially since he hadn't judged him. He had wondered, however, if Jeffrey had a whole lot of insight into his afflictions. Jeffery had always been a quiet soul, not saying much. He was genuine though, and Reverend Church was thankful he'd been to visit him almost daily while also taking care of his eldest boy, and he hoped, dealing with all that financial mess. The one thing that gave him a little hope was hearing Gerald seemed to be having a few days of clarity.

"Penny for your thoughts?" Jeffrey appeared worried, but masked it well.

"Jeffrey! Good to see you. I was just daydreaming." Reverend Church tried to prop himself up in the bed, and groaned again.

"Here let me help you," Jeffrey stepped forward quickly.

"No, no, thanks. I'm okay," Reverend Church shrugged him off.

Jeffery withdrew his hands, and stepped back.

"Where's Sandra?"

"In radiation," Reverend Church replied. "How's Gerald doing?" he asked, changing the subject quickly.

"Theo, he's doing really, really well," Jeffrey said, with happiness in his eyes. "I'm telling ya, He's had a real encounter with the Lord. When he's ready, you're going to hear all about it."

"Why hasn't he come to see us, yet?"

"He'll probably come today. We had a uh, eventful day yesterday."

"Hmm." Reverend Church studied Jeffrey eyes. "I'd love to hear all about that too."

Jeffrey nodded with a deeper acknowledgement. "Soon."

"So what's up? Shouldn't you be at church?" Reverend Church changed the subject.

Jeffrey smiled and pulled a chair up to the side of the bed. "Would you believe I skipped this morning?"

"What? How can a fixture miss a service?" The bed creaked as the great man shifted his weight.

"I know, I know, I've never had to set an alarm to wake up for church before, and I slept until ten-thirty! I guess I was exhausted from yesterday's adventures."

Reverend Church examined Jeffrey's face again. "That's understandable. You've definitely been busy, and seemingly preoccupied with something this week?"

Jeffrey nodded and examined a painting on the wall. "Your buddies will be up in a second. I saw all three of them downstairs. Apparently they all decided to preach the early morning services, so they could see you."

"Larry, Curly and Moe?"

Jeffrey laughed, "Yes."

"Don't know if I can handle them today, to be honest. I love those guys but they're really getting under my skin."

Jeffrey agreed but bit his tongue.

"On the bright side, God's doing something Theo. I don't have the full picture yet, but He's moving."

Reverend Church turned his head, and stared out the window.

"Trust me, there are things I'll have to tell you soon, but not yet. I don't want to stress you out but you should remain strong. God is working it all out for you."

Jeffrey winced from the sting of the silence. He was between a rock and a titanium wall. He didn't want to stress his friend out, but he was really beginning to wear thin at juggling this entire situation. Jeffery could understand Reverend Church's pain and confusion but if he was honest with himself, he'd been surprised at some of the Reverend's self-justifying words. Moreover he was concerned about the man's church. He had a disturbing sense that the man's sheep and congregation were the ultimate target of this attack. He'd been praying all morning, in the shower, during the drive, walking to the hospital room; the entire way. Jeffrey had been praying desperately for wisdom. He still didn't sense a release to reveal what was going on with Reverend Black.

Another knock made both men sigh. Bishop Davis was the first to poke his head into the room.

"Y'all awake?" The short, rotund man wore a dapper charcoal suit with a thigh-length jacket, which boasted wide, red pinstripes. The other two were almost equally decked out as they poked their heads around the door above him, like school kids checking if the coast was clear.

"Hey you guys," Reverend Church said, barely hiding his lack of enthusiasm.

"Where's Sandra?" Pastor Baker furrowed his brow.

"In radiation," Reverend Church replied, his shoulders drooping.

Reverend Williams shook his head and walked to the side of the bed, while Pastor Baker and Bishop Davis grabbed chairs from the other side of the room, "How'd you sleep brother?"

"So so," Reverend Church replied, looking up at Reverend Williams.

"Well, we continue to pray for healing and insight for you," Reverend Williams said, with a slow pat on Reverend

Church's shoulder. "In all areas," he added. It was as though he couldn't resist the touch of smugness.

Jeffrey groaned and shook his head. Reverend Church kept looking right into Reverend Williams' eyes,

"Not today Henry. I can't do it today okay?"

"Theo?" Reverend Williams protested, as he looked at his two cronies in mock astonishment. Pastor Baker shut his eyes and shook his head in agreement that the snub was uncalled for.

"Respectfully, the man is tired, Reverend Williams," Jeffery interjected. "I know in a strange way you mean well, but it's the condescending attitude that's getting under his skin."

Reverend Williams snorted, "Oh, forgive me Jeffrey, I didn't realize you were such an authority on the human condition."

Jeffery stared at Reverend Williams, not with a look of anger but more of disappointment, but he held his tongue.

"He's right Henry. I'm tired of the misplaced judgment all three of you have heaped on me," Reverend Church said firmly.

"Aw, c'mon Theo... why do you think we've taken so much time to see you?" Bishop Davis smiled widely. "We're just trying to help you."

"That's truly appreciated Jim, but you guys have to admit you've been pretty judgmental." Reverend Church remained steadfast.

"I know we all have slightly varying doctrines, but you've laid it on me pretty hard. And I have to say, I still believe I have yet to see a convincing argument for my guilt in these afflictions. In fact, since we're getting into this again, and I was just thinking about it all, hear me out."

Reverend Church inhaled deeply, as the three men braced themselves with stubborn faces.

"In over thirty years, I haven't even so much as looked at another woman inappropriately.
I haven't cheated on my taxes, or in the slightest way been deceitful regarding finances. I have given generously to the church, and to many people.
I have treated every single one of my staff and colleagues with the utmost respect and I've treated them fairly. I have paid them the very best I could, while striving to manage the church's funds as a wise steward of God's money.
I have provided for the poor of this city, and have begun outreaches to take care of the elderly, orphans and homeless.
I have not loved money, and have had my family go without many times than be accused of corrupting the gospel.
I have forgiven those who have opposed me, and have mourned and shown respect when those who have hindered God's work and made themselves my enemies, encountered tragedy.
I have walked as righteously and as blamelessly as I possibly could ever since I entered the ministry as a young man. I have followed God as closely as possible for *decades*, yet I am suffering as the worst sinner. It's one thing to say "the Lord giveth and the Lord taketh away, blessed be the name of the Lord," but there has to be a reason *why*. And He's not answering me. In fact, more than anything I wish God would respond to me and in His fair judgment, He would even write a book of my case. I would carry it on my shoulders, and tape it to myself like a crown. I would approach Him in the confidence of a political ambassador, and let Him thoroughly examine me. That's how confident I am. If I have done anything untrue, or other than what I have said here today, let the Lord curse my blessings and remove them all. I'm telling you all right now, I would *love* God to weigh me

in the scales. Now I am done! This is the last thing I have to say on the matter. My words are ended."

The three friends seemed to contemplate Reverend Church's words, but their expressions were ones of dramatic agony. They just *knew* Reverend Church had some hidden sin in his life, and was suffering for it. The three of them had discussed it at length, on their own of course, and all of their agreed theology pointed to the same conclusion: Reverend Church had to have sin in his life that was causing his woes. His apparent lack of acknowledgement of that fact, was bringing him dangerously close to death.

Suddenly, a voice boomed from next to Reverend Church's bed. It was Jeffrey Lee's, but gone was the quiet, patient tone. Instead, he was now standing next to his chair, and his voice rumbled with authority. The three men's attention had been seized.

"I am a relatively young man in the ministry, and I'll admit you all are very experienced! That's why I have waited a week to hear y'all speak, and have not yet voiced my opinion.

I respectfully believe age should speak first, because your greater years truly should have given you more wisdom." Reverend Church was silent in shock, staring wide-eyed at Jeffrey. He'd never heard him speak like this, with such authority, but he turned his attention to the three men and continued,

"I can say boldly the Holy Spirit gives a man wisdom, and elders are not always wise, nor do they necessarily understand justice. So please listen to me, since I heard y'all out. I waited and paid close attention to you, yet not one of you have convinced Reverend Church of his alleged wrongs, so please let me get this off my chest.

What I have to say has been burning in my heart for days, and the Holy Spirit now compels me. I will burst if I don't speak, so again, please don't interrupt me, but hear me out completely!"

Jeffery took a deep breath, turned back to Reverend Church and said, "Reverend Church, please pay close attention; I am a man just like you, yet I assure you I am speaking by the Spirit of God. Listen to my words, and decide if you can oppose what I am saying. You want a spokesperson to present your case before God? Allow me to lay it out. I heard you say 'I'm innocent. I am without transgression, and there is no sin in me, yet God is treating me like the wicked, and He haunts my every step.' My dear friend, you are correct. You are righteous in everything... except this one area: God is greater than man. Do you honestly believe you are more righteous than God? Do you truly believe He has no cause to allow affliction upon us if it serves His greater purpose in some way? If even to simply purify you of this deception that you are so righteous you are beyond God's correction? Haven't you read the scripture 'All have sinned, and fallen short of the glory of God?' How can you, as a man of God, say He is unjust in not delivering you instantly from these sufferings? We all deserve eternal punishment my friend, it is God's grace alone that has delivered us. How can we now say we are beyond suffering in this world? In fact, God may have to allow your enemy to attack you so you can be saved from such a deception, to save you from the pit.

If you wonder why God has allowed this sickness to come upon you, and these terrible tragedies in your family despite His promises that you are healed by the stripes of Christ, consider that a sinful attitude of self-righteousness may be an open door for your enemy. But if you recognize this as a wake-up call and repent, surely the Lord is gracious and will heal you and your family, and the Lord will have joy in you again.

What do you say, Reverend Church? Do you hear me? If you have anything to say, please respond. Speak, because I really want to vindicate you."
Jeffery watched his older mentor intently but the man could only sit and listen.

"Okay then," Jeffery continued. "So you four knowledgeable men, keep listening to my words and test them to see if they are good. Reverend Church has accused God of removing his justice. Seriously, I have never in my life heard a person drink such contempt for God, like gallons of water. Reverend Church, you're basically aligning yourself with sinners because you say 'It doesn't benefit us at all to follow God.'"
Reverend Church winced and averted his eyes.
"Understand that sin cannot touch God. Will God pervert justice? If God ultimately governs this world, can he hate justice? As a mere man, can you condemn God who is most just? Would it be appropriate for you to say to a king, 'You are worthless, or you are wicked?" Yet God places and removes kings. Can anyone say they have been disciplined enough, and will never sin again? Or are you willing to have God actually repay you according to any sin you've committed? Please let me know?"
Reverend Church remained silent.

"So my esteemed elders, of much theological knowledge, let's discuss your judgments. You three have judged Reverend Church, God's servant. Yet Reverend Church, in defending yourself you have proclaimed yourself righteous, because you have said 'What benefit is it to have followed the Lord, instead of living a life of sin?'
Let me answer that question - if you sin against God, can you hurt Him? Or if you're completely righteous, what do you give Him that He can't get a million other ways? No, your sin affects you and only you, as does your

righteousness. Do you think this makes the Lord want to jump to answer your empty words, Reverend Church? No I assure you He will not. He won't even regard them, but because of His patience, and His longsuffering with your rebellious words, you continue to multiply them without any intelligence, nor thought of consequence."

Reverend Williams shifted uncomfortably on the other side of the bed, and for a moment it appeared as though he might say something but a direct gaze from Jeffery quickly vanquished the idea from his mind. Instead, Reverend Williams raised his nose in the air, and kept his arms folded. "Oh, bear with me gentlemen, I have a little more to say on behalf of the Holy Spirit. If my words are righteous, it is only because of my Maker, so I assure you my words are not false. Or prove to me out of scripture, how I am wrong" Jeffery chastised, with even more authority behind his words.

"Don't you understand although the Lord is almighty, He despises no one? He does not preserve the life of the wicked, but truly He instead brings justice to the oppressed. He doesn't forget about His righteous people, but He has seated them with Christ forever. If His children are afflicted and in some sort of bondage, He will tell them what they're doing wrong if they seek Him. He shows them they've acted defiantly, and opens their ears to understand instruction. If they listen, and turn from their stubbornness, they will live out their days in prosperity and joy. If they continue to disobey Him, they will die without knowledge. But a hypocrite stores wrath like a trust fund. The hypocrite will never cry for help when God handcuffs him; no he'll die in youth and his life will end among the perverted people of the world. Yet God continues to deliver the poor in their affliction and opens their ears in oppression."

Jeffery took a deep breath, then continued, "Reverend Church, God would have brought you out of this trial into restoration but you are filled with the wicked's judgment because you have chosen sin rather than enduring this affliction. Did you hear what I just said? You would rather sin by murmuring against God than patiently endure your trial in faithfulness. Be very careful Reverend Church, because there is nothing that could save you if God decides to destroy you with one blow. Truly, who has ever accused God of doing wrong?"

Jeffery squinted his eyes as if grasping the outer edges of an enormous concept that had been revealed to him. None of the four men dared say a word, but Reverend Williams, thankful for the pause, shuffled over to where his two friends were sitting and perched himself on the room's coffee table. Abruptly, Jeffery continued, "Reverend Church, remember to focus on God's great works, about which I know your very choir sings every Sunday. The entire world has seen it, and non-Christian nations even acknowledge His works from afar. God is exceedingly great and we do not know His depths, nor can the number of His years be discovered. He gathers the clouds together and distills rain from the mist. Then He rains it on our crops, and our fields and our parks and gardens, to give us food and water and flowers and joy in abundance. But if He chooses to shoot lightning from His hands, the animals even know it's His doing, and our heart's tremble when it thunders. His voice roars greater than this thunder, with majesty and He controls every element of nature, whether snow or win or rain, or hurricanes or tornadoes."

Jeffery stood as though he preached a sermon. "Listen to this Reverend Church; lie there in stillness and consider the wondrous works of God. Have you spread out the skies like Him? Do you control the delicate balance of nature as

He does? Teach us Reverend Church, what should we say to God? Should He be told a man demands an audience with Him? Even if he agreed, if a man were to speak with God, without no doubt, he would be entirely consumed. You cannot even look directly into the sun, yet the Lord will come from Heaven in a golden splendor, so bright you wouldn't survive His glance. God's majesty is awe-inspiring and He is mind-bogglingly excellent in His power and work. He is more than competent in judgment and shows exceeding justice. He does not oppress, Reverend Church, therefore men fear Him. And He doesn't even show partiality to those who are truly wise in heart."

Jeffrey completed his sentence suddenly and as though he were exhaling his last breath. He stood next to his chair staring out the window for what felt like an hour. He turned to study the three men who were staring at him speechless, then looked over to Reverend Church. He stepped to the hospital bed with an unnatural stillness and squeezed his friend's hand.

"Be strong Theo," was all he said, then he lifted his chair, and carried it to the coffee table, nodded to the three other men and left the room.

24

THE LION'S MOUTH

When Jeffrey excused himself from the hospital room, the silence that lingered was the most uncomfortable any of the four men had ever encountered between themselves. Reverend Williams began to say something, but when he opened his mouth, his intended words became confused and jumbled, so he just remained still. Bishop Davis tried next, prefacing his statement with a goofy smile, but as he went to begin his signature anxious small talk, the words failed him. Pastor Baker wisely remained silent, while Reverend Church looked out of the window.

Before long, to the relief of the three men, a nurse came in and announced Mrs. Church would be returning from radiation therapy, and it was probably a good idea for the guests to give her some recovery time. The three men said hurried goodbyes to Reverend Church, who ignored them, after which they scrambled out of the room like kittens running from a vacuum cleaner. Once they had left, the nurse checked Reverend Church's I.V. levels, and chart, and asked the pastor how he was feeling. When he appeared to ignore her too, she walked over to the side of the bed, and attempted to make eye contact. She repeated the question. He still made no response, but kept staring vacantly out of the window.

"Mr. Church, are you feeling okay?"

Silence.

She eyeballed his diaphragm and saw it was rising and falling, but she still leaned over cautiously and announced somewhat loudly, "Mr. Church, I'm going to check your pulse, okay?"

No response.

She checked his pulse, and it was a little high, but within the normal range. She moved her face right in front of his, and asked again, "Mr. Church...." she patted his arm. "Reverend Church, can you hear me?"

He didn't even blink.

The nurse had a sinking feeling, and hurried out of the room to find the doctor, to report the strange behavior.

***

Reverend Black was no stranger to the *Mecklenburg County Jail*, sometimes visiting sons, daughters and even nieces and nephews of his congregation members. For several years, Reverend Black's concern was legitimate, and his visitations were genuine. When "the change" began to occur, Reverend Black simply didn't feel up to compassionate duties and would send an associate pastor to visit the family's loved ones. For a year or two, his associates would walk the inmates through the whole prayer, counseling and admonition routine, but one day Reverend Black saw opportunities at the looming complex of giant white, juxtaposed buildings.

"Harvey Black!" a heavyset, female officer barked from behind a bulletproof window. His head jerked up, as his deep thought was interrupted. He stood up, straightened his suit and ambled over to the counter.

"Yes," he replied as he reached the counter.

"You using a surety bond for Demarius Terrel's bail today?" the woman asked with disinterest.

"No," came the curt reply. Everything about the woman, from her appearance to her attitude to her uniform annoyed Reverend Black, as his pastoral facade wore extremely thin.

"How you payin' then?" her droopy eyes rose to meet his.

"Cash."

She cocked her head and raised her eyebrows as if to say, *Well? Show me the money.*

Reverend Black just stared at her. He wanted her to ask for it.

"That'll be fifteen thousand dollars, *sir*."

He glared into her disaffected eyes and pushed a stuffed manila envelope into the sliding box, under the window. She gave a little snort, pulled the drawer to her side of the window and opened the package.

"I want you to count that in front of me, and I want a receipt *before* Mr. Terrel is released."

She gave him no response, but shouted loudly, "Denise, I'ma need the cash counter!" Then she slowly took each stack of hundreds out of the envelope. Reverend Black kept an eagle's eye on her hands. After too long, Denise sauntered up with a counting machine and threw Reverend Black the unsettling combination of a judgmental look and a flirty glance. He gritted his teeth as the women proceeded to discuss their weekend while the cash was counted.

An hour and a half after the red tape was untied, the door leading to the jails opened and out strolled Sugar with a wicked smirk."Rev," he greeted Reverend Black, as they gave each other the bro handshake-slash-arm hug.

"You alright? They treat you okay in there?" Reverend Black asked, eyeing Sugar up and down.

"Oh yeah Rev, just like a Hilton up in here."

Reverend Black grinned. "How long till you can spring your boys?"

Sugar sucked his teeth, "If these dirty cops haven't jacked my cards outta my wallet, we can do it now."

"Alright, let's do it. We're gonna need 'em."

"Hmmm," Sugar screwed up the corner of his mouth.

Reverend Black leaned in close to Sugar and whispered, "While we're filling out the paperwork, you may want to call our pal, Jeffery and tell him you want to meet. Say you have some info on the wicked ol' Reverend Black that he will be very interested in. Maybe tell him you're considering making a plea or something, but you want him to corroborate your story since he has the evidence."

"A plea or *something*? He ain't gonna buy that, and you know it."

"He will if you tell him you know how to decode my diary."

"He'll call the FBI and wear a wire."

"Not if you tell him you have to meet him today. Wait until your boys are out, and say you have to meet in an hour. One time offer. Tell him you're not planning on sticking around if he doesn't want to play ball, and he'll never get another shot at nailing me, or getting the church's money back."

Sugar had a look in his eye of both respect, and distrust of a man who called himself Reverend, yet was so good at malevolent calculation. "Rev, you know this is gonna cost you, right?"

Reverend Black sneered. "Like betting fifteen large to spring you doesn't tell you how serious I am?"

"Okay, okay," Sugar's throaty voice boomed. "Let's do it," he shrugged.

***

While the nurse was finding a doctor, Sandra returned from radiation therapy. She was exhausted, but when she found her husband blankly staring just past her bed she became hysterical. The nurse had to lightly restrain her when she took Reverend Church's head into her hands, and was half-shouting into his face to wake up. Only when the doctor walked in, did Sandra Church give up her spot to the doctor, with anxious eyes.

"Reverend Church!" the doctor called loudly. There was no response. The doctor slapped his arm lightly, but to no effect.

"Oh my God, what is wrong with him?" Sandra cried.

The doctor called out again, and then felt for Reverend Church's carotid pulse. After a minute the doctor muttered to himself, "His pulse is normal." He waved his hand in front of the man's eyes. No response. Suddenly he smacked his hands together in front of Reverend Church's face. Not even a flinch. Finally he took his finger and closed one of Reverend Church's eyes. Eerily, it remained shut while the other was still open. The doctor opened the eye again, but it closed again of its own accord. The doctor shook his head, and closed Reverend Church's other eye. Sandra began to cry in dismay.

"He's okay, Mrs. Church," the doctor said quickly. "Well, I mean, he's okay for now. I want to run more tests on him, but it appears he's slipped into what is called a catatonic coma, for some reason."

"Catatonic coma?" Sandra yelled. "Why? Why would that happen? What's wrong with him?"

"Well, I'm afraid that's the tricky part. I don't know," the doctor replied calmly, but with obvious concern.

"Typically, and if this *is* in fact catatonia, it usually results from a disturbed mental or neurological state. His pulse is too high for *bradycardia*, which is catatonia onset by a weak heartbeat..." The doctor's thought trailed off.

"So what now?" Sandra asked fearfully.

"Well, I want to run a few more tests, but... we can try benzodiazepines. His other symptoms don't fully line up with it, but if it's a hysterical coma, benzos will sometimes pull them out of it, and there's no real harm in trying."

By now, Sandra was wringing her hands, and her breathing had become rapid. The doctor cast her a concerned look.

"Mrs. Church, perhaps it would be best if we move you to another room, while we run some tests on your husband."

"Absolutely not," she replied immediately, with a flash in her eyes that completely discouraged the doctor from trying any further.

"Ok, Mrs. Church, but please get into bed and try to rest. It won't do your husband any good if he wakes up and you're in worse condition."

The "*if*" hung in the air like a death sentence.

"What do you mean *IF*?" she squealed.

"Nancy, prepare six mils of Lorazepam, I'll be back in a minute," the doctor ordered quickly, and left the room. Nancy nodded, and scuttled out of the room, following the doctor. Only one nurse was left to manage the awkward silence with Mrs. Church.

Sandra Church looked as if she would throw up but instead, shuffled back over to her husband.

"Mrs. Church, please, get into bed. What are you doing?" the nurse darted over to her.

"Ma'am, please do not get in my way," came the terse reply. The nurse hovered uncomfortably for a second, not knowing what to do, but soon relented when Sandra would clearly not relinquish her spot beside the bed. The nurse moved out of her way as she walked over to her husband and spoke to him.

"Now Theo, you listen to me. You wake up right now! I feel so alone already, and I refuse to lose you. I've been trying to pray, but my words feel emptier every time." She took his face into her hands, and drew hers within three inches of his.

"I ask questions, but it appears that God isn't giving answers. My faith is slipping, and I don't know how to stop the slide. Theo, I cannot lose you! I couldn't recover if I did. You come back right now! Do you hear me?"

Her voice had risen to a wail and the nurse was becoming distressed. She put a gentle hand on Sandra's shoulder.

"Mrs. Church, please." Her hand was shaken off abruptly.

"Theo!" Sandra cried sharply. "Theo, wake up!" This time she shook her husband's head.

Suddenly moisture welled up in Reverend Church's left eye, and from this tiny pool, a lone tear trickled down his cheek. Both women gasped.

"Theo! You hear me! Theo!" Sandra Church shook her husband's face again.

The hospital door opened unexpectedly, and the nurse whirled around, relieved that the cavalry had arrived, but concerned because she had failed to get Mrs. Church in her bed. But it was neither the doctor nor Nancy. Instead, what looked like a raggedy bum stepped into the room.

"Sir?" the nurse turned to Sandra Church, wondering if this man was possibly a church member. The bum ignored the nurse, and walked straight over to Reverend Church with a disarming air of authority. Sandra was surprised at herself when she released her husband's face and stepped back toward her bed, unwittingly giving the homeless man access to her husband. The man, placed his hand squarely on Reverend Church's forehead, which jolted Sandra to her sense, and she shouted "What are you doing?!" She gave the homeless man a little shove backward, and put herself between him and Reverend Church.

"You get out of here before I call security!"

The man ignored Sandra and kept his focus on Reverend Church. Like a drill sergeant he spoke loudly, "Theodore Church, you have been crippled, and your son's life was taken in a terrible accident."

Sandra's eyes widened, "Get out of here! Now!" she screamed. The nurse was frozen in the corner of the room, knowing she should get help, but unable to move.

"You have a son who, until yesterday, had been a slave to drugs, lust and love of himself more than love of God," the man continued.

Sandra Church covered her mouth, "How... how did you...?"

"You have a wife that's dying of cancer." The homeless man glanced at Sandra who was now speechless. He turned to the Reverend again.

"Your church and life's work is under investigation by the government for embezzlement."

Reverend Church lay still and his eyes remained closed. The homeless man paused for a second, then said loudly, "Theodore Church! How strong is your faith?"

Sandra's eyes swung from the homeless man to her husband. For several seconds he lay motionless. Then Sandra's mouth dropped open. Reverend Church's hand began to tremor and twitch. Suddenly the door swung open, and Nancy and the doctor walked in. They both stopped suddenly, taking in the room's strange scene.

"Is everything okay in here?" the doctor asked, casting a glance at the anxious nurse in the corner. Sandra and the homeless man ignored him, and the doctor quickly realized Reverend Church's hand was slowly rising. The doctor tried to step toward the bed but couldn't for some reason he couldn't fathom. With eyes still shut, Reverend Church's forearm slowly raised, and with tremors and shaking, his fist slowly clenched. Everyone except the homeless man wore a stunned expression.

Sandra broke free of the moment first, and grabbed her husband's fist in both of her hands.

"Theo! Open your eyes honey," she kissed his face. Her husband's eyes remained shut so she turned to the homeless man, who looked back at her with no emotion. Suddenly jarred back to his sense of duty, the doctor barked, "Nancy, the Lorazepam!"

"Yessir," Nancy jumped forward with a syringe and small vial.

The homeless man quickly turned and positioned himself between the doctor and nurse. He raised his hand and slowly shook his head.

"Sir! Whatever you did, thank you for your help but we'll take it from here," the doctor ordered.

The homeless man just stood there with a stony expression.

"Doctor..." Sandra began. "I think we'll skip the-whatever that concoction is in the vial, for now."

"Mrs. Church, we have a small window to bring your husband out of this coma. Please let me do my job," the doctor replied, without taking his eyes off the homeless man.

Sandra glanced at the man, who turned his head to her, and again, shook his head.

"No, doctor. You do not have my permission. We are going to wait," Sandra replied firmly.

"Mrs. Chur-"

"I SAID NO!" Sandra shouted. "And that's final!"

"Fine, but you take responsibility for his condition," The doctor threw his hands up in the air, visibly annoyed. "And as long as he's in this hospital, I have to attach some monitors to your husband. An aid is on his way, to set them up."

"That's fine, but do not put anything else into my husband's body. Something is happening here that is bigger than medical science."

The doctor just shook his head. The homeless man gave Sandra the faintest smile and a small nod then turned from the bed, and walked out of the room. Slowly Reverend Church's fist lowered back to the bed.

***

After four rings, Jeffery picked up the phone, despite not recognizing the number. For some reason, he suddenly had an anxious feeling in his stomach, but shrugged it off as nervousness about the Sergeant Stone situation.

"Hello?"

"Jeffrey Lee, my name is Demarius Terrel. Some know me as Sugar. I am a former acquaintance of Reverend Harvey Black."

Jeffrey swung his head to Gerald, who in spite of Jeffrey's protests, insisted on eating cereal for lunch. Gerald saw his surprise and frowned while crunching his cornflakes, as if to say *What's up?*

Jeffrey mouthed the word SUGAR. Gerald's eyebrows arched.

"What can I do for you, Mr. Terrel?"

"Hehe. *Mr. Terrel*. You sound like the five-o. Listen carefully. I just got sprung from the joint and word on the block is you've given ol' Rev a good run for his money. So respectfully, I have a proposal for you."

"And what kind of proposal would that be?" Jeffrey sat down while Gerald abandoned his cuisine and jumped over the back of couch, landing next to Jeffrey. Jeffrey put a finger over his lip and mouthed *Ssshhh!* dramatically.

"Well, it looks like I got two choices right now." Sugar cleared his throat loudly. "I can run and hope for the best, or...I try to bargain with the D.A., and maybe make a plea. Seems they'd been setting me up for months, due to some sloppy mistakes by our dear Reverend Black."

"What does this have to do with me?" Jeffrey asked suspiciously.

"Well, apparently you have a certain notebook in your possession. I believe I have the missing pieces to decrypt the codes in that diary. With that information, I can make a deal for serving up the Rev, fresh and tasty, while you get to watch him pay for all he's done to you and yours."

"Hmm..." Jeffrey replied, thoughtfully. Gerald was motioning wildly to find out what was going on, but Jeffrey ignored him. "Mr. Terrel, can you hold for just a moment?"

"For sho'" Sugar boomed.

Jeffrey double checked he had put the call on hold, then placed the phone under a cushion, and turned to Gerald, "Sugar wants to meet," he whispered. "Says he can decode the diary, and wants to work with me to nail Black."

"Whaaat?" Gerald replied in a stifled yell. "Uncle Jay, you know he's settin' us up, right? Who do you think bailed him out?"

Jeffrey waved Gerald to shush, "We don't know who bailed him out," he said in a terse whisper.

"Aw come on man, I know dang right who bailed him out."

"I don't know Gerald. He sounds legitimately ready to bargain. He's facing some real time."

"Jay! Don't be foolish bro, you'll be walking into a trap. Sister Whatserface is bound to turn up soon. You even said she'll know how to decrypt that notebook."

"Even if I am walking into a trap, I believe God will deliver me from the lion's mouth. We don't even know why Sister Willis fell off the grid, and I'm really trying not to assume the worst."

Gerald just shook his head in disbelief, but Jeffrey motioned for him to be quiet. He clicked the phone back into the call. "Demarius?"

"Yo!"

"When do you want to meet?"

"In exactly one hour. Not a second later. If you flake on me, I'm gone. You'll never get this shot again."

"I'm not sure I can meet in an hour."

"Okay, well that sounds like a personal problem."

"WAIT, hold on. Okay, if I can meet, where do you want to meet?" Jeffrey was startled the man had called his bluff so quickly, and easily. Sugar meant business.

"We gonna meet at *Holy Light*."

"At the church? Why there?"

"There's something I want to show you. It's related to Reverend Black's scheme. More evidence."

Jeffrey was alarmed. Meeting at Reverend Church's sanctuary was a weird twist. The whole scenario definitely didn't feel right but what if there was evidence?

"There'll be people there. Staff... people who know me."

"Naw, the church will be empty in an hour. They've already set up for evening service. I have a key, and know the alarm codes. Let's just say Sister Willis is a former associate too."

Jeffrey's heart sank. It annoyed him that this entire wicked crew had access to Holy Light. Still, he prayed silently that

Sister Willis was safe, and sound. Now he knew he had to go.

"Okay. I'll meet you at *Holy Light* in an hour."

"Alright then," Sugar boomed. "Oh, and Jeffrey?" he continued.

"Yeah?"

"If me or my crew even catches a whiff of anyone but you or Gerald, it's going to go real bad for y'all."

The line clicked and Jeffrey turned to Gerald with genuine fear in his eyes.

25

SOW THE WIND

The air at the Carolinas Medical Center was deathly still. Reverend Church's eyes fluttered, then slowly opened. At first, he had no idea where he was; the white ceiling tiles slowly came into focus above his head. He tried to sit up, but groaned from the stiffness. It felt like he'd been lying in the same position for days. His mouth was parched, and his lips were chapped; his eyes desperately searched his bedside table desperately for a glass of water. Laboring, he gathered the strength to turn his head. He had no idea what time, nor day it was, but from the positions of the shadows outside, it appeared to be early afternoon.

Reverend Church forced himself to slowly turn his whole body to face Sandra's bed, his arms and hips finally obeying. Her bed was unmade but empty. *Where could she be?* He wondered. *Where is everyone for that matter?* He looked around the room, and realized his I.V had been removed. *What is going on?* he thought, resisting a pang of anxiety. "Nurse!" he tried to call, but his cry came out as a crackle. Slowly he pushed himself up on his pillows. He searched for the cable that had the emergency button attached, and felt it hanging behind him. He reached back, pulled the cable down and pressed the button. Instantly a loud crack shot through the air, making Reverend Church jump so violently the entire bed swayed. Pain shot through him like a hail of bullets ripping into his body. He looked outside and noticed the sky had darkened to an ominous, deep-ocean green, with the wind rapidly picking up.

Weird, he thought. *That must have been lightning. Sounded like it pretty much hit the building!* As he finished his thought the large windows flexed inward and groaned as a sudden blast of wind buffeted them. Reverend Church suddenly realized he'd seen weather like this before; well at least on homemade YouTube footage. In 2011, Reverend Church and his congregation, along with many other local churches, had come together to provide support and relief in the aftermath of the *two dozen* tornadoes that cut through North Carolina, leaving a wake of destruction, and twenty-four people dead. His stomach lurched with panic and his thoughts jumped to his wife. *I have to find Sandra!*

He began to fight his fatigue and agony, slowly drawing the covers and blankets off his legs. It seemed with every movement, the room darkened and the wind assaulted the building more fiercely. When he was finally able to drop his legs over the bed and lower himself to the cold floor, the sky outside was nothing but a wall of black and green, the sun completely gone. Rain, branches and debris were now whipping past the hospital windows and Reverend Church began to fear for his safety. He had seen, in Fayetteville, what flying debris could do to buildings...and to human bodies.

The wind had risen to a dull roar and Reverend Church began to panic, wondering if he had been forgotten in a hospital-wide scramble to get to shelter. As he shuffled forward as fast as he could, another deafening crack of lightning made a direct hit on the entire wall of hospital windows, exploding the window panes into flying shards. Reverend Church screamed and recoiled, shielding his face. What the lightning revealed in an instant drained every bit of strength from him.

Not even a hundred feet in front of the now-destroyed hospital window, a giant, seething, sickening wall of clouds churned. It was so wide he could not see the outer edges, and without a doubt, the largest F5 tornado on record roared directly in front of him. As he stood frozen in awe and terror, with rain, wind and debris stinging his face, Reverend Church knew he was a dead man.

For a moment, Reverend Church thought the wind carried a voice; faintly calling his name. It sounded like Sandra, but when he listened closely all he could hear was the dull roar. For the first time, something struck him as a little surreal; flashes of lightning illuminated the tornado from within its rushing, boiling walls while Reverend Church realized that strangely, although violently turbulent, the tornado appeared to be churning in the same spot.

He stepped closer to the window and saw the parking lot was empty too; the landscape completely devoid of life. No sirens, no ambulances, no law enforcement. Just Theo Church and the tornado. He took another step in wonder, while the building creaked and groaned, and debris and plant life swept past the windows. The rain, however, no longer stung his face, and he seemed immune to all but the dread of the colossal force of nature in front of him. Then, as if his mind had finally taken the path of his diseased body, forming from the roar of the tornado came something between the roar of a thousand Niagara Falls and the sonic boom of a hundred 747s. The voice uttered a single word: "THEODORE."

***

It was all Sandra could do, to keep from screaming. The machines attached to monitor her husband, screeched and flashed furiously, while the doctor and nurses scurried around Reverend Church, checking his temperature, pulse and preparing a stainless steel tray of an assortments of medical cocktails and syringes.

"His pulse is rocketing," the doctor shouted. "Nancy, thirty cee cees of Amiodarone, stat!"

Nancy snatched up a blue vial, and poked the syringe's needle into the lid, extracting the appropriate amount. She presented it to the doctor, who injected it directly into

Reverend Church's arm. The monitors kept shrieking, and flashing, but suddenly, Reverend Church's torso and neck appeared to convulse and spasm.

"Get the paddles on standby!" the doctor shouted.

Sandra knew enough to know the doctor was expecting a cardiac arrest, and she could no longer keep her cool, "THEO!" she screamed. "You don't die on me! You have work to do, and a family down here. I cannot lose a son and a husband in the same week! YOU WILL NOT DIE IN JESUS' NAME!"

The machines maintained their cacophony, and while the doctor was trying to remain calm, he cast two of the nurses a glance that was unmistakable.

"Mrs. Church, I think it would be better if we took you to another ward for the moment," Nancy began. "Your husband is in good hands, but it might not be benefici-"

"I'm staying right here!" Sandra growled.

"Mrs. Church, please try to remain calm," the doctor said, over his shoulder.

"I'm calm," she said, shrugging the nurse's hand off her shoulder. "I know what to do though," she muttered, and bowed her head and began praying fervently from the other side of the room.

***

As Reverend Church stood before the storm, when he heard the Voice, he felt as though his very bones were about to melt to liquid, and he collapsed to his knees in sheer terror. Through the howling, whipping wind, the tornado roared again, this time unmistakably: "THEODORE!" This time, Reverend Church knew in his heart, he was kneeling before his Maker. Yet he couldn't utter a word.

"WHO IS THIS WHO DARKENS COUNSEL WITHOUT KNOWLEDGE?" the cyclone boomed. Reverend Church bent his head over, and shook violently.

"STAND UP AND GET DRESSED THEODORE CHURCH. I AM ABOUT TO GET SOME ANSWERS OUT OF YOU."

Reverend Church was sobbing, but he wasn't about to disobey. He struggled to his feet, and waddled over to the hospital room closet and as fast as he could and put on the pair of pants, the collared shirt and the pair of shoes Sandra had brought him in anticipation of leaving. He was surprised at how loose-fitting his clothes were after only a few days in hospital. He hustled back over to the window like a death row inmate before the judge. His eyes were glued to the floor, too terrified to gaze into the monstrous storm.

"WHERE WERE YOU, THEODORE CHURCH, WHEN I LAID THE FOUNDATIONS OF THE EARTH? SINCE YOU KNOW SO MUCH, EXPLAIN TO ME HOW ITS DIMENSIONS WERE MEASURED, AND WHO MANAGED ITS CREATION?"

Reverend Church's heart felt like silly putty in a microwave, as he swayed under the force of word's blast.

"ANSWER ME! WHAT SUPPORTS THE EARTH'S FOUNDATIONS? WHO LAID ITS CORNERSTONE AS THE ANGELS OF HEAVEN WORSHIPED AND SANG IN JOY? WHO DREW UP THE BOUNDARIES OF THE OCEANS, WHEN THEY GUSHED FROM THE DEPTHS OF THE EARTH? WHO DRESSED THE SEAS WITH CLOUDS AND CLOTHED THEM IN DEEP DARKNESS? WHO CONTAINED THE OCEAN'S SHORELINES, COMMANDING THEM 'THIS IS HOW FAR YOUR PROUD WAVES MAY COME, AND NO FURTHER?'

DO YOU HAVE POWER OVER THE DEEP, THEODORE CHURCH?

If he wasn't frozen in horror, Reverend Church would have screamed at the top of his lungs. The dreadful Voice seemed to be increasing in wrath as it spoke.

"HAVE YOU EVEN ONCE COMMANDED THE MORNING TO DAWN, AND THE SUN TO RISE IN THE EAST? HAVE YOU INSTRUCTED DAYLIGHT TO SPREAD AND END THE WICKEDNESS OF THE DARK NIGHT? HAVE YOU DISTURBED THE ACTIVITIES OF EVIL MEN AND HALTED THEIR ARM, RAISED TO STRIKE?

HAVE YOU EXPLORED THE ORIGINS OF THE SEAS, OR WALKED THE FOUNDATIONS OF THEIR DEPTHS? OR HAS THE LOCATION OF THE GATES OF HELL BEEN REVEALED TO YOU, THEODORE CHURCH? DO YOU UNDERSTAND THE DEPTHS OF THE EARTH?

TELL ME THEODORE CHURCH? I AM LISTENING.

TELL ME WHERE THE LIGHT COMES FROM? AND HOW DO YOU GET THERE? OR TELL ME ABOUT DARKNESS? WHERE DOES IT COME FROM? CAN YOU FIND ITS PERIPHERIES, OR FIND ITS SOURCE?

BUT OF COURSE, YOU ALREADY KNOW ALL THIS BECAUSE YOU WERE BORN BEFORE IT WAS ALL CREATED, AND YOU ARE SO VERY QUALIFIED."

Reverend Church managed a whimper but couldn't utter a word. It was at this point, and the mention of Hell, that his deepest fear was voiced. In that moment, he knew he had to have been under some sort of temporary insanity to have spoken so arrogantly claiming injustice at God's hand. He also completely understood, knowing full well the implications, that he deserved Hell. Reverend Church wished he'd never been born.

**

"He's not responding!" the doctor yelled. On every display, Reverend Church's vital signs were going completely haywire. His heart rate was still through the roof, and his nervous system had appeared to lock up his entire body in a spasm. The doctor muttered for the third time he'd never seen anything like it, and despite administering enough sedatives to knock out a horse, the effect was exactly zero.

"Doctor you get my husband back!" Sandra wailed, barely

able to remain in an armchair at the other end of the room. "You get him back! He has work to finish on this Earth!"

The doctor whirled around in exasperation, "Mrs. Church, I'm sorry to say, I have to hold you responsible for what is happening to your husband. We should have given him the Lorazepam while he was somewhat responsive, but now it may be too late. "

"It's not too late Doctor!" Sandra cried. "It's never too late! He's going to be okay! He's going to be okay! "Her words trailed off in a sob as she desperately tried to believe them. *Who was that strange homeless man? What was going on? Has all this been part of God's plan, or am I about to lose my husband to foolishness?* Her head pounded as these thoughts ballooned in her head. She decided all she could do was double down and cling to God, so she wiped her eyes and kept praying, refusing yet again the nurse's pleas for her to leave the room. She suddenly realized she needed backup, and with her phone clutched in her hands, she typed up a text blast to all of the church's most faithful prayer warriors, explaining the situation and pleading for prayer.

***

"DO YOU STILL WANT TO DEBATE THE ALMIGHTY?" God roared from the tornado. "OR WILL YOU FINALLY SUBMIT, THEODORE CHURCH? AS MY SEVERE CRITIC, DO YOU HAVE THE ANSWERS?"

Reverend Church was quivering where he stood, sure that

any moment he was about to lose his mortal life and enter eternity, not by any means in the Almighty God's good graces. Up to this point, he could not even look up at the blast of the tornado, from which God was speaking. Somehow he knew intuitively, he had to reply. He knew this question was not rhetorical, because he was too afraid to *not* answer.

"Lord," he stuttered, his voice weak and frail in the storm. "I confess I am absolutely nothing. I have no hope of ever finding these answers." He paused, and struggled to find more words. "So I'm putting my hand over my mouth to be quiet, Lord. I've said too much already."

This did not appease The Almighty.

"STAND STRAIGHT THEODORE CHURCH, AND BRACE YOURSELF FOR WAR. I'M ASKING YOU AGAIN, WILL YOU DISCREDIT MY JUSTICE, AND CONDEMN ME, ONLY TO JUSTIFY YOURSELF?

ARE YOU AS POWERFUL AS THE ALMIGHTY? CAN YOU ROAR LIKE ME? WELL THEN, PUT ON YOUR FINEST SUIT, YOUR FINEST TIE AND OSTRICH SKIN SHOES. RELEASE YOUR ANGER THEODORE CHURCH. LET IT CRASH OVER THE ARROGANT. DISGRACE THE PROUD WITH ONE LOOK; STOMP ON THE EVIL ONES WHERE THEY STAND. CRUSH THEM INTO DUST, LEAVING THEM STONE-FACED AS THEY DIE. HERE'S THE DEAL; IF YOU CAN DO THAT, I WILL AGREE WITH YOU YOUR OWN POWER CAN SAVE YOU."

Reverend Church felt as though every bone, muscle,

nerve and fiber of his being was decaying toward death. His stomach heaved and his muscles twitched and stiffened violently. He was paralyzed with panic, but still felt every wave of anxious terror. He didn't even want to think how much longer this would last; his greatest fear was it would be for eternity.

"ANSWER ME NOW: CAN YOU STAND BEFORE THE WILD AND MIGHTY ELEPHANT, OR THE GREAT HIPPOPOTAMUS AND LIVE? CAN YOU TAME THEM WITH YOUR BARE HANDS AND TRAIN THEM? FOR I HAVE CREATED THEM TOO. CAN YOU CATCH THE GREAT WHITE SHARK OR A FEROCIOUS CROCODILE WITH YOUR HANDS? I PROMISE YOU THEODORE CHURCH, IF YOU TRY, YOU WILL NOT FORGET EITHER OF THOSE BATTLES. IF YOU CANNOT STAND BEFORE THESE CREATURES WHICH ARE MY HANDIWORK, HOW CAN YOU HOPE TO CHALLENGE ME?

ANSWER ME THEODORE CHURCH! CONSIDER MY WONDERS THAT SCIENCE HASN'T EVEN BEGUN TO FULLY COMPREHEND; WHERE IS THE HOME OF THE EAST WIND? WHO DETERMINES THE PATH OF LIGHTNING, CAUSING THE RAIN TO FALL ON BARREN DESERTS? YOU MAY HAVE SOME UNDERSTANDING OF HOW FROZEN WATER BECOMES ICE, BUT WHO COMMANDS IT TO DO SO? WHO COMMANDED THESE LAWS OF PHYSICS INTO MOTION?

OR TAKE THE STARS IF YOU PREFER? CAN YOU STOP THE EARTH FROM SPINNING, SO THE CONSTELLATIONS REMAIN STILL? CAN YOU ENSURE THE PROPER SEQUENCE OF THE SEASONS, OR DO YOU KNOW HOW THE LAWS OF

GRAVITY AND MOTION WERE CONSTRUCTED? CAN YOU
SHOUT TO THE CLOUDS TO MAKE IT RAIN, OR CAN YOU
MAKE LIGHTNING STRIKE WHERE YOU DESIRE?

WHO GIVES INTUITION AND INSTINCT THEODORE
CHURCH? WHO IS WISE ENOUGH TO NUMBER ALL THE
CLOUDS? CAN YOU CONTROL THE WEATHER, LET ALONE
THE CONSISTENT SPIN OF THIS SPECK OF A PLANET IN THE
UNIVERSE? ARE YOU MORE MIGHTY THAN GOD, THEODORE
CHURCH? IF SO, PROVE YOURSELF AND I WILL HEAR YOUR
ARGUMENT AGAINST ME. NOW YOU HAD BETTER ANSWER
ME."

Reverend Theodore Church swayed and staggered
before the rage of the storm, and braced himself as the
lightning flashed and crackled in the heart of the tornado.
While the gale ripped past the hospital windows, he knew
this was his one and only opportunity to escape the well-
deserved wrath of Almighty God. It was now clear his
confidence in the injustice of his own suffering was utter
madness. He had believed, to this point, he was a righteous
man. He had walked, in what he told himself was the most
upright way possible. But now, before the living God, he
knew every single success in his life was purely by Almighty
God's grace. And he knew he'd been ridiculously arrogant.
Excruciatingly arrogant. Yet he had felt secure because God
was protecting him in His great mercy; but now, standing
before the One who inhabits eternity, he was nothing more
than a worm. If he knew anything, he knew he could never
hope to justify himself before such a holy, and pure all-
powerful Creator. Instead, Reverend Church humbled

himself.

"Lord, I know you can do anything you want and no man or woman could ever hope to try to stop you." He swallowed hard, and fought himself to remain standing. "You asked who it was that so stupidly questioned and denied your provision and grace. I confess, Lord, it is me, Theodore Church. I admit I spoke foolishly about things of which I knew nothing; things too wonderful and profound for me to understand." Reverend Church paused. "Lord, You are demanding answers of me but all I can say is I thought I knew You, but now it seems as if I had only read and heard about You." Reverend Church lowered his head. "Lord, but now that I have seen you...I despise myself, and I repent and if I had any with me, I would throw dust and ashes over my head and entire body to mourn my foolishness."

***

Two doctors and three nurses now worked feverishly to bring Reverend Church's spasming and deteriorating body under control, while Sandra Church sobbed and prayed in the corner of the room. Suddenly, his entire body relaxed, and fell back into the bed and his vital signs slowly began dropping from their sky-high numbers.

"He's stabilizing!" the doctor cried. "What did he respond to? What did we give him last?"

Sandra looked up, fearing to hope. The machines were still beeping but one by one, they dropped off, and the Reverend's vital signs were soon within normal range.

While she was still speechless, her phone buzzed. She glanced down and it was a text from Reverend Williams' wife. It read, "Henry is having a seizure too!!! plz pray. What is going on??" Before Sandra finished reading that message, another vibrated the phone. It was from Pastor Baker's daughter: "Dad just collapsed at a restaurant and isn't conscious! EMS on their way. God help us!" Her eyes widened, and she was about to send a reply when a third message buzzed the phone. It was Bishop Davis' wife: "Sandra, James took a nap and is having some sort of episode! It's as though he is having a nightmare but I can't wake him. EMS are on their way but please ask the prayer team to pray for him too!"

Sandra Church covered her mouth as she tried to comprehend what in the world might be happening.

***

When Reverend Church uttered his repentance, although the whirlwind continued raging before him, the apex of its fury seemed to shift to his left, and was no longer focused directly upon him. He slowly turned his head to look in the direction of the guest's corner of the room, where the armchairs and coffee table were. He had to shield his eyes again from the whip of the wind, and sting of the rain, but his jaw dropped when he saw his three friends lying prostate on the hospital floor, in front of the windows. *When did they get here?* he wondered, as God's fury was now focused on them.

"HENRY WILLIAMS," The Almighty's voice boomed from the tornado. "STAND TO YOUR FEET!"

Reverend Church didn't understand how he hadn't seen his friends in the room before. He was so sure the hospital was empty when he woke up. His heart wanted to help his friend Henry up, but he knew this was a moment the man had to face alone. Slowly Reverend Williams crawled to all fours, then staggered to his feet before the raging storm. Reverend Church felt a pang of pity for his friend, but there was no way he was going to try intervene.

"HENRY WILLIAMS! I AM FURIOUS WITH YOU AND YOUR TWO FRIENDS, JAMES DAVIS AND TOBIAS BAKER," God roared from the heart of storm. "YOU HAVE NOT SPOKEN CORRECTLY ABOUT ME AS MY SERVANT THEODORE HAS.

HENRY WILLIAMS, YOU CLAIM I PUNISH PEOPLE SOLELY ACCORDING TO THEIR WICKED DEEDS, OR REWARD THEM SOLELY ACCORDING TO THEIR GOOD WORKS. NEITHER IS TRUE. NO ONE WOULD SURVIVE IF I PUNISHED MANKIND ACCORDING TO YOUR DEEDS, AND NO ONE COULD HOPE TO BE SAVED BY THEIR SO-CALLED GOOD WORKS. YOU SHOULD BETTER UNDERSTAND THE GRACE OF MY SON, JESUS CHRIST, GIVEN YOUR POSITION AS SHEPHERD."

Reverend Williams was barely standing, wobbling in the wind with his head hung, and sobbing like a baby.

"JAMES DAVIS..." God directed His attention to Bishop Davis, quivering on the floor. "YOU CLAIM I HAVE ALLOWED THIS AFFLICTION UPON MY SERVANT THEODORE

CHURCH, BECAUSE OF THE SINS OF HIS CHILDREN. HAVE YOU NOT READ IN MY WORD, THE SONS WILL BEAR THEIR SIN AND RIGHTEOUSNESS ALONE, AS WILL THE FATHERS? YOU HAVE NOT SHOWN YOURSELF COMPASSIONATE UPON A FELLOW SHEPHERD."

Bishop Davis lay there, covering his head, shivering like a child in an ice storm.

"TOBIAS BAKER, YOU HAVE OVERSIMPLIFIED MY TRUTHS. YES, MY SERVANT THEODORE CHURCH IS GUILTY, AS IS EVERY MAN, WOMAN AND CHILD IN THIS WORLD, YET I AM LONG PATIENT, AND WAIT FOR ALL TO REPENT AS LONG AS POSSIBLE. I DO NOT PUNISH ACCORDING TO EVERY, SINGLE WORK, AND YOU HAVE DISPLAYED MERE SHOWMANSHIP TRYING TO CONVINCE MY SERVANT I AM A BRUTAL GOD TO THE WICKED. UNDERSTAND, ALL ARE WICKED BEFORE THEY RECEIVE THE HOLY SPIRIT OF MY SON, JESUS. AGAIN, IT IS BY MY GRACE, THROUGH FAITH IN HIM, YOU ARE SAVED."

Pastor Baker, too, lay hiding his face in his arms, groaning and trembling violently.

"THE THREE OF YOU WILL MAKE YOUR WAY TO THIS HOSPITAL IMMEDIATELY, AND ACCORDING TO 1 JOHN 1:9 IN MY WORD, CONFESS YOUR SINS TO ONE ANOTHER, BEFORE MY SERVANT THEODORE CHURCH, AND TO MY SON, JESUS CHRIST. THEODORE CHURCH WILL PRAY FOR YOU, AND MY SON WILL INTERCEDE FOR YOU IN HEAVEN. MY WORD CANNOT FAIL, THEREFORE I AM FAITHFUL AND

JUST TO FORGIVE YOU, INSTEAD OF DESTROYING YOU FOR YOUR GRAVE SIN; FOR YOUR DISMAL FAILURE TO SPEAK RIGHTLY CONCERNING MY SERVANT THEODORE CHURCH."

The three men's heads nodded vigorously in unison. Reverend Church was relieved his friends would be pardoned, and he turned back to the tornado as the wind began to die down, and the lightning and roar of the whirlwind ceased. Seemingly appeased, slowly the gargantuan whirlwind receded and within a minute the sun broke through the clouds; calm descending over the hospital. Reverend Church took a step toward his friends, who were still groaning and lying prostate, when he heard a faint beeping that grew louder and louder and louder. Suddenly Sandra's voice echoed loudly around him: "THEO! THEO COME BACK!"

Reverend Church's eyes fluttered open, and he jolted up in his bed. His eyes widened as his wife's beautiful but distressed face came into view. Her hands firmly grasped his face, and she, seeming more surprised than he, blinked and cried, "He's awake!" Reverend Church slowly put his hands over hers, and together they burst into tears, and she kissed her husband's face until there was no spot left untouched.

"Mrs. Church, if you could please step back for a moment, I just want to check some vitals," the doctor stepped in after a moment, seemingly very relieved, and exhausted. Sandra reluctantly stepped aside, still holding her husband's hand, until the doctor took a flashlight out of his pocket, opened the Reverend's eyes and shone the light in each eye. "Reverend?" he asked. "How do you feel?"

Reverend Church realized he was still panting, but also became conscious of the fact he felt no more pain. He pushed himself all the way up on his pillows, and didn't feel any pangs of pain. In fact, he felt pretty strong.

"Doctor...," he whispered hoarsely. "Doctor, I'm fine. I just want to hold my wife for a moment. Please."

The doctor looked over at Sandra, and nodded, stepping back. The three nurses and other physician all exchanged glances as if to say, "What just happened?"

"It's over babe," Reverend Church whispered gently to his wife. "It's over. I've been very foolish, but God is so merciful. I'm healed, I know you're healed, it's all going to be okay."

Sandra's face lit up, as she looked her husband in the eyes. She threw her arms around his neck, and began weeping with joy. "I believe it honey. I do."

26

GET THEE BEHIND ME

As Sugar predicted, the parking lot of *Holy Light* was empty. Jeffrey's Camry quietly rolled in and stopped in front of the main sanctuary doors. Off to the side of the building there were three cars parked together, two of which were not recognizable to either man, but Jeffrey recognized the third as Sister Willis's.

"I've got a bad feeling about this, man," Gerald protested.

"Me too, but I've been praying and all I feel in my spirit is a green light," Jeffrey replied.

"You'd bet your life on it?" Gerald asked, craning his neck to see if anyone was near the back of the church.

Jeffrey didn't respond.

"Man, all my spidey senses are freaking out like we're straight walking into a trap. Haven't you seen *The Sopranos*?

This is how a wack goes down."

"Well, I guess we're going to have to put our lives in the hands of the Lord then," Jeffrey replied sullenly. He felt as though he was trying to convince himself, too.

"Whew, I don't know man. We should have a contingency plan." Gerald shifted in his seat, and absently touched a cold, metallic bulge in the back of his waistband.

"Well, I guess the Lord is our contingency plan. I wouldn't usually walk into something foolish but I honestly feel led to meet with Sugar. I just felt the go-ahead in my spirit when I spoke with him. Who knows, maybe he really does have info, and wants to deal."

"Man... okay, I'm going to trust you on this one. I've already died once this week, I don't want to test the Lord's patience."

Jeffrey couldn't help but smile at Gerald's gritty sense of humor. "Hey, let's pray," he said.

Gerald agreed emphatically, "Great idea!"

They bowed their heads, and Jeffrey began, "Lord, you know what is waiting for us behind those doors." He sighed. "You know this situation, Lord God. You know these men are wicked, and only you know if this man, Demarius, truly wants to come clean. I pray he does Lord, for the sake of his soul...but if not, I pray you protect us just as you protected your servant Daniel, from the mouths of the lions, and your servants Shadrach, Meshach and Abednego from the furnace. Thank you Father that we can trust You, no matter what the outcome is. In your Son, Jesus' name we pray. Amen."

"Amen!" Gerald echoed. He lifted his head and looked at Lee, "Well, let's get this done." The men climbed out of the car, and walked over to the sanctuary doors. They paused for a brief moment, then Lee swung the great, wooden door open, and they stepped inside.

As they entered, both were a little startled to see two armed men waiting for them inside. "Step inside gentlemen," a massive man commanded. He was dressed in black jeans and a black t-shirt, and he had an assault rifle hanging off his neck and shoulder. The other man was equipped in the same way, but swung his rifle to his back and stepped toward the two. "Randy is going to pat you down. Please cooperate with him."

Jeffrey cast a quick glance of concern at Gerald, who didn't appear to share his fear. Randy patted Jeffrey down first, without incident, and then moved on to Gerald. He patted under Gerald's arms, down his sides, and then his back. When he reached the back of Gerald's waistband, he felt the cold, hard lump. Randy gripped the object and announced in a loud, professional voice "WEAPON." The huge man standing to the side instantly swung his rifle up and trained it on Gerald's chest. His expression betrayed his anger, and Gerald's lip twitched.

Randy was clearly a pro. He kept his head tight on Gerald's abdomen, hugged his waist with his biceps, as a wrestler would for a double-leg takedown, but kept one hand on the weapon and one hand on Gerald's right calf. With his right hand, he lifted Gerald's shirt, and pulled out the chrome, snub-nosed nine millimeter revolver.

"Now what in hell's fire were you going to do with that?" the giant growled.

"Hey man, y'all are packing, I'm packing. What's the problem?" Gerald replied.

"The boss told ya no guns," he replied.

"Actually," Jeffrey interjected, "...he said no cops, but he didn't say a word about no guns." The man snarled, while Randy clicked open the revolver, and spun the cylinder, shaking his head at the six rounds whirling around. "But Gerald," Jeffrey continued, "...what were you thinking?"

"Insurance." was Gerald's cold reply, while Randy pocketed the firearm and finished searching him.

"That was stupid," Randy said calmly when he was satisfied there was no inch of Gerald left that could hide another weapon. The other man kept his barrel trained on Gerald's torso at all times. "Move!" Randy barked, and shoved Gerald forward to the sanctuary. He jerked his head to Jeffrey, motioning for him to follow. Jeffrey sighed, and followed his unwise friend.

Gerald opened the door and when they entered the sanctuary both Gerald and Jeffrey were taken aback at the sight before them. The overhead lights were dimmed, but at least a hundred candles were lit on the podium, with two large white ones flickering brightly on either side of Reverend Church's pulpit. Behind the pulpit, illuminated by the eerie glow, wearing a dark suit and a sinister smile, loomed Reverend Black. He appeared to be reading Reverend Church's large sermon Bible.

"Now what interest would you have in reading that book?" Jeffrey called loudly

Reverend Black closed the Bible, and looked up with a grin, "Know thy enemy and know thyself. In a hundred battles you will never be defeated."

"You didn't get that from scripture," Lee replied.

Reverend Black walked slowly down the podium steps, and reached Gerald and Jeffrey as they reached the front. Sitting off to the right was Sugar, with a fat smirk.

"Sun Tzu, the ancient Chinese general," Reverend Black replied.

"I really appreciate the history lesson, but I didn't come for that."

Reverend Black smiled widely. "Same old Jeffery, just as serious as ever. What *did* you come for, Jeffrey?"

"Well, I came to make sure you were put behind bars where

you belong, but it appears we'll have to add your double-crossing accomplice to the list."

Sugar chuckled from his chair, "Aw don't be hurt baby, ain't nothin' personal. Y'all really think I'd sell out my boy, Rev, to ya though?" He laughed some more, and the two henchmen chuckled with him.

"You know I've been in ministry a loooong time, Harvey Black," Jeffrey wasn't intimidated. "And time and again, I've seen pride and arrogance come before a fall. I watched you and your wife make small, but critical mistakes repeatedly along the way. Instead of making adjustments, even if it meant at one point that you had to step away from the pulpit for a while, you became bitter and prideful. You've caused so much harm, you've coveted your brother's God-given success, his happy family and his church. God does not take these things lightly. And He will deliver us out of your hand."

Reverend Black's grin slowly changed to a sneer, as he produced a pistol from his waistband and raised it to Jeffrey's eye level, "You sure, you pompous little ant?"

Gerald cleared his throat nervously, but Jeffrey, unmoved, kept staring Reverend Black in the eyes.

Reverend Black's grin quickly returned, but his tone shifted jarringly, "You say I'm arrogant but the opposite is true my dear Jeffrey." Reverend Black lowered the Glock, and tucked it back into his waistband. "In fact, I'm going to make you an offer you'd be a fool to refuse. First, did you bring my notebook, Jeffrey?"

"Of course not, and there is no offer you can make me that I won't refuse."

"Uh uh uuh," Reverend Black wagged his finger. "Don't you know the Proverb 'There is more hope for a fool than for someone who speaks in haste?'" He nodded to Sugar, who depressed a button on his two way radio.

"Bring her in," Sugar's voice crackled over the two henchmen's radios. Gerald and Jeffrey exchanged a concerned glance. They looked over to a side door of the sanctuary that suddenly cracked open, causing sunlight to flood in. A third henchman walked in, shoving none other than Sister Mary Willis along. She looked tired and disheveled.

"Mary!" Jeffrey cried. "Are you okay?"

"No, Jeffery, but these animals won't get away with this." As she neared the men, they could see she had contusions on her face, and blood around her nostrils and mouth.

"You devil," Jeffrey hissed at Reverend Black. "How dare you touch a woman."

Reverend Black laughed, and Sugar joined in, followed by his henchmen. "Hey man, she was going to sell you out to the Feds, and pin the entire *Holy Light* embezzlement scheme on you. I did you a favor." The men laughed again.

"Mary, don't sweat it. They won't get away with this."

The five men cackled again, as if Jeffrey had just told the joke of the year.

"Who is going to stop us, Jeffrey? You?" Reverend Black snarled, his expressions flipping creepily.

"God will."

"WHERE IS HE JEFFREY?" Reverend Black roared. "I DON'T SEE HIM? I'M LITERALLY IN HIS HOUSE, AND HE CAN'T TOUCH ME. WHERE ARE YOU GOD?" he shouted looking around dramatically. "Naw man, He's an absent Father. If He exists, He sure doesn't care what happens to you. I know where the *real* power lies, and it's that knowledge that always puts me ahead."

Jeffrey stood silent. When Reverend Black goaded him again, he simply shook his head. "Jeffrey, don't you see? I can make you rich. I can make you powerful. This deal is merely scratching the surface. I have new insight into the markets, Wall Street, how it all works, which companies are going to take a fall, and which will rise. Without the knowledge I receive from my..." he paused, "...my guides, I might as well be gambling. But with these insights, the sky is the limit. It's tested and proven Jeffrey. The future is here, and it takes a man who was on the wrong side before, the side of blindness and ignorance, to truly devote himself to this future. This is only the beginning Jeffrey. I know what you want, a family, security, stability. I can give that all to you! And much, much more. Join me. I am forgiving and generous. We can work together, Jeffrey. And that includes you Gerald. You know how I work. Everything you want can be yours. Just come back to me."

Jeffrey stood there without saying a word but slowly began shaking his head.

"What? What are you shaking your head at Jeffrey?" Reverend Black spat.

"How did you become so blind?"

Reverend Black snarled at him again.

"No man, you're not forgiving and gracious. *God is*. And sadly, that's why you are completely inflated with yourself. You don't know the way God works, or you'd know the scripture 'He is gracious and compassionate, slow to wrath and rich in love.' Unfortunately you're a fool, so you fulfill a different scripture: 'When the punishment for a sin is not quickly executed, sinner's hearts are filled with schemes to do evil.' That's you Harvey Black. God has been waiting for you to repent, but you won't. You have the opportunity, even now, but you won't. You've fallen from grace, denied the Son, and today is your day of reckoning. I wish you would turn from your sins, but I personally don't see it happening."

"Strange way for a dead man to be talking," Reverend Black replied calmly. "You have one minute. You can join me, and prove your allegiance by driving me to the bank tomorrow and with Mary's joint signature, withdraw the rest of *Holy Light's* general offering. Alternately, you, Sister Willis and your new pet, Gerald, can all die right here, right now, and my problems are over."

No one said a word, but Jeffrey knew he would never help rob *Holy Light* of a single cent. He accepted his fate and was about to tell Harvey Black where he could get off, when Gerald raised his hands. "Okay, listen. Listen, Uncle Harvey, I don't want any part of this. Hey man, I died once this week, and I don't want to experience that again. Whatever happens I'm with you. Shoot, I'll get that cash for you, myself, one way or another."

Reverend Black eyed Gerald skeptically. "Why don't I believe you, Gerald?"

"I don't *know* why, Uncle Harvey, but you know me!" Gerald was adamant.

"Gerald, what are you doing?" Jeffrey interrupted.

"Shut up Jeffrey," Gerald and Reverend Black snapped in unison.

"Gerald, son, don't do this. He's a monster. You don't even know," Sister Willis whimpered from the sidelines.

"Nah, listen...he's just misunderstood," Gerald shrugged. "I know my uncle Harvey better than all y'all. He's dramatic but at the end of the day, he's just ambitious." He raised his hands high in the air and cautiously stepped toward Reverend Black. "Isn't that right, Rev?"

Randy and the other henchman's guns swung to aim at

Gerald's torso instantly.

"Allow me to demonstrate my loyalty, Rev," he said cautiously. Reverend Black didn't say a word, but nodded to his men to allow Gerald to keep moving forward slowly.

"Gerald!" Jeffrey exclaimed. "What are you doing man?"

Gerald ignored his friend, and when he was within a few feet of Reverend Black began to lower himself to one knee. "I'll kneel before you Reverend. Heck, I even know you were trying to kill me, and I take that risk into my own hands. Forgive me, and let me serve under you. For real this time. No illusions. I know we're all dead otherwise."

Jeffrey stood gaping at Gerald who was now on one knee, with his head bowed. Reverend Black grinned as he held out his enormous, favorite ring for Gerald to kiss.

"Take notes, boys. This is how you get in my good graces," Reverend Black chuckled, but kept his gun aimed at Gerald's head. Sugar snorted, but the two henchmen kept their rifles trained on Gerald as he reached for Reverend Black's hand.

Quick as a bird, Gerald grabbed Reverend Black's wrist with his left hand, yanked it down then cupped the Reverend's tricep with his right hand into a classic arm-drag. The move was so fast, Reverend Black failed to find the trigger to get a shot off. Gerald dropped his body weight backwards, causing Reverend Black to lurch forward head-first. This allowed Gerald to bounce up and slip behind him, as he snatched the gun out of Reverend Black's hand, throwing his left arm around Reverend Black's neck.

Gerald was so blindingly quick, the two henchmen almost pulled their triggers reactively, which would have undoubtedly killed Reverend Black. Fortunately their training restrained them, and they moved a few feet apart to get better angles on Gerald, who pulled the gun up to the man's right temple in response.

"Oh wait, I changed my mind," Gerald sneered, peeping out from behind Reverend Black's head. "Tell your dogs to chill, Harvey."

Knowing he was in trouble, at least for the moment, Reverend Black yelled angrily, "Sugar! Tell your men to lower their weapons."

Jeffrey's head turned to Sugar, who was on his feet, and already halfway to Gerald and Reverend Black.

"Stand down!" Reverend Black roared, as Gerald pressed the cold steel of the forty caliber Glock painfully into his ear.

Sugar kept his own pistol drawn, but nodded to his two men who lowered their weapons, while he pointed his gun at Jeffrey.

"Easy there, boy," Sugar growled. "You're playing in the big leagues now."

"Drop your weapon right now, or I swear this evil bastard will get it straight in the dome, and I'll use him as a human shield, taking my chances with y'all."

"See, now that's where you're frontin'. You can't hold up a two hundred pound body and shoot. Believe me, I've tried," Sugar retorted.

"Just do what he says, Sugar!" Reverend Black chided.

"I said, I'll take my chances," Gerald replied. "NOW LOWER YOUR WEAPONS!"

Sugar's men looked to him for direction. Sugar paused in thought, then swung his gun to Sister Willis, and pointed at Jeffrey with his other hand. "Nah, point 'em at him," he barked. The two men's rifles swung to aim at Lee's heart, while Sugar ordered, "You cover her too," to the third man, pointing at Sister Willis.

She shrieked "Gerald just stop! What are you doing?"

"Relax, Sister Mary, I got it all under control."

"Do you now?" Sugar grunted. Release the Reverend now and I'll kill you quickly. Otherwise both of them get it." He motioned to Sister Willis and Jeffrey.

"He ain't no Reverend, and you know it," Gerald spat back. "Uncle Jay, walk over behind me, now."

"You move, you die!" the colossal henchman screamed.

"Shut up!" Gerald roared. "Walk over to me now, Jeff, or I'm going wax this menace right now."

"Gerald." Reverend Black whispered. "Listen to me, son. You

can still be a king. You can be everything you ever wanted to be. I can and will make that happen for you."

"Shoot him, Gerald!" Jeffrey surprised himself as the words came out of his mouth.

"A king?" Gerald laughed. "You tried to ruin my life. You were instrumental in turning me away from my God. You've tried to destroy my family. You're under the control of demons!"

"Ruin your family?" Reverend Black roared. "I AM your family! I treated you like a son. I was there for you, when your so-called family was too busy with ministry to give a damn about you. I taught you what's real. Showed you the way to save yourself; you arrogant, turncoat punk!"

Reverend Black became more animated as he became angry, and reared up under Gerald's grip. Gerald responded by jamming the gun's barrel into his ear canal, making it fold over like a flower. Reverend Black winced in agony.

"Give me an excuse," Gerald growled.

"It's through me, Gerald. You know you're who you are through me."

"That sounds so poetic, except I saw who *you* are Harvey Black, and more importantly, where you're headed. Yeah man, I died. My heart stopped, ask Uncle Jay over here. I saw what is waiting after this life without God. I saw what you have given yourself over to."

Harvey Black struggled and Gerald jammed the barrel back into his ear, making him grimace again.

"I've been given a second chance, and I will fulfill my calling in God. Satan has tried his best to derail God's plan for my life, but just like his lackeys, he's lost this battle and he's lost the war. Now we're going to start walking to the exit, and so help me God, if your men so much as breathe wrong, I'm going to send you to that nightmare I saw when I died."

"Gerald, this is your last chance," Harvey Black said, in complete confidence. "Take my hand. Pledge allegiance to your true calling. To your true salvation."

"The only salvation is through my Lord and Savior, Jesus Christ. Now walk."

Sugar's two henchmen still had their rifles aimed at Jeffrey's center-mass. He looked back anxiously at the two men, then looked back at Gerald. Gerald took a few small steps toward the exit, and pulled Harvey Black with him.

"GERALD!" Sugar bellowed. "I swear I will execute both of these people right here, right now if you take another step!" Sugar nodded to his henchmen.

When Gerald glanced at Jeffrey, he saw his companion was truly panicking. Gerald tightened his jaw, narrowed his eyes, and gave a near-imperceptible nod toward his gun. Jeffrey's face betrayed his dread, but after a small sigh, he gave the slightest nod back to Gerald. Sugar noticed it and began to shout but before he could get the warning out, Gerald swung the gun from Reverend Black's head and fired rapidly at the two henchmen.

Without thinking, Sugar's gun swung to Jeffrey, and fired wildly. Jeffrey dove toward Gerald as both of the henchmen's gun erupted in bursts of fire, bullets thudding into their bodies. Sister Willis screamed and dropped to the floor in terror, crawling behind the pews. Her guard momentarily froze, not sure if he should shoot her, or aim his fire to the front. None of them expected Gerald to be so bold.

Reverend Black recoiled violently from the deafening blast, and momentarily exposed, Gerald fired two more shots. Randy doubled over and stumbled backward. The other man screamed in pain, involuntarily dropping his rifle as his right shoulder exploded in a grim mess of blood, bone and flesh. Sugar turned his on Gerald and fired repeatedly.

"STOP!" Reverend Black screamed, but Gerald fired back, causing Sugar to dive sideways. Gerald wrenched Reverend Black's neck with his left forearm and shouted to Jeffrey,

"Grab my gun off the floor, and get behind those pews!" In the mayhem, Gerald's gun had fallen from Randy's waist, and lay on the floor in front of the two men. Jeffrey snatched it up as he hobbled to a spot behind the pews that offered cover. Gerald dragged his captive toward the pews as well, while Sugar leopard-crawled over to his two men. Their guns were now silent, and they were groaning and wailing in agony.

"Give me that rifle, you fool!" Sugar hissed as he pulled the firearm off his henchman's bloody neck. He looked over at Randy who was writhing on the carpet, groaning and clutching his abdomen. Sugar could see a thick syrupy crimson oozing between his fingers onto the carpet. He knew his man was as good as dead. Sugar loaded the rifle up to his shoulder and motioned to his third man who had made his way to the center of the sixth row, to crawl between the seats and flank Gerald, and Lee.

"You okay?" Gerald gave Lee a visual once-over as they hunkered down behind the pews. He noticed a few globs of blood carpet.

"They definitely got my leg," Jeffrey grimaced, holding his right thigh. Gerald now saw the thick crimson seeping through Lee's jeans. "Oh man, feels like fire."

"Dear Jesus. Here, put pressure on that Uncle Jeff." Gerald was trying to sound confident, but for the first time he was really scared.

"Gerald!" Sugar screamed. "I counted seven shots. That makes you either empty or real light on ammo. Give it up you amateur"

Gerald dropped the magazine out and saw one round in it. He knew there was one more in the chamber.

"Gettin' real light G-Dub," Reverend Black taunted.

"Shut up!" Gerald ordered.

"Here let's trade," Gerald held out the Glock, but Jeffrey was reluctant. "Take it. There are two rounds left. Protect yourself if it comes down to it, just shoot straight. Trust me, I have a plan," Gerald assured him. Jeffrey handed over the revolver.

While they were talking Sugar kept his rifle trained on the area his enemies had ducked behind, but saw his third man pop up as he made his way to the end of the pews. The man motioned that Sister Willis was possibly escaping and Sugar angrily motioned to forget about her. The third man ducked behind the pews, and began moving behind Gerald and Jeffrey.

"You're gonna die today, Gerald," Reverend Black grinned.

"No, I'm not Satan. Now I told you to shut up." Gerald replied. Reverend Black gave another sinister laugh.

Gerald took another quick look at Jeffrey's leg, and tried to hide his concern at the growing pool of blood. "Man, stick your finger in that bullet hole if you have to, but keep pressure on that wound okay?" Gerald whispered. "Now, listen...if this clown even breathes wrong," he nodded to Reverend Black. "...just pop him. We don't need him alive, and he will kill you if he gets the chance. Comprende?" Jeffrey nodded grimly.

"You're a dead man!" Reverend Black snickered again.

"I told you to get behind me devil," Gerald replied, as he began crawling over to the left end of the row of pews.

He figured they'd be watching for his position above the pews, but not at ground level. He was suddenly really grateful he'd played so much *Battlefield* on his PC. He reached the end of the pew and lowered his head to the carpet. He realized it really smelt like feet, and he was a little grossed out despite the precarious situation.

Man, Daddy's congregation got some stanky feet! he grinned to himself. He poked his head out for half a second, but saw nothing in the aisle.

"WE'RE IN ROW TWO, MIDDLE RIGHT SECTION!" Reverend Black shouted, making Gerald almost jump out of his shirt. He whirled around to glare at Jeffrey, who was mid-swing in giving Reverend Black a hearty thud on the back of the neck with the Glock. Reverend Black yelped, and grabbed his head.

"So help me God, do that again and I'll execute you, Harvey," Jeffrey snarled through gritted teeth. "Look into my eyes and tell me I'm bluffing." Reverend Black quickly declined to call any potential bluff.

Great! Gerald, thought. *Now they have the jump on us.* Then he had a crazy thought. Gerald darted his head out of the row again, and saw no one. He'd played enough online first person shooters to assume Sugar and his third guy had to be trying to flank them from either side. His heart was pounding crazily out of his chest, but something still and quiet inside his heart gave him a deep peace. Quick as he could, he crawled on all fours across the aisle and to the third row. He prayed neither Sugar nor his goon were in any of the third row pews, or he really was a dead man. He reached the other section, and hunkered down, pointing his gun to the right then to the left, just in case. It seemed for the moment, the coast was clear.

Sugar had heard Reverend Black's directions, and was, indeed, crawling toward the end of the fourth row in the same section as Gerald, only one row behind him. The third gunman had also heard Reverend Black, and had reached the edge of the sanctuary. Aiming his rifle forward, he began creeping his way to the second row, flanking these jokers from the left and shutting them down permanently.

Gerald tried to quiet his breathing, and listen above the sound of his pounding heart. He cocked his head, thinking he heard something in the aisle right behind him. His heart sank as he realized Sister Willis had probably dropped behind the pews too. Surely she wouldn't crawl toward the action? But what if it was her? He had to be cautious.

The third gunman inched his way past the third row, and slowed his leopard-crawl as he reached the second. The man was a disgraced Czechoslovakian Joint Forces rifleman. His former rank was something akin to that of a well decorated U.S Marine. He'd been hired by Sugar after showing him some combat footage he'd recorded with a digital camera in the Serbian war. Technically it was more of a civilian genocide than combat footage, but it landed him the job. He continued his crawl, with the rifle pointing forward and his finger on the trigger. He reached the edge of the second row, and came up to one knee. He inched back about a foot, so his head and rifle barrel could pop around the corner at the same time. He inhaled deeply but quietly as he prepared to round the corner, and swiftly strike the enemy.

Jeffrey was so paranoid he wanted to be sick. The rows of pews, like many churches, were not perfectly straight, and had a slight curve to them. This caused Jeffrey to not be able to actually see all the way to the outside aisle of the second row. Reverend Black was between him and the middle aisle, and the space was too narrow for him to risk a switch with Reverend Black, so he had to simply keep the gun trained on his captive.

The third gunman popped his head and rifle around the corner, his keen eye sighting right down the barrel. At first the gunman saw nothing because of the curve of the row. He kept his eye focused through his sights, and squatting, he slowly and silently stepped his body to follow his head into the row. Moving forward, within seconds his target came into view. The soldier smiled as he drew the back of Jeffrey's head perfectly into his sights and inhaled deeply again, knowing to pull the trigger on the second half of the exhale. This would guarantee zero sight bounce, and at that distance the man would surgically be killed.

At the same time, Sugar and Gerald unknowingly edged closer to each other. Within seconds their paths would cross just one row apart. If either man stopped crawling for just a second, there would be no mistaking the sound of the other moving.

Jeffrey was now feeling unnaturally tired, and his hands and feet were terribly cold. He knew he had already lost a great deal of blood, so he bowed his head forward, still training the gun on Reverend Black who appeared to be sneering at him. Keeping watch on his captive, he prayed silently, *Lord Jesus I praise You right now, and believe You will deliver us out of this truly desperate situation.* Behind him, the Czech exhaled slowly. The back of Jeffrey's skull hung perfectly in the center of his sights. His finger slowly began squeezing the trigger.

A giant air conditioner right above the Czech's head kicked off loudly, and startled him as he squeezed off the round. Jeffrey jumped at the noise of the A.C unit, his head banging painfully into the pew. A millisecond later, he heard a loud pop behind him and a bullet thudded into the pews on the other side of the aisle. Without thinking Jeffrey whirled around and squeezed the Glock's trigger rapidly. The first round grazed the man's t-shirt, close to his ribs as he was re-sighting for a second shot. The second bullet entered the top of the Czech's head, just above his left eyebrow. The soldier's head spun back and his body collapsed instantly on the carpet. Jeffrey kept dry-firing the trigger in horror.

Both Gerald and Sugar jumped at the pop of the first gunshot, but it was Gerald who banged his gun against the wooden pew. Sugar immediately pointed the AR15 assault rifle at direction of the sound and fired four shots, in an even spread. Gerald screamed as a round caught him at the top of his thigh, just below the hipbone. The impact of the second shot shattered Gerald's left collar bone, and caused him to spin onto his back, flat on the floor.

As he heard Gerald scream, Sugar jumped up and aimed his rifle over the pew, wanting to finish off his enemy while he was wounded. Gerald, lying on his back, saw the rifle barrel come over the top of the pew first and lifted his gun but quickly realized his hand was shaking so much he couldn't aim properly.

Meanwhile, Reverend Black had dropped to the carpet after the first shot from the Czech's rifle zinged by his head. He cowered down in the ensuing volley from both Jeffrey's shots and Sugar's burst of fire. In the two seconds of silence, he whirled around to see Jeffrey dry-firing an empty gun. Reverend Black jumped to his knees, snaked his way to Jeffrey with astonishing speed, and punched him viciously in the back of the head. Jeffrey's head bounced forward and he groaned, dropping the gun in a total daze. Reverend Black pushed past him, and Jeffrey realized what he was going for and feebly grabbed his arm, but Reverend Black gave him another elbow for good measure, banging Jeffrey's head into the wooden seat of the pew. Reverend Black crawled over to the dead Czech and pulled the rifle out from under the man's bloody corpse. He swung it around, and aimed it squarely at Jeffrey's head.

In a crazed fury Sugar jumped up from behind the pew, his rifle barrel leading the way. Gerald saw him coming up and squeezed the wobbling gun's trigger rapidly. One of Gerald's first three shots penetrated just below Sugar's left floating rib, but the raging man barely felt the nine millimeter slug penetrate his body, and kept firing wildly. Two more 5.56 millimeter rounds pierced Gerald's chest, almost perfectly in line with each other. Gerald felt the thuds and the sting like a thousand volts of electricity through his body, but adrenaline kept him firing. The first two shots whizzed by Sugar's torso but the third entered Sugar's left cheek, splintered the bone and lodged squarely in the man's brain. Sugar's rifle clattered off the pew, as the man dropped heavily to the ground, stone dead.

Gerald's didn't even take a moment to be thankful his would-be killer was dead. His next thought was to check on Jeffrey. He tried to prop himself up on his right elbow but a wave of nausea flooded him, almost causing him to throw up. He tasted blood in his mouth too and looked down at his abdomen, noticing two holes in his shirt, flowering rapidly into crimson pools.

"Oh Lord Jesus, help me. I've repented Lord God of every sin, and I believe you are the only begotten Son of God. Save me and accept me into your Kingdom Lord," he prayed in fear.

"Oh Jesus, don't let me die here today." As his strength fled, Gerald became terrified, certain he was about to die. Still he couldn't stop thinking about Jeffrey. He tried again to lift himself, but his entire body convulsed in agony, and the world faded to darkness as he fell back to the carpet.

"SUGAR!" Reverend Black shouted. He was still hiding in the second row, his rifle zeroed on Jeffrey's head. "YOU STILL WITH ME?" Reverend Black had dropped to the carpet when Sugar and Gerald's second volley of fire began. He'd waited quietly in that position, with his rifle aimed at Jeffrey until it was over.

"GERALD!" he shouted. He didn't hear anyone but knew from the volley of shots fired, Gerald was either out of ammo or within a round or two. Jeffrey's head was now laying on the floor and he was motionless, so Reverend Black weighed up his options, deciding that best case, Jeffrey was too weak to go very far. Reverend Black took his chances and leopard-crawled back out the row, up the side aisle to the fourth row, and began making his way to the center aisle. Before he was two-thirds down row four, he saw a body in the row on the opposite side of the aisle. He froze and pointed the rifle toward it. He crawled a little closer, stopping every few seconds to listen intently, in case Gerald got the jump on him, but he couldn't hear a sound. As he reached the center aisle he could see it was the bulky body of Sugar. Reverend Black cursed quietly.

Suddenly rage filled him to where he decided he'd had enough and he sprang up to his feet. He placed the rifle butt firmly in his shoulder, with his cheek resting on the stock, ready to mow down anything that moved. He was sick of this fiasco, and wanted nothing but all of these idiots to die. Reverend Black crouched and slowly made his way to Sugar.

When he saw Sugar's lifeless body in a pool of blood, rage burned in Reverend Black's chest. All he could think about was snuffing the life out of Gerald and then ending that plague named Jeffrey. He already had his alibi figured out if he couldn't make his getaway; Gerald brought a gun to a business meeting, he pulled it and things went haywire. He would figure out the details later, but one thing he needed to do as well was find Sister Willis. She would definitely not be making it out of this alive, no matter what happened. If she'd already run, he'd find her, kill her and make his way to the Cayman Islands, incognito and start a new life.

Suddenly a pair of sneakers came into sight. He aimed the rifle at the second body in the row just behind Sugar's, and knew it was Gerald. *Looks like they took care of each other* he smiled to himself. He walked a little closer to watch for Gerald's chest rising and falling, and saw his former protégé was also lying in a pool of blood. *Oh man, he's toast, even if he ain't dead yet,* he smiled to himself. Then Reverend Black swung the rifle to movement on his left, coming within a split hair of pulling the trigger.

"JEFFREY!" he screamed. "I NEARLY KILLED YOU!" Jeffrey was feebly trying to drag himself toward the door behind the stage, and stopped in defeat when he heard Reverend Black's voice.

"Now, I wouldn't want to kill you without giving you one last chance to join me, Jeffrey," Reverend Black walked to him, and loomed over the man with his rifle, "You know I am a merciful leader, Jeffery ."

His former deacon resumed his crawl.

Reverend Black strolled up to him, and placed his ostrich skin shoe squarely on Jeffrey's back. He stomped him to the floor.

"Jeffrey!" he said in demented disappointment. "You gonna do me like that? After all I've done for you? I'm giving you a chance to pledge your allegiance to me, bro. This is how you thank me? Just help me get that money, and we're all good. I'll let you live, we can figure out a story about this whole mess...otherwise you just die right now man. Where's the sense in that?"

"Get thee behind me Satan..." Jeffrey whispered hoarsely, struggling to raise his body from under his assailant's foot. "...for you are an offense to me."

"SO THAT'S HOW IT IS?" Reverend Black screamed crazily. He raised his rifle and rammed the barrel tip into the back of Jeffrey's head. His victim didn't even wince, but buckled under the force of barrel and collapsed to the ground.

"Father accept my spirit..." he breathed gravelly, accepting his demise.

"Stubbornness is stupidity boy! See ya in the next life

sucka." Reverend Black stepped back and aimed the rifle at Jeffrey's back. He knew enough to be able to say Jeffrey was going for a gun, so he had to shoot him in the back, and not have it look like an execution.

Two shots rang out in rapid fire and Jeffrey gasped as everything turned black.

***

After what felt like hours of peaceful sleep, Jeffrey felt himself ascend weightlessly. Strong hands carried him up so that he felt as though he was floating. He heard a rustle like wings and the excited chatter of various voices. He thought he heard Gerald's among them and smiled. *The kid made it.* Jeffrey wanted to view this, and forced his eyes to flutter open. He found himself still staring at the overhead lights of *Holy Light's* sanctuary, as his eyes focused. He, somehow, seemed to be floating down the center aisle.

A strong face came into view. A stern face. A familiar face.

"He's with us!" the man in the grey suit barked. "Mr. Lee, you've lost a lot of blood, but you'll be okay if you hang in there, do you hear me? Hang in there. Nod if you can hear me."

"Agent...Willoughby?" Jeffrey croaked. This was a strange turn of events. He wondered if he had indeed died, and this was some sort of purgatory. *Nah, I don't believe in purgatory,* he thought to himself.

"Yes. Don't talk Mr. Lee, save your strength. You're going to need it buddy." The FBI agent managed a smile, and patted Jeffrey's arm. "You're gonna be alright, just stay strong, okay?"

Jeffrey desperately tried to find the strength to speak again, but struggled with how massive a task this seemed. Agent Willoughby saw him struggling and lowered his ear, "What is it pal?"

"G-Gerald?" he whispered.

The agent stood up and said nothing, but his furrowed brow spoke volumes. "Just rest Mr. Lee. It'll all be okay." A lone tear welled up in Jeffrey's eye.

He slowly turned his head to perhaps get a glimpse of Gerald as his eyes closed, but he couldn't see the young man. Instead, for a strange, fleeting second he wondered why that homeless guy who stepped out from the alley was at the back of the church.

27

HOW STRONG IS YOUR FAITH?

After the shooting, the attendance at both *Holy Light* and *New Day* spiked due to gawkers, busybodies and those who "church-surfed." Although attendance remained relatively high overall, it had thinned in original attendees since what everyone was calling, "the craziness." After local, and even a few national, news crews descended on both campuses like buzzards, and the internet blew up with visceral opinions from all sides, more than a few congregation members felt it was just too much publicity for them and found membership elsewhere. Especially those at *New Day* since the role of pastor had been vacant since "the craziness."

For twenty-one days *Holy Light* was cordoned off by the F.B.I as a federal crime scene. Once the sanctuary was released back into the church's custody, it took another sixteen days to clean, measure, order and lay new carpets.

Several pews also had to be patched, and various damages from the "craziness" had to be repaired. Many vocal onlookers had to be fended off the property by police, who had a presence on site until the federal investigation was over. The three Sundays following the "craziness," the *Holy Light* congregation met in a local high school gymnasium, and needless to say, the church went through some trying days.

During this time the opinions of *New Day's* members regarding the astonishing revelations about Reverend Black ranged from sorrow, to disbelief to "I knew it all along." For the next three weeks, two of the original board of elders (who had largely been disbanded by Reverend Black,) and one of the Sunday School teachers took turns in preaching and teaching the congregation, while the search for a new pastor was underway. A flood of hopefuls applied, likely due to the extensive media coverage, but most were written off as too inexperienced, under-qualified, or simply not a good fit. The few remaining elders grouped back together to narrow the selection down to a few candidates, but it was after an inspired idea from the longest-sitting elder, that *New Day* discovered their new pastor.

It was a warm, bright Sunday morning when *Holy Light* reopened, but despite the drop in attendance, not an empty seat was left in the sanctuary, and three overflow rooms were filled as well. Live feeds of the service were projected onto giant screens in these rooms, with live audio feeds over the ceiling speakers. *Holy Light's* reopening had its share of curious .spectators but it was also due to *New Day's* leadership announcing the church would meet in support of *Holy Light* for a joint service. After a vibrant forty-five minutes of electrifying praise, and heartrending worship it was time for the service to begin.

To thunderous applause that threatened to require restoration to the roof and walls of the sanctuary as well, Reverend Theodore Church, looking significantly leaner, and donning a striking grey pinstripe suit and blue satin tie, walked with his head bowed from his seat in the first row, up the steps and pointed to the heavens.

"It's Him y'all. It's all Him. Let's give Jesus all the praise and honor and glory today!"

This time the older members of the congregation looked around nervously, sure the walls would begin cracking and crumbling down from the shake and roar of the congregation.

Eventually Reverend Church quieted them down, but had to take a moment to gather his emotions, "My, my, my! What an awesome God we serve." The church threatened to roar again but Reverend Church shushed them with a broad grin and a wave of his hands.

"My precious family, my loved ones, from both *Holy Light* and *New Day*, I want to welcome you all today, and thank you for joining us as the grand reopening of our sanctuary." Several in the audience hooted and hollered, but they let the good Reverend continue. "I especially want to welcome and thank the board of elders, and leadership of *New Day Church of Faith* for joining us, and all our work together in the past couple of weeks." Reverend Church turned and nodded to the row of New Day leaders seated as special guests on the stage behind him.

"Before I continue," he said, as the crowd still buzzed. "I have to testify of what the Lord has done for me personally." Instantly the crowd hushed in anticipation. "You all know my family and I have been through some terrible times over the past few months, with that one week in particular being the worst."

A couple of "Dear Lawd's" and "Help us Jesus's" echoed throughout the building.

"I want to let you all know that although God may allow us to go through trials, even severe trials. He promises to use it for our benefit IF we let Him." The church fell silent. "I want to ask you today, church, *How strong is your faith?* It's been almost three months since the devil had his grip on me, but he couldn't close the deal. *How strong is your faith?* When times are hard. *How strong is your faith?* I didn't come to preach today, but I want you to take this with you: *how strong is your faith?*"

The church was still.

"Even a seasoned pastor is prone to blind spots, weakness and sin, so I have confessed before our elders, and I confess before you today, the sin of self-righteousness and of unseen pride. I believe the Lord allowed me to endure these afflictions so He could bring these issues to light and refine me." Reverend Church paused, and seemed to be considering his next words carefully.

"In spite of suffering the worst tragedies in my life, I want you to know the Lord has used it all for our good, and has blessed me more than I could ever hope for since then. I want to testify that as of this day, I am in perfect health, In fact, much better than before, "he chuckled, rubbing his flatter belly, to the amusement of the congregation.

"What's more is my beautiful wife, Sandra." he motioned to her in the front row. "...has made nothing short of a supernatural recovery. As of Wednesday this week, she is entirely cancer free!"

The crowd erupted again in a volley of praise and hoots and hollers, with half the church jumping to their feet in expression of their joy. If Reverend Theo Church was their spiritual dad, Sandra Church was undoubtedly their spiritual mom, and a leader among women in the community.

After a long while the crowd died down, and Reverend Church continued, "Friends, faith and faith alone is the reason I am still here today. I want to especially thank all of you who have been praying around the clock for my family and I, and this church. Your prayers truly have a direct audience with the Lord, and it's a testimony to the mountains we can move with prayer when we put our minds to it." More "Amens and a "Preach" rang out.

"Furthermore," Reverend Church began. "I'd like to

announce yet another miracle in our lives. Most of you know my precious daughter Jewel and our beloved son-in-law Dexter."

Reverend Church waved to the couple sitting next to Sandra in the front row. "Stand up please, you two. I want to brag on you a little. It's a daddy's right," he smiled. Jewel and Dexter stood up turned to the congregation, and waved shyly.

"Those of you who are close to them, know Jewel and Dexter have been trusting God to bring them a child for a long time now." Reverend Church faltered a little, and needed to take a moment a moment to gather himself. Jewel was unable to do so, and graciously accepted a Kleenex from her mom.

"I'm pleased to announce that my baby girl, Jewel," Reverend Church choked back tears. "...and her dear husband Dexter are expecting their first child in eight months, and the doctor says everything looks great."

Again, pandemonium broke out and the church shook from deafening applause and cheers of the congregation. Reverend Church bowed his head and squeezed his eyes shut tightly, pinching them with one hand, while the other was raised in agreement of praise with his congregation. Jewel dropped her head into Dexter's chest, while tears formed in his eyes and he raised one hand in worship, while the other embraced his wife.

"What's more." continued Reverend Church, above the

noise of the crowd. "What's more is Dexter has signed up for Bible School classes, and will be working toward his diploma at Seminary!"

It took the church longer each time to quiet down, but no one cared at all. It was a time for celebration and joy, and everyone was ready to let loose and give God the glory. After a good deal of revelry, Reverend Church gestured to Jewel and Dexter that they may be seated if they wished, and he began to speak again.

"God is so good! Today is truly a day of blessings! Today, we're going to have a unique sort of service...as many of you may have heard, and voted on," he winked, to the laughter of the crowd. "...the elders and leadership have, after much prayer and deliberation, found the perfect candidate to lead *New Day Church of Faith* into the future. I thought it respectful that *New Day* leadership announce their new pastor, however, the *New Day* leadership asked if I could present their new shepherd. I said it would be an absolute honor." Reverend Church cleared his throat, and paused for effect, but his face was beaming as he continued.

"You see there is another announcement I want to make, along with the leadership of *New Day*," he nodded to the row of elders behind him, who stood from their chairs, and walked up to form a row right behind him. Reverend Church stepped back between the men, into their line and continued.

"The first thing we are so excited to announce is that *New*

Day Church of Faith has decided to become part of the *Holy Light* network of churches and bring their talents, gifts, skills and deep experience in blessing this community to our family of churches. I can say I haven't been so excited about anything in years." The crowd erupted again in another deafening roar, as both churches displayed clear support of the union.

When everyone quieted down again, Reverend Church added, "It only makes sense, right?" More applause rippled through the congregation.

"Now guaranteed, there will be some birthing pains, and some things to work out." Reverend Church raised his eyebrow like a knowing father.

"Which brings me to the second announcement. The man you, the elders and myself agree is the only logical person to lead the flock at the *New Day* campus is a man I quite literally trust with my life. He is a man of immense wisdom, lives with the utmost integrity, and is astonishingly brave. He is as humble as he is effective, which says a lot in both regards. Without further ado, I would like to present to you the honorable Reverend Jeffery Lee as pastor and shepherd of *New Day Church of Faith*!"

This time, the ground literally did shake as several thousand people stomped their feet and shouted and bellowed their zeal for the new pastor. Two ushers scurried to the front row to help Pastor Lee to his feet, but were quickly shrugged off as he insisted on limping up to the stairs on his own. The men hovered behind under the watchful gaze of Reverend Church until Pastor Lee had made it up the stairs, and received a microphone. He and his friend, Reverend Church hugged for a long time as the crowd went wild, and the worship team burst into a spontaneous, soulful soundtrack for the moment. When the two men of God released their embrace, Pastor Lee's eyes were wet with tears, but his face shone brightly. He hobbled down the line and shook each elder's hand in respect, and thanked them sincerely. He was then guided to the pulpit by Reverend Church, and addressed the congregation:

"My dear family, I cannot tell you how humbling this moment is," he almost succumbed to emotion before he started. He bit back the tears, and continued, "Man, the enemy has tried to destroy two beautiful doves, these two precious churches, with one evil, fiery arrow. But he has lost, and he will keep losing, and keep losing." The crowd went wild again.

"I pledge to you, I swear it on my life, I will lead *New Day* with every ounce of integrity, wisdom and devotion I have, and I will work diligently to bring you the Word, and the Spirit, in submission to the vision of the *Holy Light* leadership under our highly anointed Reverend Church, and the board of elders."

Pastor Lee looked around the church, shook his head and wiped more tears from his eye.

"I want you all to know this is a war we're in. We were born into it, and it's real and there are real casualties. I served under Reverend Black for years, and witnessed firsthand, the creeping changes in his life. The enemy attacked him relentlessly, and he finally dropped his guard. The enemy is a *coward*. He'll attack your wife first, your kids, your husband, whoever is the weakest, he'll attack them to get to you. If you allow him to get a foothold, you'll literally have a hellish time rooting him out. My family, don't let him get a foothold. This isn't a game."

Every ear listened intently, and not even a baby murmured in the back.

"Two fellowships are uniting today, and there will be adjustments to be made. Walk in love, and go the extra *ten* miles for your spiritual family. Pray for your leadership, don't criticize us. Please, we're human, and as you have tragically seen, we are fallible too. We don't teach you to pray, and study the Word for no reason. It is to protect you and your families, and to help you to serve the Lord effectively. Our goal has, and always will be changed lives, and as much as there are casualties in this war, there are victories. Awesome victories! Those victories are what we aim for, and what keeps us going.

We know the Lord intended good to come from Reverend Church and his family's sufferings, and those are powerful testimonies. The most powerful testimony of all according to scripture though, is when a lost sheep returns home. Today, I want to share one of those victories with you. When I thought I was helping him, this young man helped me in so many ways, I can't even begin to recount them to you.

With deep concern, I watched this man be led astray for a number of years, and offered many prayers with many of you for his safety and return to the Lord. We know our God is faithful, and this young man was raised in the Lord, so when he was older, he had to return to God. Now, the Lord will get a person's attention, even if it means in ways they would have preferred not to learn, but in light of this, it is with so much joy, I would like to announce Gerald Church will be going through a period of restoration, and has expressed interest in assisting in leading the Outreach and Evangelism team for the *New Day* campus."

The church was just waiting for the next excuse to unleash their excitement, and broke into happy pandemonium again as Pastor Lee called Gerald up to the pulpit, over the roar.

Gerald's hip injury still required him to walk with a crutch, and he graciously accepted the help of the two ushers as his lung function was still somewhat impaired. Pastor Lee's words about the reality of this spiritual war rang home soundly as they had seen first Pastor Lee, now the formerly athletic young man, walking with great difficulty up the stairs.

The elders all surrounded Gerald, and shook his hand so he didn't have to walk over to them. Gerald then hugged his father who was now weeping openly. Finally, Gerald embraced Pastor Lee for a good while, who then squeezed his shoulder, handed him the mic and walked him to the pulpit.

"Wow, wow, wow!" was all Gerald could say at first, shaking his head as cheers and "Praise God's" rippled through the church. The crowd fell silent quickly, eager to hear what this young man had to say.

"First, I too want to thank our precious, precious God for His faithfulness, even when we are not faithful. Most of all I can't thank Him enough for what He has done in my life, saving me from certain hell." Gerald stiffened up, and appeared to struggle with the next sentence.

"You see, I speak of hell not figuratively but very, *very* literally. As you know, I became the proverbial prodigal son. I could say I was lured away, and that may be partially true, but I had my own issues, and I allowed myself to be deceived because I was resentful of various aspects of having parents in ministry. But God allowed me a very unique but extremely terrifying experience. In an attempt to quiet the pain I'd given my life over to, I injected what I thought was a standard dose of heroin into my arm. Turns out, it was from a new source in town, and was almost fifty percent more potent. Long story short, thanks to Pastor Lee's spiritual discernment, and no small amount of supernatural intervention, I was rushed to the hospital. I flat-lined on the operating table.

During what I was told was several minutes, I found myself being dragged down into the Earth, down, down, down, seeing my hospital room as a dimming light far, far above me. I could somehow hear the doctor and nurse's frantic conversation, as well as my Uncle Jeffrey's prayers." Gerald froze up again, and had to regain his composure. He bit his lip, and stuttering slightly, he forced himself to continue.

"Sheer terror gripped me like I've never experienced before. It is impossible to explain, but if you can imagine the complete and utter absence of goodness, love or hope, that's what was down there. Pure malevolent, psychotic evil emanated from behind huge, looming iron gates, which I could only make out from the dim light of distant flames, from what was a gigantic pit, *billions* of screams were just assaulting my ears. The stench of rotten sulfur burned my sinuses, and scorching heat bore down on me from every side, suffocating me, although I couldn't die.

I sensed a particularly malicious presence behind me, and turned to see the most hideous creature standing about ten feet tall, looming over me, glaring menacingly into my eyes. It grabbed my arm, talons ripping into my flesh, and I screamed. Somehow, I knew as soon as the gates opened, it was going to hurl me into the pit of flames beyond."

At this point, Gerald suddenly needed to take a break, and cleared his throat. He looked up to a completely silent crowd, and quickly looked back down at the pulpit. Everyone was mesmerized, and shocked.

"The monster shook me violently, like I was a washrag, and emitted a deep, horrible half-roar-half-screech and the gates began to creak open. In that moment, paralyzed in pure terror I did what I never thought possible-I screamed out to Jesus Christ that I repent and turn from my sins, and I begged Him for another chance."

The crowd's ears corporately perked up as they hung on Gerald's every word.

"At first nothing happened, and the demon, even more enraged took a step toward the gates, dragging me along like it was in a rush or something."

He cleared his throat. "Man, I screamed and screamed for the help of Jesus." He paused again. "Suddenly the brightest, whitest light I'd ever seen, brighter than the sun, pierced the gloom above us. The creature wailed, dropped me to the ground and ran into the shadows, cowering from the light. I heard a loud voice boom from above, in a language I didn't understand but I felt the rage and contempt emanating from somewhere behind the gates.

I was startled to begin ascending again, toward the light and as I did, the gates began closing. I could see the demon in the shadows cursing and hissing, clearly wanting, more than anything, to jump up and drag me back down, but it was terrified of the Presence behind the light. I ascended a little more, then I was suddenly conscious back in my body, with the doctor and two nurses trying to restrain me. That was my first near death experience."

Gerald waited for a moment, expecting a response from the congregation but none came. The entire church was captivated by his account, so he continued.

"As you know, I was severely wounded in a shooting right here in this church, in the third row right there," he pointed to the section just left of the center aisle, from his point of view. "I was defending my life, as was Pastor Lee, and for whatever reason, maybe because I brought a gun into the mix, and didn't fully leave it to God, we took some hits."

A slight murmur of realization spread through the crowd.

"Yeah, that was a pretty rough week," Gerald grinned, breaking out of his somber tone. A ripple of laughter spread through the church.

"I left my body again, as I lay right there on the carpet. I was lifted upright, and then rose, and rose, and ascended through the rafters, through the ceiling and through the roof. I was surprised to see several squad cars outside, as I wasn't yet aware the FBI agents had been alerted by Sister Willis, and were surrounding and entering the building.

Now this is God's honest truth, at a certain point, I saw a giant man - an angel - in my blind spot, clothed in dazzling white. He didn't move his lips, but he smiled and said to me, 'Have no fear. You're going home.' I suddenly shot forward at what was like, you know in the Star Trek movies how they do warp speed? Like that, just flying through space and galaxies and nebulas and it was just beautiful and spectacular." Gerald became lost for words as he went back in thought.

"Finally, I arrived Heaven, and I have to tell y'all, there are gates there too. But these are giant, beautiful iridescent gates. And strong. Nothing will penetrate those gates that shouldn't get through. And from behind these gates there emanated a joy and love and peace and, imagine the most chill day at an ocean resort, with not a care in the world, all expenses paid, all your family and loved ones with you, your soul mate at your side, I can't even explain it. It's paradise. It's total peace and joy. "Gerald stared off into the distance for a few moments shaking his head slightly.

He drew himself back, and continued, "The angel motioned and the gates opened for me, and I was escorted through. Far off in the distance, like maybe a mile or two away, I could see the glow of a city and I could hear celebration and music and, like a huge party. The biggest, baddest party you can ever imagine."

Several of the younger people broke their silence with an excited laugh.

"I knew in my heart, it was the New Jerusalem. It's our eternal home, and man, it's just so beautiful. But in front of me was the most beautiful nature I've ever seen. Like, the discovery channel has nothing on this. Picture Switzerland, but this place make Switzerland look ghetto, for real. I mean, the stuff artists can't even imagine, snow capped mountains, the greenest grass, fruit trees, flowers, just color and life and energy all around. I heard the babbling of a river nearby, and I turned to see coming from this direction my b-"

Gerald voice cracked and he bit his lip. Tears welled in his eyes, and he momentarily became overwhelmed with his feelings. His father stepped forward, who also had tears in his eyes and put his arm around his son, who turned into his dad's shoulder and sobbed for a about thirty seconds.

The church remained hushed, but whispers and prayers went up throughout the building as the congregation waited in awed reverence to hear the rest of the young man's experience. After about a minute, Reverend Church whispered into his son's ear, encouraging him, and Gerald wiped his eyes, and lifted his head to continue. His dad stepped back again.

"M-my baby brother, Tavaris, was walking up to me," he began, as his voice cracked again and the tears flowed once more. But Gerald's face was filled with joy. He continued speaking in a jerky voice as little rivers streamed down his cheeks.

"My baby bro came walking up with, y'all know that swagger of his," Gerald laughed, and by now half the congregation were crying as women dug in their purses searching frantically for Kleenex.

"We ran up to each other and man, I lifted that kid up off the ground I hugged him so hard. We laughed and laughed, and he said he was so happy to see me. It's weird, but he said he was expecting me. I kinda still don't understand it, but he said he was having a blast, and there was so much he wanted to tell me but he said that for now, I shouldn't stay.

The weird thing is it seemed like the choice was mine, but he encouraged me to go back.

I looked at the angel who had accompanied me there, and he agreed, 'There is much work left to do on Earth, but it is your decision.'"

Gerald sighed and wiped his eyes again, "Whew, me and my bro talked about a lot of stuff. He was the same in a way, but different too, I've never seen him like that. Happy isn't the right word. He was filled with pure joy, and he was so...mature. One thing he told me that stuck out, though, he said that I couldn't understand it now, but there was a reason he went home early. He's right, I don't understand it but I can tell y'all, that boy is having a good time up there. He told me he was going to talk to the Apostle Paul soon, and he was most excited about that."

Behind Gerald, his father shook visibly as he wept tears of joy, surrounded by the elders of *New Day*, and *Holy Light*, while his mother, Sandra, had given up on her makeup, and she too wept openly, with her daughter and son-in-law surrounding her.

Gerald pointed to a young man who had been quietly sitting next to Dexter in the front row, quiet as a lamb until this point, "Smoke!" Gerald smiled. "I've told you this already, but in front of the whole church, T said you gotta join the Worship Team and serve God! He says you have a potent calling on your life bruh."

Smoke nodded emphatically, rocking forward, and wiping

away his own tears. He dropped his head into his lap and put his face in his hands, and Dexter leaned over and hugged the kid, while Jewel reached over and rubbed his head lovingly.

The congregation continued in praise and celebration for way longer than scheduled, but no-one cared at all. Several of the elders testified of the great works God continued to do in their various ministries, and eventually, although most would have stayed all day and all night, babies had to be fed, appointments had to be kept, and life had to move forward. The elders called the entire Church family up, as well as Pastor Lee, and also Reverend Williams, Pastor Baker and Bishop Davis. The elders surrounded the men and women, and prayed a long, powerful prayer for all of them, to close the service.

As large as their church had grown, Reverend Church and Sandra still went and stood at the front of the church every Sunday, to shake the hands of church members. This Sunday was no different. Pastor Lee stood with them, along with Gerald, Jewel and Dexter, and several of the elders. The atmosphere that day was one of pure revival and Reverend Church wondered ecstatically if he would get calluses on his hands from all the enthusiastic shaking.

At least seventy percent of the attendees gathered to greet them, and offer their own, special blessings. The Churches lovingly spoke to each member, and were truly overjoyed to be able to stand in that line, and do so.

Toward the end of the line, a finely but modestly dressed lady patiently waited her turn, then walked up and greeted the Churches warmly.

"Mary! How are you doing? So good to see you!" Sandra exclaimed, giving her a keen hug.

"Hi Sandra, my doll! Wow! You look totally radiant. I *love* the short hairdo!"

"Oh, thank you!" Sandra beamed.

"Sister Willis!" Reverend Church smiled, and extended a hand. "Anything new with our new Fed buddies since Thursday?"

Sister Willis shook Reverend Church's hand, and sighed, "No, nothing new yet, but we're still praying. Still trusting God I'll just receive probation, but I'm ready to bear whatever comes down the pipe."

"No, we're trusting with you, and as I said before, we'll testify of your character. You made a few mistakes, but you're family and as long as you're committed to the restoration process, I know God will come through for you."

"Amen! Thank you Pastor, I receive that in Jesus' name."

"I have to tell you how much I appreciate you, Mary. Without your bravery and your call to the FBI agents, my son would be dead," Sandra said, placing her hand on Mary Willis' arm.

"Oh, Sandra," Mary became emotional. "I just wish I had the strength to speak up sooner."

"Hey, all things work together for good, for those who love God, right?" Sandra replied.

"Yes, they do," Sister Willis said shyly.

"Say, how did the FBI get there so quickly, anyway?" Sandra asked. "Theo won't tell me anything."

Sister Willis laughed, "Oh I wouldn't mind if y'all discussed what happened at all. Basically the agent had a GPS tracker on mine *and* Deacon-I mean *Pastor* Lee's car, since we were both suspects in the investigation, *and weren't laid up in the hospital*. When he got the alert that both of our cars were at the church on a Sunday afternoon, he was ready, and was hoping to catch us in the act of some fraud, and had a few of his men meet him there. He was surprised to get my call as he was pulling up to the church."

"No way!" Sandra cried, and looked at her husband, who nodded somberly.

"Yeah, and I guess that explains some of how Pastor Lee and Gerald were exonerated in the car chase by Sergeant Stone. The surviving officer's testimony was very different to what the GPS tracker on Pastor Lee's car and Sergeant Stone's cruiser showed."

"Wow!" Sandra replied. "God's ways are so much higher than our ways! Praise God, He even uses FBI tracking devices!"

"Yes, He does!" Sister Willis agreed. "And tell me Jeffery-sorry, Pastor Lee," she smiled. "Tell me again what happened with you and Reverend Black. I've only heard rumors?"

"Oh, well it's another miracle," Pastor Lee inhaled, and wondered where to start. He didn't really like telling this part of the story. He didn't like telling any part of the story in fact, and had only recounted the full version for the police. Still, he knew God received glory when he told this part, so he obliged Sister Willis. "Agent Willoughby was the first one in the doors and ran in with his weapon drawn. But as he came in, he saw Reverend Black fire four shots, point-blank at my head and back."

Sister Willis placed a hand over her mouth.

"The weird part, as the agent tells it though, is that right after the shots were fired-or right as they were fired, he can't be sure...a tall homeless man stood at the front of the church and stretched out his hand. Reverend Black then fell to the ground, stone dead."

"My Lord!" Sister Willis whispered.

"Yeah," Pastor Lee nodded. "Pretty wild. To make it stranger, according to the agent, the homeless man started to speak in an unknown tongue. What appeared to be an image or shadow started to rise from Rev. Black's body. Then before the agent could react, everything went pitch dark and there was a deafening, screeching cry."

Sister Willis shook her head in disbelief.

"On top of that, there were four AR15 slugs found in the carpet beneath my body, but none of those wounded me. Two of the medical team have testified that the slugs were beneath my body when they turned me over."

"Wow!" Sister Willis was blown away.

"Yep. Agent Willoughby said he's seen some pretty weird stuff, but he's never seen anything like that homeless guy, the shadowy ghost, and seeing Black fire those rounds, and the slugs under my body while I was unharmed by them. Oh, and the homeless dude and the shadow just vanished. The lights came back on and they were gone."

"Oh my gosh," Sister Willis said, fanning her face. "I have goosebumps!" The others nodded, knowing exactly how she felt. "Praise God," she said. "Wow!"

"Praise God," they all agreed.

As the line was drawing to a close, a large, *vibrantly* dressed lady waddled up, almost bumping Sister Willis out of the way, "Oh 's'cuze me sister!" she grunted, eyeing Sister Willis up and down disapprovingly. "I like the new accessories!" she chirped, bobbing her head at Sister Willis' ankle adornment.

"Ah, yes, Sister Haywood, my monitoring device." Sister Willis laughed. "Matches my hat, doesn't it?" she winked at the portly lady, who huffed and turned away. Sister Willis giggled and waved goodbye to the Churches and Pastor Lee, as Sister Haywood thundered forward and grabbed Sandra's hand, shaking it vigorously.

"Aw I just got to come in for a hug, Sister Sandra, I just got to!" Sandra laughed as she embraced Sister Haywood tightly.

"Aw as soon as I heard you had the cancer, I dropped to mah knees, Sister Sandra" she rattled off like machine gun fire. "I said nuh-uh devil, you ain't snatchin' away our lovely Pastor's wife! She too lovely!"

Much to the amusement of all around, Sister Haywood pantomimed with her finger, showing an invisible devil she was just not having it. "I'm tellin' ya, I felt it, I felt my prayers break through, I said Lawd, we can't have the devil beat up on this lovely Pastor's wife now, that cancer got to GO in Jesus' name!"

Sister Haywood was now highly animated, her voice getting louder and louder. Sandra thoroughly enjoyed the show, which only egged Sister Haywood on, as she feigned a more dire concern. "Mm, mmm, we got prayer warriors up in this church right here. We love our Pastors, yes we do."

"Thank you so much, Sister Haywood," Sandra smiled graciously, still giggling. "Truly, you're such a blessing to us."

"Oh thank you Sister Sandra. You and Pastor Church over

here are such wonderful blessings to me." She sidled up to Reverend Church, and looked up at him with puppy dog eyes. "My, my, the Lawd sure has blessed us with such a fine Pastor. Mmm such a fine man, and looking so healthy and lean?" She eyed his newly trim torso, and shook her head in appreciation.

"Sister Haywood," Reverend Church nodded nervously and cleared his throat. He extended a hand, much to the mischievous glee of his wife and children. The rotund lady looked at his extended hand as if it were an insult, and replied,

"Aw naw, Pastor, I got to get me the real thang. I need some of that anointin' to rub off on me!" She promptly pulled the pastor into a full body hug. Reverend Church squirming, patted her formally on the back and after two seconds, wriggled to free himself.

Sandra lost her composure, and hid her face in Jewel's shoulder, shaking with laughter at her husband's fear. After way too long, Reverend Church broke free from Sister Haywood's unnaturally strong grip and offered his warm wishes to her and gave her the handshake slash please-keep-moving pat on the back. She grudgingly relented, and eyed him adoringly as she waddled off down the line, to find another victim.

"Dear Lord help me. Sandra, are you kidding me? No help at all? None?" Reverend Church protested. Sandra and her daughter and pretty much all those around her were in hysterics. After a stern few seconds, Reverend Church couldn't help but smile, and just shook his head, "Y'all are a mess. A complete, hot mess, you know that right? Leave a man to be afflicted like that. After all I've been through."

The group cackled even louder.

"I'm taking notes, Rev," Pastor Lee smiled, as he squeezed his friend's hand.

"Hey, you need a wife don't you?" Reverend Church winked impishly.

"Hey now, I can handle crazy gangsters and rogue reverends, but Sister Haywood's in another league Rev," he laughed. Reverend Church laughed too.

"Rev, I just want to say again, how privileged I am to be serving under you. I believe there are truly good things ahead for us."

"I know my dear brother. And I can't thank you enough, for having my back even when it meant your life. You saved my son, you saved our church's funds, you're a true man of God. A *hero* Jeff."

Pastor Lee shrugged and grinned. "Hey, as you said, it was all God. I could never have orchestrated that pharmacy stock that Black had stashed the money into, getting an unprecedented *two-hundred* percent return almost overnight. And I definitely couldn't have orchestrated the judge awarding the church everything in the account, even the increases."

Reverend Church's eyes welled up again. "I know, brother, I know. It's a miracle. It also really helped that Sister Willis gave up all the codes in that notebook, and cooperated with the FBI. It'll be good for her too."

"Oh yeah," Pastor Lee agreed.

"And did I tell you *The Three Musketeers* gave generous gifts to the church as well?" Reverend Church added.

"Nope, they did really? Williams, Baker and Davis?"

"Yep. They've also learned a lot in this time, and their hearts have really come around. Thanks to your boldness too! Now they're *even* talking of joining the *Holy Light* network as well," he half-whispered out of the side of his mouth, as if someone would overhear. "Wouldn't that be something?"

"Yes it would! How generous were their gifts?"

"*Exceptionally* generous!" Reverend Church raised his eyebrows. "Like six figures generous, each. And they gave me personal gifts. I didn't want to accept them, but they insisted."

"Whew," Pastor Lee whistled. "Praise God! We're going to be able to do some big things in this city when Gerald's ready."

"Yes, we are my friend. Yes we are. The devil has no idea

how much he's gonna pay."

Pastor Lee grinned widely and nodded, then threw his hand up for a bro-hug. He embraced Reverend Church and then chuckling, hurried off to rescue another of the elders from Sister Haywood.

Reverend Church put his arm around his wife and daughter, and leaned over to squeeze his son's shoulder. He looked around him, at the beautiful site of people laughing, celebrating and enjoying a mighty victory and quietly thanked his God for how blessed he was. He was entirely in his element at that moment, a true shepherd just happy to be surrounded by his sheep, especially the lost ones who had returned home.

As his heart brimmed over with joy, a man standing at the edge of the parking lot caught his eye. He was tall. Remarkably tall, and striking in appearance. He wore a perfectly tailored charcoal suit, and his hair and beard were neatly combed. It was his piercing eyes, however, that Reverend Church recognized immediately. The men held each other's stare for a long moment, a thousand unspoken thoughts flying between them, but they all ultimately boiled down to only one: Reverend Church raised his fist and clenched it tightly. The angel smiled, raised his fist, and clenched it tightly too. Then he nodded slightly, turned and walked away.

ABOUT THE AUTHOR

David T. Brown and his wife Stacey are strong devoted believers in Christ. David is intrigued by the natural response of Christians as they endure various trials, tribulations, and storms set forth by almighty God. As a young adult David strayed from the church for many years before following the path back to his Lord and Savior. Within those years he witnessed many things that made him question how strong his faith truly was. Although at the time it seemed as though he might lose his faith entirely, in time many of the things David experienced have strengthened his belief that his savior, Jesus Christ would never leave him, nor forsake him. It is upon this primary premise that *How Strong Is Your Faith?* is written.

Keep in touch! Like David's Facebook page at

www.facebook.com/How-Strong-Is-your-Faith . Follow him on twitter at https://twitter.com/howstrongfaith.

Visit David's website at www.davidtbrown.org.